Arafat Madi Shoukri is Director of the Council for European-Palestinian Relations (CEPR). He has participated in many conferences on the issue of Palestinian refugees and is a regular commentator in the media about the current affairs of the Palestinian refugees. He holds a PhD from the School of Oriental and African Studies (SOAS), University of London.

INTERNATIONAL LIBRARY OF MIGRATION STUDIES

Series ISBN: 978 1 84885 225 9

See www.ibtauris.com/ILMS for a full list of titles

1. *Migrating to America: Transnational Social Networks and Regional Identity among Turkish Migrants*
Lisa DiCarlo
978 1 84511 646 0

2. *Homelands and Diasporas: Greeks, Jews and Their Migrations*
Minna Rozen [Ed]
978 1 84511 642 2

3. *The Iraqi Refugees: The New Crisis in the Middle East*
Joseph Sassoon
978 1 84511 919 5

4. *Immigration and National Identity: North African Political Movements in Colonial and Postcolonial France*
Rabah Aissaoui
978 1 84511 835 8

5. *From Egypt to Europe: Globalisation and Migration Across the Mediterranean*
Leila Simona Talani
978 1 84511 669 9

6. *Critical Diaspora: Women, Art, Migration*
Suzanne Chan
978 1 84885 337 9

7. *Refugee Status in Islam: Concepts of Protection in Islamic Tradition and International Law*
Arafat Shoukri
978 1 84885 390 4

8. *Compensating Palestinian Refugees: Legal Economic and Political Perspectives*
Rex Brynen and Roula al Rifai (Eds)
978 1 84885 727 8

REFUGEE STATUS IN ISLAM

Concepts of Protection in Islamic Tradition and International Law

ARAFAT MADI SHOUKRI

I.B.TAURIS
LONDON · NEW YORK

Published in 2011 by I.B.Tauris & Co Ltd
6 Salem Road, London W2 4BU
175 Fifth Avenue, New York NY 10010
www.ibtauris.com

International Library of Migration Studies 7

ISBN 978 1 84885 390 4

A full CIP record for this book is available from the British Library
A full CIP record for this book is available from the Library of Congress

Library of Congress catalog card: available

CONTENTS

ACKNOWLEDGEMENTS

The origin of this book is a thesis written to complete a PhD program at the School of Oriental and African Studies (SOAS), University of London, in 2007. This thesis was the first, to the best of my knowledge, to treat this topic comprehensively.

Having reached the final stage of my work, I am indebted to many people. I was honoured to have my thesis supervised by Dr. Stefan Sperl, who sensed the importance of this topic from the very beginning and worked enthusiastically to read, discuss and guide me to reach this point. I wish to express great gratitude and thanks to him.

I also wish to express my gratitude to my mother, whose prayers and encouragement were a source of empowerment throughout the years, and my wife and friend, Mariam. I will remember and appreciate Mariam's patience, support and sacrifice for the rest of my life. Without her, I would never have been able to finish this book. Likewise, I extend my thanks to my children Albara, Almuthanna and Jana, who missed their father during my research and were a constant source of joy and pleasure.

Finally, being a full-time employee and student at the same time was extremely tough, and without the understanding and support of my manager at the time, Majed al-Zeer, it would have been much more difficult. The same is true for all of my friends and colleagues who supported and helped me in many ways.

All of the above individuals deserve a share of the credit for this work. However, any faults or weaknesses are my responsibility.

INTRODUCTION

By any measure, the issue of refugees occupies an important place on the contemporary international agenda. Millions of people around the world have become refugees as a result of wars, natural disasters and other circumstances.

The challenges facing international agencies such as the United Nations refugees agency (the UN High Commissioner for Refugees – UNHCR) are many and include 'the plight of tens of millions of internally displaced people; widespread confusion over migrants and refugees; tightened asylum policies and growing intolerance'.[1]

A quick survey of elections, be they in the developed or developing world, shows just how sensitive the refugee question is. Parties of all political hues have a position on this issue. A considerable number of developed societies are witnessing 'the re-emergence of racism, xenophobia and that brand of populism which always tries to generate confusion in the public opinion between refugees, migrants and even terrorists'.[2] The governments of many developed countries are seeking to reinterpret articles of international law relating to refugees in an attempt to circumvent their duties and free themselves of the refugee burden.

Arab and Muslim states are not exempt from this problem. On the contrary, according to António Guterres, the head of UNHCR, 'the majority of refugees worldwide are Muslim'.[3] Despite this, some UNHCR operations 'in the Muslim world have been systematically underfunded … [and] the generosity of host countries has not been matched by that of the international community'.[4] Moreover, 'only a few of them possess domestic legislation which deals with refugees or migrants' (Elmadmad, 1991, p. 462). In fact, only 35 out of 57 member states of the Organization of the Islamic Conference (OIC) have ratified the 1951 Geneva Convention and the 1967 Protocol.[5]

The appeal that Guterres issued at the 127th meeting of the League of Arab States (LAS) Council of Ministers of Foreign Affairs in Cairo in March 2007 is very telling. He appealed to 'the Muslim world, and in particular the Arab world, to play a greater role in the discussion, formulation and implementation of international refugee policy'.[6]

Given this reality, and the ambiguity of the Islamic position on such issues, this research is especially relevant. Broadly, this book aims to clarify the attitude of the Islamic tradition towards refugees and establish whether this tradition has any views, principles, rules or regulations on a range of issues including the definition of the term refugee and the rights and duties of refugees and host states. In this sense the book will hopefully underline the relevance of the Islamic tradition concerning refugee status and will contribute to the international legislation regarding this issue.

This research also aims to collate relevant sources on refugees in Arab history in the *jāhiliyya* (pre-Islamic period),[7] such as the concept of *jiwār* (protection). The book will further examine concepts related to the refugee status in the Islamic tradition, for example the term *hijra* (migration) and *amān* (safe conduct). Together, these sources comprise a vital store of information for future researchers seeking to examine Islamic parallels to contemporary regulations relating to refugees.

The significance of this research also derives from the fact that it is the first occasion since the endorsement of the 1951 Geneva Convention relating to refugees that a study has attempted to examine the interface between the Convention and the Islamic tradition, with a view to identifying the similarities and differences between the two.

Remarkably little has been written on this topic from an Islamic perspective. In view of this, I hope this book with the huge amount of scholarly opinions it includes will fill a gap in the Islamic library and provide experts and legislators in Islamic states with a guide to interpreting the law on refugee issues into modern legislations.

Chapter 1

THE *JIWĀR* IN THE *JĀHILIYYA*

Introduction

When addressing the status of refugees in the Arab and Islamic tradition, writers often refer to the issue of *jiwār* among Arabs in the Arabian Peninsula before the advent of Islam. They consider *jiwār*, in essence, to be the equivalent of the modern concept of refuge as it meant granting protection and welfare to the needy and the fleeing person. The importance of this principle also derives from the fact that tribes in many modern Arab states still adhere to and preserve this customary practice.

Existing works on this subject, despite its significance, fail to convey the importance of *jiwār* to Arabs in the *jāhiliyya*. Those that have elaborated on *jiwār* do so only from a narrow perspective, where mention of it is limited to one particular context only.

For this reason, the research begins with a study of the principle of *jiwār* in the *jāhiliyya* as an introduction to the main topic. It should be noted that the scale of this research is limited to the Arabs who lived in the Arabian Peninsula in the period before Islam, which is the period Muslims later called the period of the *jāhiliyya*, 'the age of ignorance'.

The fact that so little has been written on this issue makes the task more difficult. Hence, to form a complete and uniform picture of *jiwār* before Islam, a range of texts, including history, literature, poetry, language, biography and genealogy have been consulted in an attempt to collate the scattered evidence and produce a more complete picture of *jiwār* as observed by Arabs in the period before Islam.

The definition of *jiwār*

Looking up the three-letter root of the word; that is *jawara* (Jım-Wāw-Rāʾ), we find the following in the language dictionaries:

'*Jāwar Banī Fulān*' sought *jiwār* of Banī so-and-so: became sacred, i.e. protected due to their *jiwār* تـحَرَّمَ بجوارهم *jār* and *mujīr*: 'he is who protects and grants you *jiwār*' هو الذي يمنعك ويجيرك (Ibn Manẓūr, 1956, vol. 4, p. 154). Al-Farāhīdī (1980, vol. 1, p. 490), however, defines the *jār* as 'your neighbour in dwelling, who has contracted your *jiwār* and protection'. So, the term *jār* could be used to mean the protector, the *mujīr*, or the protected, the *mustajīr*. For the sake of clarity, I will use the term *mujīr* to mean the protector and the term *mustajīr* to mean the protected.

Thus, *jiwār* could in essence be defined as a contract between two parties where one asks for protection and the other grants it to him or her.

In fact, the right to grant *jiwār* was reserved solely for the true-blooded members of the tribe (al-Jumaylı, 1972, p. 198). It was their premier right and the most perilous, because as a result the tribe would take in foreigners and bear the consequences of their actions, even if that meant war or a loss of wealth or even lives. Granting *jiwār* was therefore a serious decision for anyone other than the freemen of the tribe to take.

Protection and welfare

Granting *jiwār* by definition meant providing protection and welfare to the *mustajīr*. The relationship between the two, however, 'varied according to circumstances. Sometimes it was quite temporary, and other times it was permanent and even hereditary. At one time the protector only promised to aid his *mustajīr* against some particular enemy; at another time he undertook to protect him against all enemies' (Smith, 1903, p. 51).

By and large, the protector would do his utmost to provide protection to his *mustajīr*. Some of them took pride in the fact that their *mustajīr* was in a safe and elevated position in the tribe so that no one could harm him. Marwān Ibn Abī Ḥafṣa praised Man Ibn Zāʾida, and his tribe by saying (al-Andalusī, 1987, vol. 1, p. 122):

هم يمنعون الجار حتى كأنما　　　لجارهم بين السماكين منزل

They protect the *jār*, until it is as though
their *mustajīr* has a place among the Samākayn[1]

Others went even further in honouring the *mustajīr*, considering him equal to the *ṣihr*, the relative by marriage. Ibn al-Arabī says: 'Muṣhir is said to one who is given sanctity by marriage, blood relation, or *jiwār*' (al-Zamakhsharī, 1979, p. 268).

The extent of their generosity and the honour in which they held him sometimes made the *mustajīr* feel that he was one of the tribe's true members, such that his lineage would be dissolved into the lineage of the tribe to become one of them (Ibn Khaldūn, 1900, p. 50). To praise Banī Shaybān the poet Yazīd Ibn Ḥamān al-Sakūnī described them as follows (al-Marzūqī, 1953, vol. 1, p. 301):[2]

ومن تكرمهم في المِحَلِ أنهم لا يعلم الجار فيهم أنه الجار

حتى يكون عزيزاً من نفوسهم أو أن يبين جميعاً وهو مختار

And of their honouring of the *mustajīr* during the hardships that
he does not know that he is a *mustajīr*
until he becomes a noble one of them
or goes away out of free choice.

In addition to extending physical generosity, some tribes were also concerned with the psychological state of the *mustajīr*. They took account of his feelings and made him feel as if he was close family, while disregarding his faults and mistakes and listening to him attentively, so that he would not feel a stranger far from home and family. The poet Qays Ibn Āṣim al-Minqarī describes them (al-Marzubānī, 1935, p. 324):

لا يفطنون لعيب جارهم وهم لحسن حديثه فطن

They do not sense the fault of their *mustajīr*
and they are in observing his protection, alert.[3]

Moreover, some tribes cared so much about the *mustajīr* that they would continue to care about him even after he left them for other places. Umayr Ibn al-Ayham al-Taghlibī praised his tribe, saying (al-Qazwīnī, 1998, vol. 1, p. 340):

ونكرمُ جارنَا ما دامَ فينَا ونتبعهُ الكرامة حيثُ مالا

And we put up well our *mustajīr* amongst us
and follow him, honouring him wherever he goes.

In some cases, protecting the *mustajīr* took extreme forms and the *mujīr* had to pay a heavy price in order to keep his *mustajīr* safe. One such example is the famous story of al-Samawʾal, who kept the shields of Imruʾu al-Qays with him. When al-Ḥārith Ibn Ẓālim came to take them from him, al-Samawʾal took refuge in a fortified position. Al-Ḥārith took al-Samawʾal's son hostage, demanding the shields in return. al-Samawʾal refused to hand over the wealth of his *mustajīr* and break his trust. Al-Ḥārith swung his sword and cut the boy in half, while al-Samawʾal looked on. On this occasion, he said his famous verses (al-Aṣfahānī, 1983, vol. 12, p. 116):

وفيت بأدرع الكندي إنـي   إذا ما خان أقوام وفـيت

I am true to my promise for [keeping] shields of the Kindī
if people betray, I fulfil.

In other verses he depicts the moment of decision to protect the shields of his *mustajīr*, and sacrifice his son (Ibn al-Athīr, 1884, vol. 1, p. 235):

فشك غير طويل ثم قـال لـه   اقتل أسيرك إني مانع جـاري

So he pondered little then said to him
kill your prisoner, I'll protect my *mustajīr.*

For this great sacrifice he became the subject of the popular saying on observing trust: 'More faithful [to his promises] than al-Samawʾal' أوفى من السموأل (al-Maydānī, 1987, vol. 2, p. 441).

Protection was sometimes even extended to include beasts and roaming animals. Mudlaj Ibn Suwayd al-Ṭāʾī, for example, gave protected status to the locusts in his vicinity, and prevented his people from collecting them, and thus was called 'Protector of the locusts'[4] مجير الجراد (al-Andalusī, 1987, vol. 1, p. 122). The significance of these extremes is that they are considered a sign of power, chivalry and warrior spirit. If locusts could not be hunted on tribal lands, then people taking refuge there would surely be protected, and anyone thinking of harming the tribe or any of its members would be advised to think again.

To show their status, power and strength some tribes even went so far as to build a special dwelling for those who requested their *jiwār*. The tribe of Banī Abd al-Mudān, for instance, 'built a dome of adobe they called Kaʿba. If entered by a seeker of *jiwār* they would grant him their protection and if entered by a person with any need like food, water or money they would give him what he is asking for' (al-Aṣfahānī, 1983, vol. 12, p. 7).

Using the word Ka^{c}ba for that dwelling was probably to give a sense of sanctity to the place, as was the case of the Ka^{c}ba in Mecca. For this reason, Arnaout says that *jiwār* was 'essentially religious' (Arnaout, 1987, p. 11). In fact, even the normal tents in which the Bedouin lived had a certain sanctity and inviolability, such that it was sufficient for the *mustajīr* simply to touch a tent or its ropes to be considered a legitimate request for *jiwār* (al-Aṣfahānī, 1983, vol. 3, p. 57).

The family of Muḥlam Ibn Dhuhal, nobles in the *jāhiliyya*, built a dome in the valley of Awf and called it the Dome of Mu^{c}ādha. Whoever sought refuge in it would be protected (Ibn Durayd, 1958, p. 358). In the same vein, al-A^{c}shā took pride in saying (Ibn Jinnī, 1913, vol. 1, p. 389):

لنا هضبة لا ينزل الذل وسطها   ويأوي إليها المستجير فيعصما

We have a mount, no humiliation comes to it
the *mustajīr* comes to it for refuge and he will be protected.

Obviously, the issue of *jiwār* assumed grand dimensions in the customs of the Arabs before Islam, to the extent that a person would sacrifice himself, his family and property to defend his *jār*, as we have seen in the above examples. Protection of *mustajīr* was strongly related to the preservation of honour and respect. Additionally, granting protection was also very much connected to the status of the tribe in that harsh environment. The level of protection a tribe was capable of offering was an indicator of its ability to protect itself and its members. Moreover, there were religious reasons for granting *jiwār* – as was apparent in their observance of the sacredness of the Ka^{c}ba and the refugees who came to seek asylum there.

The reasons for asking *jiwār*

The reasons for asking *jiwār* were various but one of the main factors in formulating *jiwār* was *khal^{c}*, which means abolishing all sorts of lawful responsibilities placed on the relatives or the tribe of the outcast person. If a man commits a crime after *khal^{c}*, he should be solely responsible for that and nobody would protect or defend him. The expelled person was left, in most cases, with no option but to seek *jiwār* from other tribes or prominent figures in the vicinity.

Still, there were other motives that drove people to seek *jiwār*, such as protection from drought and hunger. The harsh desert conditions were sometimes merciless and people sometimes struggled to find any kind of sustenance for their families or their animals. Such conditions forced some people to seek *jiwār* of other rich and powerful tribes. Al-Ḥuṭayʾa, the well-known poet, sought refuge with Banī Muqallad Ibn Yarbūʾ when he suffered hunger and poverty. They granted him *jiwār* and when the difficult times passed, he left saying (al-Aṣfahānī, 1983, vol. 2, p. 150):

جاورت آل مقلدٍ فحمدتـهـم إذ ليس كل أخي جوارٍ يحمد

I stayed with Banī Muqallad and am grateful
for not all those granting *jiwār* are worthy of gratitude.

Some, however, would seek refuge during the winter months only, when the need was great, and leave for their own home and tribe when the season was over. The *mujīr* was obliged to treat such a visitor with honour, take care of his needs, protect his wealth, if he had any, and compensate him for any loss during his stay with them (al-Marzūqī, 1953, vol. 1, p. 302).

Some would seek *jiwār* for protection from certain harsh environmental conditions, such as strong winds. Ibn al-Mujāwir (1954, p. 165) reports that a group of people asked *jiwār* of Ḥijr Ibn al-Muhalhal from the wind. After accepting them, he built them a wall from stone and mortar to protect them from the wind.

Such examples demonstrate the impact of the harsh environment on the custom of *jiwār*. They also indicate that asking *jiwār* was not a complicated process, nor was it shameful. If someone needed help, he would not hesitate to seek it from the wealthier and more powerful members of that society.

Exacting vengeance was another reason which led some people to seek *jiwār*, especially when that person was weak and unable to achieve his goal unaided. He would seek the protection of someone else until he could exact his revenge, as Imruʾu al-Qays tried to do when Banī Asad killed his father Ḥijr al-Kindī (al-Aṣfahānī, 1983, vol. 9, pp. 87–91).

This type of *jiwār* is an example of a very politically motivated request for *jiwār*, since Ḥijr al-Kindī was a king when he was killed. Revenge by his son was a way of regaining honour after taking his father's place. Nevertheless, *jiwār* in general always had a political dimension, either to highlight honour and prestige or to show the power of the tribe to protect the weak and needy as well as the members of the tribe itself.

Protecting the trade caravans was another valid reason for seeking *jiwār*. This type of *jiwār* covered wealth rather than its owner. Even if the owner was safe, if his goods were passing through insecure territory he might be forced to request the protection of a tribe to safeguard it. After al-Nuᶜmān Ibn al-Mundhir killed the brother of Balᶜāʾ Ibn Qays, the latter attacked his caravans in Tihāma and robbed them twice, so al-Nuᶜmān had no choice but to 'ask protection for his caravans from the Arab tribes there' (Ibn Ḥabīb, 1985, p. 45).

More interestingly, some people went even further and asked *jiwār* from death, knowing that nobody could ever stop death. The idea behind this is illustrated in the incident of al-ᶜAshā and ᶜĀmir Ibn Ṭufayl. Al-ᶜAshā came to ᶜĀmir Ibn Ṭufayl asking *jiwār* from *jinni* (spirits), men and death. When Ibn Ṭufayl accepted, the astonished al-ᶜAshā asked 'how would you protect me from death? He said: "If you die while in my *jiwār*, I will send to your family your blood-money".[5] He said: Now I know that you have protected me from death. So, he complimented ᶜĀmir and insulted ᶜAlqama in his poetry [for refusing to protect him from death]' (al-Aṣfahānī, 1983, vol. 9, p. 117).

Some people would even seek *jiwār* from poets so as not to become the subject of their contempt and derisive poetry, as this story illustrates: 'When al-Farazdaq composed poetry maligning Banī Jaᶜfar Ibn Kilāb, a woman feared he would mention her name and insult her. To escape this severe threat she sought refuge at the grave of his father, Ghālib Ibn Ṣaᶜṣaᶜa. As al-Farazdaq knew this, he accepted her *jiwār* and did not mention her name or lineage' (al-Mubarrad, 1956, vol. 2, p. 87).

The examples above demonstrate the general relationship between *jiwār* and poetry. The incident involving al-Farazdaq and the woman is significant in the sense that it exposes the direct relation between *jiwār* and poetry. The influence of poetry in the life of the Arabs at the time is clear. This gives justification to the unhesitating nature of the decisions to grant *jiwār* to whoever sought it, despite the heavy price they might pay as a result.

In the above examples, some tribes not only gave protection to the *mustajīr* but were exceedingly proud of their actions and extended their hospitality to the extent that the *mustajīr* became one of them. In all previous examples, the *mustajīr* used his ability to compose poetry praising the *mujīr* highly. This praise was extremely important to the *mujīr* as it would spread all over the Peninsula and would be transmitted for generations.

In general, poetry played a significant role in strengthening and maintaining the custom of *jiwār*, as it was the strongest medium of communication and the best way of spreading news among the Arab tribes. Both praise and ridicule could be spread rapidly all over the Peninsula through verses of poetry.

Granting *jiwār* necessarily entailed the ability to provide protection and welfare. As a demonstration of power and strength, spreading news of *jiwār* could be very beneficial to the tribe. This was particularly so in that environment, where power could mean survival and freedom from slavery.

Thus, *jiwār* was basically an exchange of bounty between the *mustajīr* and *mujīr*. While the *mustajīr* got the material help and protection needed, the *mujīr* received praise, fame and high status among the tribes. This status would certainly mean an increase in power and would reduce the likelihood of raids and attacks: a tribe that was ready to defend foreigners would definitely fight fiercely to protect its own members and property.

Other factors that made the custom of *jiwār* so entrenched in the lives of the Arabs were the nature of their personalities and the structure of the tribe. The *ṣuraḥāʾ* of the tribe were usually distinguished by their bravery, generosity and protection of the weak. 'They considered nothing worse than subjugation and oppression' (Ḍayf, 1960, vol. 1, p. 69). Therefore, defending and protecting the *mustajīr* was the source of much pride and praise amongst them. One of the highest forms of praise was to depict somebody as follows: 'He is protective of the *mustajīr* and defender of morals' منيع الجار حامى الذمار (al-Andalusī, 1984, vol. 1, p. 86).

It seems that the Arabs generally took pride in this issue among other nations. According to al-Andalusī (1987, vol. 1, p. 278), when al-Nuʿmān Ibn al-Mundhir came to Khosru, king of the Persians, while many emissaries from Rome, India, and China were praising their kings and lands, al-Nuʿmān showed great pride in the Arabs and held them above all other nations for their protection of their *jār*. He noted that: 'One of them [the Arabs] may hear news that a person who had sought his protection had been harmed, perhaps far away from his land. Then he would not be content until he annihilate the tribe which had harmed the seeker of his protection or his own tribe be wiped out.'

On the other hand, mistreatment of the *mustajīr* or refusing his *jiwār* was very shameful and such persons or tribes would be subject to costly ridicule and derision in poetry. When al-Ḥuṭayᵓa wanted to insult his stepfather, the worst that he said of him was that he was from a tribe that did not protect their *mustajīr* (al-Aṣfahānī, 1983, vol. 2, p. 135):

قبَح الإلهُ قبيلةً لم يمنعوا   يوم المجيمر جارَهم من فقعسِ

May God cast ugliness on a tribe who did not protect
their *mustajīr* from Faqᶜas on the day of Mujaymir.

Abu Wāsiᶜ from Banī Asad Ibn Khuzayma derided Ibn Ḥassān in verse, saying that not only did they not protect their *mustajīr*, but he lived in fear of their treachery (al-Aṣfahānī, 1983, vol. 15, p. 91):

وما للجار حين يحل فيكم   لديكم يا بني النجار حام

يظل الجارُ مفترشا يديه   مخافتكم لدى مَلث الظلام

When the *mustajīr* comes to you
Banī al-Najjār, he finds no protector.
The *mustajīr* sleeps on his hands
in fear of you, when night falls.

The poet al-Burj Ibn Muṣhir insulted Banī Kalb after he left their *jiwār* saying sarcastically (al-Marzūqī, 1953, vol. 1, p. 359):

فنعم الحي كلبٌ غير أنا   رأينا في جوارهم هنات

فإن الغدر قد أمسى وأضحى   مقيماً بين خبت إلى المسات

The best of neighbourhoods is [the tribe of] Kalb, except that
we saw in their *jiwār*, problems.
Treachery has resided night and day
between Khabt [name of place] and al-Masāt [name of place].

How *jiwār* was contracted

If we can use the term 'contract' to describe this customary relationship, then *jiwār* as we have seen, was contracted by a clear request and answer, or by acting in a manner by which it was understood that this relationship now existed. However, the most prominent actions undertaken to request *jiwār* were tying the camel to the tent pole,[6] lowering one's spears in front of the *mujīr* until *jiwār* was granted,[7] tying the end of one's clothes to the tent,[8] mentioning the name of the *mujīr* even if that person was not present[9] and seeking refuge by the grave of a famous person.[10] The entanglement of a bucket with that of the others in the well,[11] or using the rope belonging to the others[12] sometimes obliged *jiwār*.

At times, to affirm this contract, the *mustajīr* would eat the food of his protector – as Muᶜāwiya Ibn al-Ḥārith did when he ate some dates from al-Bajlī after the latter had granted him protection (Ibn Ḥabīb, 1942, p. 208).

The contract of *jiwār* required little in the way of ceremony. The process was simple, like the lives of the Arabs in general. As soon as the *mustajīr* asked *jiwār* of a person, and the other was able to bear the consequences, he was quick to take it on, stimulated by chivalry and noble manners, and fearing ridicule and contempt if he were to refuse (Ḍayf, 1960, p. 69).

Announcing *jiwār*

As they did when disowning a member of their tribe, the Arabs would also announce their protection of individuals. The protector would announce this in the presence of an assembly, so that everyone was clear on the matter. Henceforth, that individual was in his custody and protection, equal to his blood relatives and afforded the protection of family or tribe. The tribe would ratify this in line with the individual's right to grant *jiwār*, so the *mustajīr* was now deserving of their collective protection. People would avoid harming him in any way, out of respect for the force of his protection. The announcement would usually be made in the markets and other places of assembly. To give the bond sacredness and strength people would sometimes go to the Kaᶜba and declare their *jiwār* publicly (Ibn Abī Ḥadīd, 1959, vol. 15, p. 231).

In Yathrib, as Medina was known in the *jāhiliyya* period, if a person asked their protection, they would give him an arrow and say to him: '*Qawqil*,[13] cavort with this where you will, you are safe. They may say to him *qawqil* to the top of the mountain, so this group were called the *Qawāqil*'[14] (Ibn Hishām, 1990, vol. 2, p. 280).

Rights and duties of the *mustajīr*

It is apparent that the custom of *jiwār* was a comprehensive and recognized law practised by many people in the pre-Islamic Arab world, even though no written text existed detailing this law with respect to the party seeking *jiwār*, or the party granting it. Each party knew their rights and responsibilities and abided by them. If they violated them, they understood the consequences.

Generally, the contract of *jiwār* comprised a number of rights for the *mustajīr*, guaranteed by his benefactor. Even though these rights were not written down, the Arabs were meticulous about discharging them in the best manner possible. The rights of the *mustajīr* as a result of this *jiwār* included:

- Protection: This included protection of his person, family and wealth. Hāniᵓ Ibn Masūd, head of Banī Shaybān, summarized them when he granted *jiwār* to al-Numān Ibn al-Mundhir saying: 'I am obliged to protect your honour, and I shall protect you from that which I protect myself, my family and my children, so long as there is a man left in my tribe' (al-Aṣfahānī, 1983, vol. 2, p. 104). In other words, he was taking it upon himself to protect him, even if that meant his family and tribe were wiped out, that wars flared and many were killed. The Arabs witnessed horrific wars caused by aggression against the *mustajīr*, like the war of al-Basūs which lasted 40 years.[15]

  In view of the serious consequences some tribes would decline to grant protection, when they knew that they were not able to afford it (Ibn al-Athīr, 1884, vol. 1, p. 257). Even the *mustajīr* may decline offers of protection, if he found that this was beyond the resources of his benefactors (al-Aṣfahānī, 1983, vol. 2, p. 104).
- Blood vengeance for the *mustajīr* if killed: The Arabs would seek retribution for the killing of the *mustajīr* as they would do if he was one of the true-blooded members. The tribe would seek redress from the killer even if he was one of its own *ṣuraḥāᵓ*.[16] When Qays, the brother of ᶜAwf Ibn Maṭar al-Māzinı killed the *mustajīr* of Awf treacherously to get his wife, ᶜAwf killed him in revenge for his *mustajīr* saying (Ibn Ḥabīb, 1942, p. 348):

  إني، إبْنَتَ العمرْىّ لا ثوب فاجر   لبست، ولا من غدرة أتقنع

  سعيت على قيس بذمة جاره   لأمنع عرضي إن عرضي ممنع

  I, O daughter of al-Amrī, not clothes of the corrupt have I
  put on, nor from treachery turned blind eye.
  I went against Qays with the revenge of his *mustajīr*
  to defend my honour, my honour is well-guarded.

- Seeking *diyya* [blood money] and paying it to the family of the *mustajīr*, if he was killed: *Diyya* is an amount of money paid by the killer as a fine, in punishment for his crime. This is payable if capital punishment is waived by the family of the victim. The *diyya* for the *mustajīr* was asked by the tribe in the same way as it would demand it for one of its own members (al-Balādhurī, 1996, vol. 1, p. 81).
- Preserving their wealth and recovering what had been stolen: If the *mustajīr* was wealthy and his possessions were stolen or harmed the *mujīr* would bear responsibility and compensate him for his entire loss.[17]

In return for the protection and welfare the *mustajīr* received from his benefactors while among them, he had to respect the limits of good conduct in his actions, so as not to bring the tribe that protected him into disrepute. Generally, the *mustajīr*'s personality was subsumed in that of the tribe and he become one of the tribe: 'He rises when it rises, without asking why' (Shalabī, 1974, vol. 1, p. 150); he was even sometimes attributed to his new tribe and given their name, especially if his stay was long. He had to carry out all the tasks that fell on him as an individual member of the tribe so long as he was their *mustajīr*. In other words, the *mustajīr* observed the laws of the tribe that protected him, and submitted to it as long as he was with it.

Persons from whom *jiwār* may be requested

As we have seen, *jiwār* was requested from the strong who were able to provide the protection and welfare needed by the *mustajīr*. Those who were not able to, did not take the obligation upon themselves. However, as al-Nuwayrī (1988, p. 1812) and al-Aṣfahānī (1983, vol. 22, p. 47) report, we do find some cases where *jiwār* was requested from women, especially if they belonged to powerful tribes. It was considered a compliment to the tribe's status and power, that a woman was able to provide the protection of *jiwār*.

On rare occasions people even asked for the protection of boys, due to the sheer power and status of their tribe, as al-Ḥārith Ibn Ẓālim did of the son of Abjar al-ᶜIjlī (al-Aṣfahānī, 1983, p. 1216). Such stories show the strength of this tribe and its status, where a young boy could make such a grave decision as granting protection with his tribe bearing the consequences of this decision, whatever they may be.

There are also interesting stories where a conquered tribe seeks the protection of the victorious tribe to save them from further harm and humiliation. Muḥammad Ibn Naṣr Ibn ᶜUyayna describes such a situation (al-Ṣafadī, 1931, vol. 5, p. 127):

فما برحت سمر الرماح تنوشهم　　　بأطرافها حتى استجاروا بنا منا

Points of dark spears continued to eat them
until they sought our protection, from us.

Here the poet points out that there was no tribe more powerful than his tribe, and so the conquered tribe was forced to ask their *jiwār*, even though they were enemies. In other words, this meant the complete surrender of that tribe to the victorious one.

Some people even went so far as to ask *jiwār* of *jinn* (spirits), especially when travelling in an unknown place. Al-Aṣfahānī (1961, vol. 4, p. 630) reports that when one of them 'feared the *jinn*, he would say in a loud voice: "I seek the protection of the master of this valley", and this would be for him protection'.

It seems that this case of *jiwār* was more psychological than physical, for this *jiwār* of the *jinn* would not prevent a highwayman from attacking him, killing him and taking his money. It does demonstrate, however, just how deep the principle of *jiwār* was embedded in their psyche. Wherever there was danger, it was natural to seek protection from the party able to provide it. Some went even further: when the beast of burden belonging to one traveller wandered off and he was left alone in the darkness of the night, he sang out (al-Baghdādı, 1998, vol. 5, p. 20):

تجاوزتْهُ في ليلةٍ مدلـهـمّةٍ　　　ينادي صداها ناقتي يستجيرُها

She moved past him in the dark night
he calls to her echo, my she-camel, seeking its protection.

He sought the protection of his she-camel from the night closing in on him; he needed its company to feel safe, as if he was asking her for *jiwār*. This emphasizes the psychological aspect of the custom, and the ease with which one could ask *jiwār* from those with the power and ability to give it.

The termination of *jiwār*

The tie of *jiwār* was in general temporary and not permanent. It would be dissolved for various reasons, for example when the *mustajīr* left the tribal territory, or when he gave back the protection and absolved his patron from it in public or if he did something shameful to the tribe's honour or trespassed on one of its prohibitions. In the case of aggression against the former *mustajīr*, the protector no longer carried responsibility for him (al-Andalusī, 1987, vol. 6, p. 19).

When they wished to end the *jiwār*, the tribes would give the *mustajīr* three days notice to prepare himself to leave the tribal territory. The Arabs would say he gave his *mustajīr* three days, i.e. he allowed him three days before the end of *jiwār* (al-Andalusī, 1987, vol. 6, p. 19).

Despite the chivalry and nobility demonstrated by the Arab tribes in supporting the *mustajīr* and the particular care and concern for him, his family and wealth, there are some examples of various tribes betraying the *mustajīr*, for example by stealing his money[18] (al-Baghdādı, 1998, vol. 11, p. 186) or taking revenge on him (al-Aṣfahānī, 1983, vol. 21, pp. 247–9).

Examples of such betrayal are rare compared to the vast number of examples of fulfilment, nobility, and sacrifice for the sake of the *mustajīr* and his rights. Whoever broke the contract of *jiwār* faced the worst possible criticism and ridicule in poetry, scorn, and contempt from a society that held good reputation and history in very high regard.

The continuity of the *jiwār* to the modern age

The custom of *jiwār* is still preserved and respected to some extent among Arab tribes in many parts of the Arab world. In his valuable book, Dresch (1993, p. 108) deals with this issue and reports incidents in Yemeni society which are very similar in essence to the stories detailed here. Peristiany (1966, pp. 254–5) also elaborates on the issue of honour and shame and its impact on *jiwār* in the life of the Arab tribes of western Egypt. His work makes it clear that there are great similarities between the way the Arabs of the *jāhiliyya* dealt with the issue of *jiwār* and the way the contemporary Arab tribes do so.

However, *jiwār* in the *jāhiliyya* was a common customary practice, which continued afterwards. But how did the Prophet and his companions deal with this custom? Did they fight against it? Or adopt it as an Islamic tradition? The next chapter is dedicated to answering these and other questions.

2

JIWĀR IN THE ISLAMIC TRADITION IN THE MECCAN PERIOD

The essence of *jiwār* in the *jāhiliyya* was the provision of protection. Indeed, were we to undertake an examination of asylum throughout history, the provision of protection would surely emerge as a core issue and common factor in all such cases. However, it is crucial to find out how the concept of *jiwār* was affected by the advent of Islam in Mecca through the practise of the Prophet and his companions.

The Prophet was born an orphan and badly needed protection throughout his thorny mission. God provided His Prophet with His protection from birth, through the people who surrounded him in the different stages of his life, not through miracles. The Prophet, however, after the revelation, tried to gain protection from the Arab tribes, for example through his migration to al-Ṭāif, the migration of his companions to Abyssinia and the collective migration of the Muslims to Medina.

Heaven's protection of the Prophet

Prophecy by its very nature requires a comprehensive revolution in people's beliefs, visions and fundamental principles. Such revelations are usually met with varying degrees of rejection, depending on the society and the ideological, economic, political and social conditions.

Very often this rejection was translated into different forms of insult, abuse, offence, torture and, in some extreme circumstances, death, as the Qurʾān (3:21) tells. Therefore, it was essential for those who undertook this tremendously thorny mission to be psychologically, spiritually and physically qualified to cope with the potentially harmful consequences.

For His part, God, the divine source of the prophecy, would prepare the conditions and qualify His prophets for the mission they were to undertake. God not only protected and took care of His prophets during their mission, but also during their childhood. For example, God protected the prophet Moses from Pharaoh, who would kill the newborn children of the Israelites, by making the Pharaoh himself the guardian and protector of Moses (al-Ṭabarī, n.d., vol. 1, pp. 231–6).

In the case of the Prophet Muḥammad, God began His protection of him by preparing the conditions for his mission long before his actual birth. Choosing him to be from among the noblest families in Mecca and a descendant of the prophet Ibrāhīm was the beginning.

The genealogical tree of the Prophet Muḥammad stretches back to the prophet Ismā^{c}īl, the son of Ibrāhīm. This was emphasized in the *ḥadīth* narrated by al-Ḥākim (1990, vol. 2, p. 602): 'I am the son of the two slaughtered.' The two slaughtered to whom he refers are his father ^{c}Abdullah and the prophet Ismā^{c}īl.

The issue of genealogy played a significant role in Mecca's hierarchical society in the time of the Prophet. Some of the masters in Mecca rejected Islam on the grounds that it treated masters and slaves as equals. As the Qur'an records (26:111): 'They answered: "Shall we place our faith in thee, even though [only] the most abject [of people] follow thee?"'

This hierarchical system played an important role in protecting the Prophet from the polytheists of Mecca on many occasions.

The story of the Prophet's father, ^{c}Abdullah, and his father, ^{c}Abd al-Muṭṭalib, was not far removed from the preparations God had arranged for His Prophet. ^{c}Abd al-Muṭṭalib made a commitment to slaughter the tenth child should God give him ten children. When God gave him what he wanted, he was obliged to fulfil his promise. The tenth was ^{c}Abdullah, the father of the Prophet, the most beloved of his children. The elite of Quraysh – the tribe to which the Prophet belonged, and a dominant tribe in Mecca – rescued the situation by advising him to slaughter 100 camels instead. After this incident the love of ^{c}Abdullah increased not only in the heart of ^{c}Abd al-Muṭṭalib, but in the hearts of all people in Mecca. Therefore, when ^{c}Abdullah died in Medina at the age of 25, ^{c}Abd al-Muṭṭalib was 'saddened very much' as Ibn Sa^{c}d (n.d., vol. 1, p. 99) narrates. When the Prophet was born months later he was already an orphan, but all the love of his father was later transmitted to him and eventually played a significant role in his life, especially in protecting him after the revelation.

Even before the Prophet was born, heaven was caring for him and his mother. As his mother told, she felt no tiredness during her pregnancy. 'All she noticed, and by which she knew she was pregnant, was that her period interrupted and somebody came to her while she was half asleep and asked her whether she was pregnant and she said I do not know, then he told her that you are pregnant with the master and the Prophet of this nation' (Ibn Sa^c^d, n.d., vol. 1, p. 98). When she gave birth to the Prophet, a flood of light came out with him and lit between east and west (Ibn Sa^c^d, n.d., vol. 1, p. 102).

God's blessings continued to surround the Prophet after his birth and into the foster period. The Arabs in Mecca at that time would send their newborn baby boys to women fosterers in the desert, believing that the children would grow up stronger, sharper in their intelligence and more eloquent. It was also said they did this because they considered it shameful that the mother only should nurture the child (al-Ḥalabī, n.d., vol. 1, p. 146).

Some of the Arab tribes in the desert were well known for their eloquence. Banī Sa^c^d, the tribe that the Prophet was raised amongst, were especially renowned for their eloquence. The Prophet later expressed his pride to his companions that he had been fostered in Banī Sad and would say: 'I am the most eloquent of you, I am from Quraysh and I was fostered in Banī Sa^c^d' (Ibn Kathīr, n.d., vol. 2, p. 277).

Thus, the choice of Ḥalīma from Banī Sa^c^d to foster and raise him was a very important qualification for the Prophet and one he would very much need in a society that valued eloquence, articulacy, fluency and poetry so highly.

As he was an orphan with no father to offer generous rewards, Ḥalīma was initially hesitant to foster the Prophet and wondered: 'What good rewards would his mother give her?' (Ibn Isḥāq, n.d. vol. 1, p. 26). Finally, though, not wanting to return to her tribe without a baby, Ḥalīma agreed to take him and it seems she began to feel the blessings of fostering the Prophet from the first moment. Her breasts filled with milk such that this baby and her own child drank till they were sated. Their goat's dug was full and even their lazy donkey became very strong and worked harder than the others for the first time in his life (Ibn Isḥāq, n.d., vol. 1, p. 26).

When Ḥalīma's husband saw this he realized that all these blessings were because of the child they had taken in. He said to her: 'O Ḥalīma, by God you have taken a very blessed soul' (Ibn Isḥāq, n.d., vol. 1, p. 26). The continuous blessings that shadowed Ḥalīma's house in particular after they returned to their tribe increased her love and care to the Prophet.

An incident which happened to the Prophet when he was two years old led Ḥalīma to decide to return the Prophet to his mother. The incident, as narrated by Ibn Isḥāq (n.d., vol. 1, p. 27), was strange by any standard. While the Prophet was playing with other children, two angels in the shape of men came and took him away. They opened his heart and took out a small black clot, then washed his heart and replaced it in his body (Ibn Isḥāq, n.d., vol. 1, p. 27).

Ḥalīma was frightened when her son told her what had happened and she decided that he should go back to his real mother. At the same time, however, she was reluctant to return him because of the blessings she had enjoyed while he was in her care. When Ḥalīma told the Prophet's mother, Āmina, what had happened, Āmina said: 'Ney, by God, the devil has nothing to do with him; my son will have a great status' (Ibn Isḥaq, n.d., vol. 1, p. 27).

The act of opening the Prophet's heart and removing the black clot, symbolizing evil, is evidence of heaven's nurturing of the Prophet to prepare him for his mission. As a result, Satan – the first enemy of the Prophet – has nothing to do with him, and has no power to seduce him or cause him to deviate from the right path. This is obviously one of the central means of protecting the Prophet. It was narrated that the Prophet said to his companions: 'None of you but has accompanying Satan. They said: and you O Prophet? He said: and me but God helped me, so I am saved' ولكن الله أعانني عليه فأسلمُ (Ibn Kathīr, n.d., vol. 1, p. 67) and in another narration there is an extra paragraph which says: 'And he does not whisper to me but good things' فلا يأمرني إلا بخير (Al-Naysābūri, 1990, vol. 4, p. 2167). In the latter narration the word فأسلَم does not mean 'to be saved', but that his Satan has become a Muslim so he whispers only good things to him.

This matter was obvious in the life of the Prophet, particularly in his youth before the mission in Mecca. God safeguarded him not only from the doing but also from the intention to do what the youth in Mecca did at that time. Al-Ṭabarī narrates a *ḥadīth* on the authority of the Prophet which confirms this fact: 'I never intended to do something of what the ignorant people used to do except two times, in which God prevented me from doing what I was intending to do' (al-Ṭabarī, 1984, vol. 1, p. 520). He mentions the two cases,[1] and after that he was never tempted to do anything wrong until he was honoured by God's mission.

The protection of ᶜAbd al-Muṭṭalib

After Ḥalīma al-Saᶜdiyya returned the Prophet to his mother, he lived with her until her death when he was six years old. It was natural that ᶜAbd al-Muṭṭalib would take care of him. Ibn Saᶜd narrates that: 'ᶜAbd al-Muṭṭalib loved him more than his sons, he used to get him close to him. The Prophet was the only person who could enter to ᶜAbd al-Muṭṭalib when he sits alone. Moreover, ᶜAbd al-Muṭṭalib used not to eat until the Prophet joins him' (Ibn Saᶜd, n.d., vol. 1, p. 118).

ᶜAbd al-Muṭṭalib's love of the Prophet was increased by something a group of Banī Mudlaj had said to him. They told him to take very good care of the Prophet as: 'We have never seen a foot as similar to the foot in *al-Maqām*[2] as Muḥammad's' (Ibn Saᶜd, vol. 1, p. 118). ᶜAbd al-Muṭṭalib also heard that the Jews said Muḥammad was the prophet of his nation and so he ordered his nurse Um Ayman not to take her eyes off the Prophet.

When death approached, ᶜAbd al-Muṭṭalib entrusted the Prophet's care to Abu Ṭālib. The Prophet was eight years old when his grandfather passed away.

The protection of Abu Ṭālib

Following the death of ᶜAbd al-Muṭṭalib, the Prophet joined his uncle's family. Abu Ṭālib acted precisely according to his father's instructions and took very good care of the Prophet. He loved him more than his sons and would not sleep unless the Prophet was beside him. When Abu Ṭālib went out the Prophet would usually accompany him. 'Abu Ṭālib [also] used to particularize him with food and special care' (Ibn Saᶜd n.d., vol. 1, p. 119).

When the Prophet was twelve years old, he accompanied Abu Ṭālib on a trading journey to Syria. On their way they met Baḥīra, the saint. When Baḥīra saw the Prophet he recognized the marks of prophecy, which Baḥīra knew very well through his readings of the Old Testament. When Baḥīra was sure that this was the expected prophet, he told Abu Ṭālib to 'take the Prophet back to Mecca and to be careful of the Jews. By God, should they see him and recognize what I recognized they would harm him' (al-Ṭabarī, 1986, vol. 1, p. 519). This incident made Abu Ṭālib more careful and vigilant than ever towards the Prophet and his protection of him continued until his death.

Even after God commissioned his Prophet with his mission, Abu Ṭālib stood by him shielding, defending and protecting him with all the means at his disposal. When a delegate of Quraysh came to Abu Ṭālib complaining about the Prophet and his preaching, Abu Ṭālib said to the Prophet: 'O my brother's son, do say whatever you like, by God I will never disappoint you' (al-Ṭabarī, 1986, vol. 1, p. 545). When Quraysh intensified their pressure on the Muslims, Abu Ṭālib called on his tribe, Banī Hāshim, to protect the Prophet.

The Prophet understood the full benefit of Abu Ṭālib's protection soon after he died. One day, while the Prophet was travelling home, a thug threw sand on him. His daughter started to cry while she cleaned the sand away, but the Prophet said: 'O my daughter, do not cry. God will protect your father. Quraysh could not reach me by something I hate until Abu Ṭālib died' (Ibn Hishām, 1990, vol. 2, p. 264).

This is perhaps the first time the Prophet mentions that God will protect him, meaning God will prevent Quraysh from killing him, but not from harming him. The offences and insults from the Quraysh escalated dramatically after Abu Ṭālib's death, so that the Prophet said: 'O uncle, how quickly I missed you' (al-Ḥalabī, n.d., vol. 2, p. 50).

These words reached Abu Lahab, the Prophet's uncle, who decided to protect him and said: 'O Muḥammad, do whatever you want as you used to do when Abu Ṭālib was alive. By Allāt and ᶜUzzā no one will harm you until I die' (Ibn Saᶜd, n.d., vol. 1, p. 210), and he protected him for several days.

However Quraysh began to goad Abu Lahab, claiming that the Prophet had said his father was in hellfire. When he asked the Prophet if he had actually said this and the Prophet said yes, Abu Lahab said: 'I will be your enemy as long as you say ᶜAbd al-Muṭṭlib is in the hellfire' (Ibn Saᶜd, n.d., vol. 1, p. 211), and he ended his protection.

The vulnerability of the Prophet, his status as orphan and his need for protection at different stages of his life ensured that the values of mercy and protection were deeply entrenched in him. Certainly, the difficult experiences he endured helped him to understand the needs of the destitute, the weak and those requiring protection. Finally, if we were to call the seeker of protection an asylum seeker then Prophet Muḥammad was the first asylum seeker in Islam.

Under enormous pressure from Quraysh, eventually the Prophet decided to go to al-Ṭāʾif in an attempt to find shelter and a protector should the people there follow him.

The journey of the Prophet to al-Ṭāʾif

With the death of Abu Ṭālib and Khadīja, the Prophet's wife, within a month of each other, 'two disasters ... gathered on the Prophet. He stayed at his home and got out rarely' (Ibn Saᶜd, n.d., vol. 1, p. 211). The Quraysh were now in a position to harm him in a way that they could not have hoped for while Abu Ṭālib was alive. The Prophet lost the safety and the economic security provided by Abu Ṭālib and Khadīja respectively. He became vulnerable and subject to torture and harassment by the non-believers in Mecca, especially when Abu Lahab ended the protection he had offered the Prophet for a few days after Abu Ṭālib's death. The suffering of the Prophet and of the Muslims was unprecedented and the Prophet named this time 'the year of sadness', as al-Ḥalabī transmits (1979, vol. 3, p. 498).

Despite the torment and anguish faced by the Prophet in Mecca, he continued to speak out to the tribes about his new religion. None of them, however, was convinced and they would say: 'His people know him better, and how would he straighten us who distorted his people?' (Ibn ᶜAbd al-Barr, 1982, vol. 1, p. 62). The Prophet then decided to go to al-Ṭāʾif, seeking protection and support.

He set out for al-Ṭāʾif in search of the help and protection of the tribe of Thaqīf, hoping that they would accept what God had sent him with. He set out by himself according to the narration of Ibn Isḥāq, while Ibn Saᶜd says he went out 'with Zayd Ibn Hāritha in the tenth year of his mission' (Ibn Saᶜd, n.d., vol. 1, p. 211).

After meeting and preaching to the three masters of Thaqīf, the Prophet asked them to convert to Islam and support him in delivering his massage (al-Ṭabarī, 1986, vol. 1, p. 554). In seeking the *jiwār* of Thaqīf, the Prophet was not looking out for his personal protection and welfare only. He was asking them to follow his religion and to fight with him against those who opposed and oppressed him.

The elite of Thaqīf understood what the Prophet was asking and what the consequences of their acceptance would be, particularly the price of supporting him against Quraysh, the most powerful tribe in Mecca. They refused to follow his religion and gave him a harsh reply (al-Ṭabarī, 1986, vol. 1, p. 554).

When the Prophet heard their answer he asked them to 'keep what happened a secret' (Ibn Kathīr, n.d., vol. 3, p. 235). He did not want Quraysh to hear about it because he feared that this would encourage them to increase their attacks on him.

However, the three masters of Thaqīf not only revealed the secret, but ordered the Prophet to 'get out of our country and go to a land where you can be saved' (al-Ḥalabī, n.d., vol. 2, p. 52). 'They feared that he would spoil their youth' if he stayed there, as Ibn Saᶜd (n.d., vol. 1, p. 212) says. They feared that some of their younger members might convert to Muḥammad's religion and eventually offer him *jiwār*. The right to grant *jiwār* was guaranteed for all the freemen in the tribe and, if it was given, the whole tribe would be obliged to defend Muḥammad and protect him.

Moreover, they urged their thugs and slaves to abuse and harass him: 'they stoned him until they had blooded his feet. Meanwhile, Zayd kept trying to shield him with his body until he was injured in his head' (Ibn Saᶜd, n.d., vol. 1, p. 212).

Eventually the Prophet managed to escape to a vineyard belonging to ᶜUtba and Shayba Ibn Rabīᶜa. Here he made an impressive, powerful prayer asking God to help him. The prayer was extremely telling and explained much about the painful and traumatic situation the Prophet found himself in (Ibn Kathīr, n.d., vol. 3, p. 136). 'No man or a woman of Thaqīf believed him', as Ibn Saᶜd says (n.d., vol. 1, p. 212) and there was no glimpse of human support, especially after his relatives became his enemies and Thaqīf refused to give him *jiwār*. There was no one left to seek *jiwār*, refuge and mercy from, except God.

This was the most difficult day the Prophet ever faced, as he himself revealed to ᶜĀʾisha when she asked him whether he had ever faced a day more terrible than the day of Uḥud (al-Bukhārī, 1986, vol. 3, p. 1180).

However, when Rabīᶜa and Shayba saw him they sympathized with him, as they were relatives from the same tribe. They sent their Christian slave called ᶜAddās with grapes for the Prophet.

After that the Prophet moved to a place called Nakhla, close to Mecca, and 'stayed there for some days' (Ibn Saᶜd, n.d., vol. 1, p. 212). One night while he was praying, a group of spirits came across him and listened to the Qurʾān. The spirits believed in the Prophet and went to their people as warners, as the Qurʾān states (46:29).

Moreover, God sent the angel of the mountains to the Prophet, ordering him to follow the instructions of the Prophet even if it was to collapse the two mountains of Mecca on the heads of its people. But the Prophet said: 'I hope that God will bring out of them who worship God and make no partner with Him' (al-Bukhārī, 1986, vol. 3, p. 1180).

It could be that God wanted to tell the Prophet through these incidents that He and His angels were with him and supported him. The message was that if the elite of Thaqīf did not believe in you, but the poor people and the spirits believe in you, then your mission is not a failure. It could also be said that God might have wanted to raise the morale of the Prophet when he was in a desperate situation after humans had let him down.

However, on their way back to Mecca, Zayd asked the Prophet: 'How would you enter Mecca after they had expelled you? (Ibn Saᶜd, n.d., vol. 1, p. 212). Although Quraysh did not force him to leave and accordingly he still had the right to return, Zayd meant (as al-Ḥalabī comments) 'their aggravation and harassment were the reason behind your departure' (al-Ḥalabī, 1979, vol. 2, p. 62). The Prophet replied: 'God will ease things and make a way out of it. God will elevate his religion and support his Prophet' (Ibn Saᶜd, n.d., vol. 1, p. 213).

Zayd's question emphasizes that the Prophet's journey to al-Ṭāʾif was considered by Quraysh as a de facto rebellion, a kind of declaration of war by seeking support from another tribe to fight his own. The Prophet knew this well, and knew that he could not re-enter Mecca without *jiwār*.

Thus, he sent a messenger called Urayqiṭ to al-Akhnas Ibn Shurayq with a clear message: 'Muḥammad asks you: Would you be my *mujīr* until I deliver the message of my Lord?' (al-Ṭabarī, 1986, vol. 1 p. 555). The message was brief but it contained two important points. The first was that the Prophet had not lost hope of convincing Quraysh of his message. He was trying to return to Mecca in such a way as to preach to them again. The second point was that the Prophet was more concerned about delivering his message than he was about his personal safety. This explains his request that the *mujīr* protect him until he had delivered God's message. To do this, the *mujīr* would have to be strong enough to face the powerful Quraysh elite.

This was beyond the powers of Ibn Shurayq, who replied: 'The *ḥalīf* of Quraysh does not give *jiwār* against the *ṣamīm*[3] of Quraysh' (Ibn Kathīr, n.d., vol. 3, p. 137).

Hence, Ibn Shurayq, the *ḥalīf* of Quraysh, could not give *jiwār* to the Prophet against Quraysh, the powerful tribe whom he made *ḥilf* with because of his need of their power. Therefore, he could not provide the Prophet with the protection he needed.

The Prophet then sent Urayqiṭ to Suhayl Ibn ᶜAmr, requesting his *jiwār*, but Suhayl replied: 'Banī ᶜĀmir Ibn Luᵓay do not give *jiwār* against Banī Kaᶜb Ibn Luᵓay' (Ibn Kathīr, n.d., vol. 3, p. 137). This again shows the nature of tribal relations and the importance of lineage at that time. Ibn ᶜĀmir could not give *jiwār* because Banī ᶜĀmir and Banī Kaᶜb were of the same origin and had the same grandfather, and therefore they could not be in a position to fight each other should there be a need to defend the *mustajīr*, as the customs of *jiwār* compel.

The third trial of the Prophet in seeking *jiwār* was to ask al-Muṭᶜim Ibn Adyy. He sent Urayqiṭ to al-Muṭᶜim with the same message and al-Muṭᶜim accepted. So, the Prophet went to him and spent that night at his home.

Next day, al-Muṭᶜim went out with his sons carrying their weapons and 'called upon his tribe that he had given *jiwār* to the Prophet' (Ibn Saᶜd, n.d., vol. 1, p. 212). Then they entered the Kaᶜba and told the Prophet to make his *ṭawāf*, circumambulations. Hurriedly, Abu Sufyān[4] came to al-Muṭᶜim and asked him whether he was a *mujīr* or a follower. Al-Muṭᶜim said: 'I am a *mujīr*.' Abu Sufyān replied: 'Then your [*jiwār*] will not be disrespected' (Ibn Kathīr, n.d., vol. 3, p. 137).

This question and answer reflect the deep and significant changes that took place in Meccan society with regard to the principle of *jiwār* after the advent of Islam. By asking al-Muṭᶜim that question, Abu Sufyān wanted to say: If you are a follower of Muḥammad then your *jiwār* is void, but if you are not, then your *jiwār* is respected and your *mustajīr* is protected.

This means that those who became Muslims would lose most of, if not all, their tribal rights and, especially, the right to grant *jiwār*. The Muslims were treated as if they were *ṣaᶜālīk* or rebels against society. They did not worship the idols of Mecca and hence they were outside society and had no rights at all, especially the right to be protected by the tribe, let alone grant protection to others.

The other point worthy of note is the central place the principle of *jiwār* occupied in this society. Despite their bitter enmity towards the Prophet, especially after his trip to al-Ṭāᵓif looking for support against them, Quraysh could not do anything to the Prophet when he received the *jiwār* of al-Muṭᶜim.

The *jiwār* of al-Muṭᶜim included protection not only against physical harm, but also verbal abuse. When they were at the Kaᶜba, al-Muṭᶜim rose on his horse and shouted: 'O the people of Quraysh, I have granted my *jiwār* to Muḥammad, so nobody deride him' (Ibn Saᶜd, n.d., vol. 1, p. 213).

Al-Muṭᶜim's noble stance was remembered by the Prophet and the Muslims in general. When the Muslims captured some prisoners of Quraysh after the war of Badr, the Prophet said in an indication of his thankfulness to al-Muṭᶜim: 'Had al-Muṭᶜim been alive and asked me to release them I would have done so' (al-Bukhārī, 1986, vol. 2, p. 305).

In seeking the protection of non-Muslims, the Prophet shows that Islam does not reject the well-established principle of *jiwār*. On the contrary, this affirms that the custom of *jiwār* was legalized by the Prophet, on the condition that this *jiwār* does not contradict the principles of Islam.

Moreover, the attempts of the Prophet to seek *jiwār* of al-Akhnas Ibn Shurayq and Suhayl Ibn ᶜAmr and their refusal to grant him *jiwār* indicate the structure of the Arab tribes and the rules governing relations between them in regard to the custom of *jiwār*. However, al-Muṭᶜim's agreement to grant the Prophet his *jiwār* and the acceptance of this by Quraysh, despite their enmity towards the Prophet, emphasize the central place the custom occupied in that society.

Nonetheless, after the advent of Islam some significant changes altered the custom of *jiwār*. The outward form of the process remained intact, but the essence of *jiwār* and the deal done between the *mujīr* and the *mustajīr* was altered. Previously, the *mujīr* would give protection, relief and care. In return he gained fame and good reputation. After the advent of Islam, the *mujīr* was offered something extra in return for his *jiwār*. In addition to fame, he was promised entry to Paradise, should he accept Islam, in exchange for his *jiwār*. This new deal was revolutionary to the tribesmen who were accustomed to receiving the bounty of their *jiwār* immediately, through verses of poetry that spread rapidly throughout the tribes.

The migration to Abyssinia

As the harassment, torture and abuse of the Quraysh increased, the search for protection by the Prophet and his companions intensified. A quick overview of the *sīra* books gives us a sense of the important role the two migrations to Abyssinia played in the life of the Muslims in Mecca. The migration to Abyssinia was the first collective migration in Islam. It was only when they migrated to Abyssinia that those Muslims could worship openly, without fear or intimidation.

The circumstances that drove Muslims to migrate to Abyssinia

Despite the fact the Prophet was safe and protected by his uncle Abu Ṭālib, he did not feel comfortable. His followers were harassed and tortured day and night and he was incapable of protecting them. Thus he gave them permission to migrate to Abyssinia saying: 'If you were to go to Abyssinia you will find a king under whom nobody is oppressed, and it is a land of truth, [stay there] until God grants an ease for you' (Ibn Hishām, 1990, vol 2., p. 164).

The Muslims fled to Abyssinia individually and in groups, to escape the torment they faced in Mecca. Some of them took their wives, while others migrated alone. In total, eleven men and four women undertook the first migration in Islam.

There is some dispute among the scholars as to who the very first migrant was, although most of them agree that ᶜUthmān Ibn ᶜAffān and his wife Ruqayya, the daughter of the Prophet, were the first to migrate.[5]

Ibn Saᶜd (n.d., vol. 1, p. 204) says that they set out to Abyssinia in the fifth year of the Prophet's mission, in the month of Rajab.[6] Once they got to the coast they found two trading ships travelling towards Abyssinia. The captains agreed to take them across the sea for half a Dīnār. Upon hearing that they had fled Quraysh followed them to the coast, but could not catch up with them.

When the Muslims reached Abyssinia, al-Najāshī gave them his *jiwār*. For the first time, they felt secure and could worship without fear. They showed their appreciation to al-Najāshī, and wished their fellow Muslims in Mecca could be with them.

The delegation of Quraysh to al-Najāshī

The news that Muslims were living in safety and security in Abyssinia was not welcomed by the Quraysh elite. They wanted to bring them back to Mecca and force them to abandon Islam. After discussing this matter among themselves, they decided to send a delegation to al-Najāshī consisting of ᶜAbdullah Ibn Abī Rabīᶜa and Amr Ibn al-ᶜĀṣ. The aim of this delegation was to persuade al-Najāshī to hand the Muslims over to Quraysh. The delegation took valuable presents not only to al-Najāshī but to all the cardinals surrounding him.

As soon as the delegation arrived in Abyssinia, they gave the cardinals their presents and revealed their intentions. The cardinals agreed to help them. When they met al-Najāshī and gave him their gifts, they started to explain their mission. They told him that the Muslims were scurrilous people who had rejected their religion and mocked their Gods, and at the same time did not follow his religion.

The king listened attentively until they had finished. He then told them that he would not hand over those who had asked for his *jiwār* and preferred his country to any other country, until he had questioned them about the delegation's claims. If they were as the delegation alleged, then he would return the Muslims to Mecca. Otherwise he would protect them and grant them *jiwār* as long as they were in his country.

When the Muslims were told they were to meet al-Najāshī for this reason, they gathered to discuss what they should say to him. Finally, they decided to tell him what the Prophet taught and ordered them regardless of whatever may happen.

This decision is significant. It shows how the principle of *jiwār* was affected by the new religion. It shows the insistence and resolve of the Muslims to say what they believed in regardless of whether or not this belief would impinge on the *jiwār*. Their faith came first for them, and whether or not this would offend al-Najāshī, the *mustajīr*, was another issue. They understood the consequences very well. They knew that al-Najāshī would send them back to Mecca if he was not happy with their answer, but they resolved to say what they believed in.

When the Muslims stood before al-Najāshī, he quizzed them about this new religion that made them abandon the worship of the idols and at the same time prevented them from converting to his religion. Jaᶜfar Ibn Abu Ṭālib, the spokesman of the Muslims there, made a powerful presentation explaining why they followed the Prophet and describing the harassment of the Quraysh that drove them to migrate to Najāshī's country to seek his *jiwār* in the hope that they would not be oppressed in his land.

Al-Najashī was deeply affected, especially after he had listened to some verses of the Qurʾān. When Jaᶜfar finished reciting al-Najāshī said: 'This and what Jesus came with, come from one lantern. Go free, by God, I will not hand them over to you (the Meccan delegation)' (Ibn Hishām, 1990, vol. 2, p. 180).

Next day, the delegation came back to al-Najāshī in a second attempt to turn him against the Muslims. They told him that the Muslims believed Jesus to be a slave of God and not a son of God, as al-Najāshī believed.

Once again al-Najāshī called upon the Muslims to explain these claims. Though mindful of the potentially disastrous consequences, the Muslims decided to tell al-Najāshī what they believed in regardless, of whether or not this would displease him.

With all his cardinals surrounding him, al-Najāshī asked the Muslims about Jesus. Without hesitation, Ja^{c}far replied: 'He is a slave of God, His messenger and His word that He cast into the virgin and worshipper Maryam' (Ibn Hishām 1990, vol. 2, p. 180).

Yet again, the Muslims emphasized that belief had priority over anything else and *jiwār* should not compromise the faith. Otherwise it should be ended – whatever the price to be paid.

The Muslims remained in Abyssinia in safety and security in the *jiwār* of al-Najāshī until they heard the story of *al-Gharānīq* and the conversion of the Quraysh to Islam. They took the decision to return to Mecca three months after their migration to Abyssinia.

When they got closer to Mecca they found out the truth. After discussions as to whether to go back to Abyssinia or enter Mecca, they chose the latter option. However, they could not do this without *jiwār* from the people of Mecca, as they were still wanted by Quraysh.

Most of them sought *jiwār* and entered Mecca. ^{c}Uthmān Ibn Maẓ^{c}ūn was granted the *jiwār* of al-Walīd Ibn al-Mughīra. Nevertheless, when he felt that he could come and go securely and without fear, while his fellow Muslims were tortured and harassed, he felt ashamed and he decided to give back *jiwār* to al-Walīd.

Al-Walīd was amazed and asked if anybody had harmed him. ^{c}Uthmān said: 'No, but I am satisfied with the *jiwār* of God and I do not want *jiwār* from anybody else' (Ibn Hishām 1990, vol. 2, p. 214). Then al-Walīd asked him to state this publicly, as he had granted him his *jiwār* publicly. When they got to the Ka^{c}ba, al-Walīd stated that ^{c}Uthmān wanted to give back his *jiwār*. ^{c}Uthmān said: 'He is right, I have found him sincere and generous to his *mustajīr*, but I liked not to ask *jiwār* except from God, so I give him back his *jiwār* (Ibn Hishām 1990, vol. 2, p. 214).

Some days later, ^{c}Uthmān quarrelled with some people of Quraysh over a matter of faith and was injured in the eye. Al-Walīd was in the area and saw what happened to ^{c}Uthmān. Indirectly, he blamed him. He told ^{c}Uthmān that this would not have happened if he had remained in a secure *jiwār*. ^{c}Uthmān replied that his second eye was in sore need of what had happened to the first eye, and that he was in the *jiwār* of the One, More Powerful and More Glorified. Al-Walīd once again offered his *jiwār* to ^{c}Uthmān, but he refused.

Clearly, ᶜUthmān did not reject the *jiwār* of al-Walīd because a new Islamic legislation had emerged. He refused it because he wanted to feel like his fellow Muslims who were being tortured in Mecca. This in itself indicates the strong bonds Islam had created among its followers. These emotional bonds were stronger than tribal ties and blood lineage. This was the real revolution that the society was experiencing.

Another important aspect of this account is the fact that the Muslims continued to deal with the mechanism and formalities of *jiwār* in the same way the Arabs had. ᶜUthmān accepted *jiwār* and later went to the Kaᶜba and publicly released al-Walīd from the responsibility of *jiwār*. In other words, the changes that Islam had applied to *jiwār* were not in the form, or the rights and duties, but in the sense that the principle itself should not contradict the Islamic faith.

Abu Bakr accepts the *jiwār* of Ibn al-Dighna

Another example of a high-profile Muslim accepting the *jiwār* of a non-Muslim is Abu Bakr. The second person after the Prophet to lead the Muslims, his faith according to ᶜUmar Ibn al-Khaṭṭāb (al-Dhahabī, 2000, vol. 8, p. 405) would be heavier than that of the whole nation if it were to be weighed.

Like the Prophet and other Muslims, Abu Bakr was harassed and persecuted by Quraysh because of his conversion. He asked the Prophet's permission to migrate and the Prophet gave it. Abu Bakr left Mecca and after two days of travel, he met Ibn al-Dighna who asked him where he was going. Abu Bakr explained that his people had harmed him and that he was leaving Mecca. Ibn al-Dighna exclaimed that Abu Bakr was a noble man who helped the needy and treated everybody well. Eventually, he offered him his *jiwār*. Abu Bakr accepted and they returned to Mecca together.

Upon their arrival in Mecca, Ibn al-Dighna announced that he had granted his *jiwār* to Abu Bakr and that nobody should do him any harm. Accordingly, Quraysh stopped harming him.

Things progressed peacefully until the elite of Quraysh complained to Ibn al-Dighna that Abu Bakr had harmed them by his prayers. They told him that the prayer room Abu Bakr had established outside his home had become a focal point for their children, women and slaves, and that they were afraid Abu Bakr would spoil them. Ibn al-Dighna went to Abu Bakr to discuss the complaint. He asked him to either pray inside his home or to give back his *jiwār*. Without hesitation, Abu Bakr renounced his *jiwār* and told him that he would be satisfied with God's *jiwār*. Instantly, Ibn al-Dighna announced that he was no longer the *mujīr* of Abu Bakr.

Again, this example underlines the acceptance of *jiwār* by different Muslims. Moreover, the Muslims adhered to the conditions of the *mujīr* and in case of dispute they were more than willing to give back the *jiwār*.

It is worthy of note that the Prophet's permission to the Muslims to migrate was an Islamic legislation of immigration to seek protection in non-Muslim countries when oppression and injustice occurred. However, this migration should not compromise the faith and if there was a contradiction between them, the faith should take priority.

On the other hand, Muslims should fulfil their promises and adhere to the conditions of the protection contract as far as these conditions were acceptable in Islam.

Another important aspect of this story is the migration of women alongside their men. Ibn ᶜAbd al-Barr (1982, vol. 1, p. 49) narrates that Ḥudhayfa Ibn ᶜUtba Ibn Rabīᶜa fled with his wife, Sahla Bint Suhayl Ibn ᶜAmr, from her father, fearing for their religion.

This indicates that women were not migrating simply because their husbands were. On the contrary, they were fully aware of what they were doing. Sahla challenged her father when she converted to Islam and challenged him again when she migrated to find a place where she could worship without fear.

This shift in attitudes to women in the *jāhilī* society, which, according to some sources,[7] considered women a property to be inherited after the death of her husband, could be attributed to the moral and intellectual revolution Islam had brought about among its followers in a very short time.

This was the first time the Arabs witnessed women migrate in search of justice. The thorough search of the sources I have conducted has not revealed an example in Arab life before Islam of a woman migrating in search of *jiwār* from another tribe.

Ibn Kathīr makes reference to another case that emphasizes this understanding, that of Um ᶜAbdullah Bint Ḥarmala. She and her husband decided to migrate to Abyssinia. One day, as she was preparing to set out and her husband, ᶜĀmir, had gone off to fetch something, ᶜUmar Ibn al-Khaṭṭāb came along. Noticing that they were preparing to travel, he asked her what was going on. Without hesitation, she replied: 'Yes, by God we will go out to a place in God's earth until God grants us a way out of this. You have harmed and oppressed us' (Ibn Kathīr, 1964, vol. 3, p. 78).

Clearly, she was fully aware of the implications of her acts. She was migrating for God's sake to find a place where she could worship without fear. This was something the Arabs had not witnessed in the *jāhiliyya*.

It can safely be concluded that the Islamic tradition rejects oppression and tyranny and calls for freedom and protection. If this protection is not available in a particular place, the oppressed should migrate to a safer place. The Prophet's order to his companions to migrate to Abyssinia formed a clear Islamic legislation of migration to non-Muslim countries. It is true that the Arabs of the Peninsula would move from one place to another due to the nature of Bedouin life, and in some cases to seek *jiwār*. But this collective migration was the first in Islam and it is the precedent that made the *jāhilī* custom an Islamic one. The Prophet, in giving permission to his followers to migrate, was legalizing the migration of oppressed people to any place where there was justice. Moreover, this legislation was not only for the Muslims at that time, but for all Muslims until the Day of Judgement.

In another sense, this legislation imposes heavy duties on the Islamic state. The early Muslims tasted torment and knew what oppression was. Their state should not only be free of any kind of oppression, suppression and tyranny, but should be ready to do whatever it could to protect the weak and the oppressed and be a safe haven for those seeking protection. Many verses and *ḥadīths* stress that God does not like oppressors: 'God does not love oppressors' (Q. 3:57). In the *ḥadīth Qudsī* God says: 'O My slaves, I have forbidden oppression for Myself and have made it forbidden amongst you, so do not oppress one another' (Muslim, n.d., vol. 4, p. 1994).

The migration to Medina

When ᶜUmar Ibn al-Khaṭṭāb convened a meeting of the elite of the companions to decide upon a system of dating, according to one account,[8] some of the companions suggested the day of revelation should be the start point while others proposed the year of the Prophet's death. Then ᶜUmar said: 'Verily, we shall start dating from the [year] of the Prophet's *hijra*, as his *hijra* was a severance between the truth and the falsehood' (al-Ṭabarī, n.d., vol. 2, p. 3). These words from the second Caliph sum up the absolute importance of the *hijra* and its significant impact on the course of history.

The *hijra* to Medina was not the first of its kind, as the *hijra* to Abyssinia preceded it by eight years. However, it was unique in the sense that it symbolized the start of the coming era, where Muslims established their own state for the first time in history, practised their religion without fear of persecution and spread Islam outwards.

The atmosphere in Mecca before *hijra* to Medina

In this period, the torture and oppression of Muslims by the Quraysh continued, making the need for a safe haven a priority. Some Muslims sought refuge in Abyssinia, while others stayed in Mecca, for various reasons, despite the dreadful conditions there.

The Prophet's efforts to convert people to Islam, especially the elite of the Arab tribes, did not stop after the experience in al-Ṭāʾif. He exposed himself to various troubles in preaching to the tribes who came to perform pilgrimage in Mecca. These tribes, in most cases, not only rejected his message but also harassed and mocked him. As Ḥamīdullah (1974, p. 54) says: 'The fifteen tribes he had approached without any result represented the whole of the Arabian Peninsula; tribes from the North, the South, the East, the West and the Centre of the desert continent.' However, this bitter and harsh rejection did not deter him. He remained confident that the day would come when all the Arabs would convert to Islam. This was particularly the case after his miraculous journey *al-Isrāʾ wa al-Mirʿāj* to heaven, where he saw the world of the unseen, Paradise, Hellfire, the previous prophets, the angels and much more.

A spark of hope comes from Yathrib

The meeting between the Prophet and the pilgrims from Khazraj who eventually converted to Islam gave hope to the Prophet that the achievement of his mission was drawing closer.

A year after this crucial meeting, a group of twelve people, nine from al-Khazraj[9] and three from al-Aws, came to meet the Prophet in Mecca. They met in Mina valley in a place called al-ʿAqaba, after which the allegiance was named *al-ʿAqaba* allegiance.

The members of the delegation stood out. The three men from al-Aws gave a powerful indication of the absolute sincerity and earnestness of the Khazrajite group who promised the Prophet they would spread the word in Medina. They not only spread it amongst their tribe, al-Khazraj, but also rose above their enmity and approached al-Aws with the new religion. Watt (1994, p. 146) describes the situation in Medina at the time: 'No formal peace was made after Buᶜāth,[10] but the combatants were too exhausted to continue the struggle actively. For the most part, the enemy groups avoided one another, but there was a state of hostility, and, if a man was careless and gave his opponents an opportunity, he was liable to be murdered.'

This could mean that the Khazrajite Muslims were taking a risk in approaching al-Aws with this religion. Once again, this demonstrates that their enthusiasm for the new religion was not a matter of political interest, as Watt says (1994, p. 1) but an intellectual convention and an emotional belonging. Otherwise, they might have restricted their preaching of Islam to their own tribe, al-Khazraj, and not spread it to all the tribes in Medina, as Hamīdullāh says (1974, p. 55).

The essence of the allegiance which the delegation came to swear before the Prophet was adherence to monotheism and the rites of Islam. The literal text of this oath, as Ibn Hishām (1990, vol. 2, p. 280) states, was: 'Not to ascribe anything as a partner to God nor to steal or to commit illegal sexual intercourse, nor kill our children, nor fabricate any calumny either by hands [or to walk into it] by feet, nor disobey him in any good'.

Should they stick to these commands and fulfil their promises, the reward would be Paradise. Otherwise, 'their fate was up to God Exalted is He, either He forgives or punishes them', as the Prophet said (Ibn Hishām, 1990, vol. 2, p. 280).

This oath of allegiance was called the allegiance of women, *bayᶜat al-nisāʾ*, because fighting was not obligatory on them. However, by this allegiance a new base for the oppressed Muslims in Mecca was in the making. To strengthen this base, the Prophet sent one of his intimate companions, Muṣab Ibn Umayr, to teach the Medinan Muslims the Qurʾān and spread Islam among the tribes.

Muṣab's mission was a great success. After only a year, there was no house in Medina that had not heard about Islam. In addition, 73 high-profile Medinan Muslims came to the Prophet to swear allegiance to him, in what is known as the second allegiance, *byaᶜat al-ᶜAqaba al-thāniya*.

The second allegiance, *byaᶜat al-ᶜAqaba al-thāniya*[11]

Accompanying 500 non-Muslim pilgrims from among their people, the three Medinan Muslims, including two women, went to Mecca to meet the Prophet. The meeting was arranged at the same place, *al-ᶜAqaba*.

Discreetly, the Medinan Muslims went along without their non-Muslim relatives suspecting anything.

The Prophet was there, accompanied by his non-Muslim uncle al-Abbās who came to ensure the quality of the deal they would strike with the Prophet. Being the first one to speak, al-ᶜAbbās, as narrated by Ibn Hishām (1990, vol. 2, p. 290) said:

> O people of Khazraj,[12] verily Mohammad is in [a unique] position within his tribe, as you know. We have protected him from our own people who do not believe in him like me.[13] He is respected within his people and protected in his country. However, he refused but to align and depart to you. Should you think that you can fulfil what you have promised him and protect him from his opponents, then it is up to you to face what you have borne. But, if you think that you may surrender him and let him down after he departs with you, then leave him now, as he is respected and protected in his country and amongst his people.

The delegation answered respectfully that they had listened and then asked the Prophet to speak and set whatever conditions he liked. After preaching and reciting some verses of the Qurʾān, the Prophet put before them his condition to migrate, as Ibn Hishām (1990, vol. 2, p. 291) states: 'I accept your allegiance [on the condition that] you protect me from what you protect your women and children.'

Obviously this was the condition for the Prophet's migration to Medina. He wanted protection, a safe haven and a base for him to set out preaching and spreading his message.

To demonstrate their sincerity and acknowledgement of the serious implications of their actions, al-Barāʾ Ibn Marūr stood proudly, took the Prophet's hand and said: 'Yes, by He Who has sent you with the truth, we will protect you from what we protect our women, so accept our allegiance O the Messenger of God. By God we are the sons of wars and the people of battle, we have inherited it from noble grandfathers' (Ibn Hishām, 1990, vol. 2 p. 291).

With this reply the *jiwār* was struck between the Prophet and the Muslims of Medina. It is a clear manifestation that the Islamic tradition accepts the contract of *jiwār* and endorses it. They promised to protect him as they protected their women and children, which meant they were ready to die, if need be, to defend him. Nonetheless, their reasons for accepting such a risky and dangerous deal were different from the motivations of ordinary tribesmen who gave *jiwār*. Their motives were not mainly fame and reputation but reward in Paradise. This kind of reward was unfamiliar to the Arab tribes. From then on, the factor of religion was present when making the *jiwār* contract.

The start of the migration to Medina

Unconfirmed news of the allegiance reached Quraysh, who intensified their torture, harassment and persecution of the Muslims in Mecca. If the news turned out to be true, then their trade would be threatened and Yathrib would provide a military base for the Muslims to launch attacks against them.

According to Ibn Saᶜd (n.d., vol. 1 p. 224), God revealed to His Prophet through a vision the permission for Muslims to migrate to Medina. The Prophet then told his companions that: 'God, Exalted is He, has made for you brothers and a home where you should be safe' (Ibn Hishām, 1990, vol. 2 p. 314). Hastily, the distressed Muslims started to migrate individually and in groups. No Muslim remained in Mecca, except for the Prophet, Abu Bakr and ᶜAlī, as well as those who were compulsorily detained and locked up, or too sick or weak to travel (Ibn Saᶜd, n.d., vol. 2, p. 224).

With the mass migration of the Muslims, Quraysh realized that their worst fears were materializing. The Prophet would join his followers sooner rather than later and consequently fight them with his zealous followers. Hence, they convened an urgent assembly in *Dār al-Nadwa*,[14] to decide how to deal with the Prophet. After lengthy discussions they agreed that the Prophet should be killed by a group of men selected from different divisions of Quraysh, so that the Prophet's tribe, Banī ᶜAbd Manāf, could not seek revenge for his killing.

This plot and the alternatives discussed in dealing with the Prophet were swiftly revealed to the Prophet by Jibrīl, the Angel (Q.8:30): 'And when those who disbelieve plot against you to pin you down, or to kill you or to exile you; they plot and plan, and Allah too plans; but the best of planners is Allah.'

This was the awaited permission for the Prophet to migrate, as al-Rāzī says (2000, vol. 16, p. 51). Divine Providence intervened to protect the Prophet. God aborted the plot of Quraysh and saved his Prophet from the fighters who surrounded his home. The Prophet then went to Abu Bakr to accompany him on his journey to Medina.

The details of the Prophet's journey to Medina and the precautions he took reveal the deep sense of insecurity he felt. His order to ᶜAlī Ibn Abī Ṭālib to sleep in his place, the choice of an unconventional route to Medina, the use of the goats that ᶜAbdullah Ibn Abu Bakr used to graze to wipe out their footsteps and the refuge of the Prophet and his companion at the Thawr Grotto during the pursuit of Quraysh, all demonstrate the Prophet's reliance on God and the employment of every possible human measure to achieve his goal. These measures also indicate the fear experienced by the Prophet and his companion in fleeing from Mecca and escaping the assassination attempt.

Whether this departure was flight or expulsion is something of a philosophical debate, as discussed by Rubin (2003, p. 44), and this is of little relevance here. It was Quraysh who created the harsh conditions and made the atmosphere intolerable for the Prophet to live there any longer, hence he had to flee, as al-Rāzī says (2000, vol. 16, p. 51). They also pursued him while he was fleeing, and in this sense he was expelled forcibly. In any case, the outcome of both flight and expulsion was the same, as both drove the Prophet to Medina, where he found protection and managed to establish the first Islamic state.

Establishing the Islamic state in Medina

When the Prophet arrived in Medina, acceptance of Islam was spreading and the Muslims there waited eagerly for the Prophet to join them. The welcome was very warm, as Ibn Hishām (1990, vol. 3, p. 20) states. However, there were a few tribes, specifically Khaṭma, Wāʾil, Wāqif and Umayya, who were called 'Aws Allah', that did not convert according to Ibn Hishām (1990, vol. 3, p. 29). The reasons for their refusal are not evident. However, Watt (1994, p. 178) tried to explain it by the fact that 'these clans were closely linked with the Jews. Their lands were apparently not in a solid block, but mixed among Jewish lands. Their position was thus weak, and it is understandable that they were not ready, without further observation at close quarters, to commit themselves irrevocably to a movement that was looked on with disfavour by their Jewish neighbours.'

Some members of these clans converted to Islam covertly, but after the killing of ᶜAṣmāʾ Bint Marwān al-Khaṭmī, who had compiled poems abusing the Prophet and his religion and inciting the men of her tribe to kill him, they openly declared their conversion without any fear.[15]

Opposition to the Prophet was not exclusive to these clans, as the Jewish tribes also kept aloof from Islam. Given that the Prophet was not from among them, as they were expecting (Ibn Hishām, 1990, vol. 2, p. 276), they were disappointed. As Watt (1994, p. 198) says: 'The great majority of the Jews did not … accept Muḥammad, but became increasingly hostile. Very soon after the *hijra* it must have become clear that few Jews were likely to accept the Gentile Prophet.'

Opposition to the Prophet in Medina also came from the *munāfiqūn*, the hypocrites, who overtly adopted Islam as their religion but clandestinely devised plots against the Prophet and his followers.

ᶜAbdullah Ibn Ubayy, the head of the hypocrites, who was about to be crowned as the king of Yathrib before the arrival of the Prophet to Medina considered the Prophet his enemy. The Prophet dealt with him gently and tried to win his heart, but with no success. On the contrary, ᶜAbdullah Ibn Ubayy kept trying to hurt the Prophet by inciting the Muslims against him, as occurred during the expedition of Banī al-Muṣṭaliq. When the Prophet heard about this he got angry but ᶜUsayd Ibn Ḥuḍayr intervened and asked the Prophet to forgive him as narrated by Ibn Kathīr (n.d.,vol. 4, p. 157). The role of the *munāfiqūn*, and especially this incident involving ᶜAbdullah Ibn Ubayy in the expedition of Banī al-Muṣṭaliq, is important to gain an understanding of the nature of Medinan society at that time.

The bond of brotherhood between the Muslims

The first step in his venture to establish the first Islamic state was the Prophet's construction of the Mosque and his dwelling within it. This mosque functioned as a place for worship, for learning the teachings of Islam and for receiving the revelations. In addition, it was the government headquarters, where policy, social affairs, foreign affairs, economic affairs, peace, war and anything else of importance to the Muslims, individually or collectively, was decided upon. In brief, Islam for Medinan Muslims as Watt (1994, p. 146) says: 'Provided an economic, social, and political system. Of this system, religion was an integral part; it may be called the ideological aspect of the system.' There is little wonder then that the mosque played such a central part in the life of the Muslims.

To ensure the survival of Islam, the Prophet made unprecedented changes in the lives of the Arabs of the time. He diminished their tribal relations and founded a new relationship called *al-muʾākhā* (brotherhood) between the emigrants – the *muhājrūn* and the people of Yathrib

– the *Anṣār*. According to Ibn Saᶜd (n.d., vol. 1, p. 238) the Prophet: 'Made them brothers on [the basis of] truth and equality and to inherit each other after death excluding their [non-Muslim] blood relatives'.

This *muᵓākhā* relationship was new to them, but they embraced its implementation. One interesting account of this *muᵓākhā* was that between ᶜAbd al-Raḥmān Ibn Awf (*muhājir)* and Saᶜd Ibn al-Rabī (from the *Anṣār*). According to the narration of Ibn Saᶜd (n.d., vol. 3, p. 126) and that of Ibn Kathīr (n.d., vol. 3, p. 228) Saᶜd told Ibn Awf: 'I am the wealthiest man in Medina, so look at half of my riches and take it. I also have two wives; have a look at them and see who you fancy more, so that I divorce her [so you can then marry her].'

This portrait of generosity exceeded the familiar boundaries and customs of the Arab tribes before the advent of Islam. Generosity was one of the characteristics the Arabs prized most highly. The poets frequently wrote verse praising the generous, and this praise played a crucial role in motivating people to help the needy either by providing them with food and shelter or by granting them protection and *jiwār*. However, the motivation here was not the poets' praise but the Prophet's praise and reward in the hereafter. This again shows that a new society based on new relations was emerging in Medina.

It is worth noting that the *muᵓākhā* was not merely between the *Muhājīrūn* on one side and the *Anṣār* on the other. It was actually between all sectors of society regardless of their position in the hierarchy at that time. The *Muhājirūn* themselves were bonded together as brothers by the *muᵓākhā*. The Prophet and ᶜAlī Ibn Abī Ṭālib became brothers and Ḥamza Ibn ᶜAbd al-Muṭṭalib, the Prophet's uncle and Zayd Ibn Ḥāritha, the servant of the Prophet, also became brothers in the light of this *muᵓākhā*. Hence, the ultimate aim of the *muᵓākhā* was not just to help the destitute and needy immigrants, but to demolish the tribal ties and relations and build new allegiances based on religion alone. This new bond aimed at strengthening the internal front and constructing a harmonized society.

The *muᵓākhā* also shows the power of Islam and its innovation in establishing strong relationships between its followers, whatever their ethnic or social backgrounds.

This was one of the rare occasions in history where there was harmony between immigrants and the indigenous people of a country. This success was due to the Islamic ideology on which the whole system was based. The *Anṣār* gave unstintingly because they wanted rewards in the hereafter, as they had been promised by the Prophet on the first day they met in al-ᶜAqaba and swore allegiance to him. Without such unity and harmony, the newborn state probably could not have withstood the challenges inside and outside Medina.

For this unique hospitality and warm welcome from the *Anṣār* towards the *Muhājīrūn*, they deserved eternal praise from God. In the *jāhiliyya*, the poem was the most effective way to praise and honour. Now it was the Qurʾān and the Prophet's sayings that took this position, although poetry continued to play a reduced role. An example of this praise was in the Qurʾanic verse 59:9:

> And [it shall be offered, too, unto the poor from among] those who, before them had their abode in this realm and in faith – [those] who love all that come to them in search of refuge, and who harbour in their hearts no grudge for whatever the others may have been given, but rather give them preference over themselves, even though poverty be their own lot for, such as from their own covetousness are saved – it is they, they that shall attain to a happy state!

The *Muhājīrūn* were also praised in the Qurʾān (59:8) for their sacrifices: '[Thus, part of such war-gains shall be given] to the poor among those who have forsaken the domain of evil – those who have been driven from their homelands and their possessions, seeking favour with God and [His] goodly acceptance, and who aid [the cause of] God and His Apostle: It is they, they who are true to their word!'

Despite the spirit of generosity, unity and brotherhood that spread across Medina, there were some isolated incidents which hint at the difficulty felt by some in relinquishing the blood-feud and *jāhily* tribal attitude. These incidents were fuelled by those representing the opposition in Medina. One of these incidents, narrated by Ibn Hishām (1990, vol. 4, pp. 254–6) occurred during the expedition of Banī al-Muṣṭaliq. It started when Jahjāh, the servant of ᶜUmar Ibn al-Khaṭṭāb, squabbled with Sinān Ibn Wabar, an ally of al-Khazraj. Sinān shouted: 'O the people of the *Anṣār*'[16] and Jahjāh shouted: 'O the people of *Muhājirūn*.' Hurriedly, two groups from the two sides gathered with their weapons, as a sign of readiness to fight. When ᶜAbdullah Ibn Ubayy heard this, he became angry and started to abuse the *Muhājīrūn* and scold his people for their hospitality towards them. He said:

> They have become more than us and confronted us in our country. By God, we and those of the low class of Quraysh have become like what the predecessors said: Feed your dog and he will bite you. By God, if we return to Medina, the honourable will expel the meaner. Then he turned to those who attended his gathering of his people and said: This is what you have done to yourselves; you opened your country to them and shared your possessions with them. By God, if you had not given them what you have, they would have turned to anywhere other than your country.[17] Part of this occurrence was recorded in the Qurʾān (63:7–8).

The *munāfiqūn* were a kind of fifth column in Medinan society. Despite this, the Prophet did not take any direct action against them, especially Ibn Ubayy. This may have been because the Prophet preferred to concentrate on building and nourishing the more positive and receptive part of society, hoping that the *munāfiqūn* would die away in the course of time. The Prophet also may not have wanted to send a negative message to the other tribes by killing ᶜAbdullah Ibn Ubayy. This was clear in the Prophet's response to ᶜUmar Ibn al-Khaṭṭāb, who asked the Prophet to kill him: 'How would it be O ᶜUmar if people propagate that Muḥammad kills his companions?' It was, then, for political reasons that the Prophet did not kill him. The Prophet was proved right, when the closest circle of Ibn Ubayy started to criticize him and stop him from saying, let alone doing, anything to harm the Prophet (Ibn Hishām, 1990, vol. 4, p. 256).

Another powerful indication of the changes taking place in the society's tribal relations was the offer by the son of ᶜAbdullah Ibn Ubayy after hearing what his father had said. He went to the Prophet and expressed his readiness to bring the head of his father to the Prophet, should he order him. The Prophet refused, however, and told him to be gentle with his father as long as he was alive[18] (al-Ṭabarī, 1984, vol. 28, p. 116).

After this incident and what followed for Ibn Ubayy, the influence of the *munāfiqūn* started to fade while the Muslims continued to gather strength and power in establishing the new Islamic state, which became a safe haven for any Muslim seeking refuge.

The integration of the migrants into Medinan society may be without historical precedent. The migrants did not only integrate fully into that society, but also became the governors of the country, not through occupation and oppression but with the cooperation of the indigenous people.

Giving *jiwār* to non-Muslims

Until the oppressed Muslims in Mecca started to migrate and build their state in Medina, they only knew one side of *jiwār*; that is, to ask for it and be *mustajīr* rather than *mujīr*. However, as the first Islamic state in Medina became capable of defending itself, Muslims began to experience the other side of *jiwār*; that is, to be *mujīr*, the one who gives *jiwār*.

Interestingly, we find in this period examples of women giving *jiwār* to non-Muslims and the Prophet himself endorsing this *jiwār*. The account of the Prophet's daughter Zaynab giving *jiwār* to her non-Muslim husband al-ᶜĀṣ is well known. As narrated[19] by Ibn Kathīr (n.d., vol. 3, p. 332) al-ᶜĀṣ Ibn al-Rabīᶜ refused to convert and stayed in Mecca, while his wife Zaynab migrated to Medina to join her father. Al-ᶜĀṣ went on a trade journey to Syria and on his way back encountered a group of armed Muslims. They took all his trade goods, money and belongings, although he managed to escape. Secretly, he went to his wife Zaynab in Medina who gave him *jiwār*. To declare it to all Muslims Zaynab shouted from the back lines, while the Prophet was leading the morning prayers: 'O people I have given *jiwār* to al-ᶜĀṣ Ibn al-Rabīᶜ.' When the Prophet finished his prayers he turned to people asking whether they had heard what he heard, and they said yes. To assure people the incident was not staged, the Prophet swore that he knew nothing about this until he heard it with them. Then he said: 'The weakest of the Muslims gives *jiwār*.'

Another well-known example of women giving protection to non-Muslims is the *jiwār* of Um Hāniᵓ to two of her brothers-in-law of the Banī Makhzūm, as narrated[20] by Ibn Hishām (1990, vol. 5, p. 72).

In these two examples we see that women could give *jiwār* to non-Muslims and that all the Muslims had to keep this *jiwār* intact and respect it. In other words it could be said that this new society, due to its history and composition, was able to feel the pain of the oppressed and refugees and swiftly provide them with the protection needed. It was natural to see the Prophet endorsing the principle of *jiwār* and even more for it to become a Heavenly obligation on Muslims through the Prophetic practice and verses of the Qurᵓān.

3

AMĀN (SAFE CONDUCT) IN THE ISLAMIC TRADITION

Research across the various sources of exegesis, *sīra*, *ḥadīth*, literature, history, poetry and linguistics suggests that three main terms were used to identify the person who sought the Muslims' protection. These terms were *mustajīr*, *muhājīr* and *mustaʾmin*. There were also other people living in the Islamic state and enjoying protection, called the *dhimmīs*. Studying the issue of *dhimma* in this context is crucial in order to differentiate between them and those who came from outside the Islamic state seeking temporary protection, such as the *mustajīr* and *mustaʾmin*.

Before delving into the definition of each term, its usage and the similarities and differences between them, it is essential to define other terms relevant to the subject, such as those relating to the land from which the *mustajīr*, *muhājīr* and *mustaʾmin* may have come. Some scholars, as we shall see, divided the world into two main categories: *dār al-ḥarb* and *dār al-Islam*. The importance of studying these *dārs* lies in the fact that each has its own rulings, and the movement of a person from one *dār* to another could have important consequences. This book is concerned with the movement of the *mustajīr*, *muhājīr* and *mustaʾmin* from *dār al-ḥarb* to *dār al-Islam* and not vice versa, so as to examine how the Islamic tradition dealt with them in the Islamic state (*dār al-Islam*).

After defining all of the terms listed above, the research will examine the Qurʾanic commentary books to see how scholars, throughout the course of Islamic history, understood and interpreted verse 9:6, which is considered the cornerstone in legalizing the protection of non-Muslims when they seek refuge in the Islamic state.

Dār al-ḥarb and *Dār al-Islam*

Muslim scholars in general divided the world into two and sometimes three categories,[1] as Zaydān states (1982, p. 18). The first category is *dār al-Islam*, the second is *dār al-ḥarb* and the third is *dār al-ᶜahd*.[2] While this categorization seems not to have any supporting evidence in the Qurʾān, the early scholars might have relied on the account narrated by al-Bukhārī (1986, vol. 5, p. 2024) on the authority of Ibn ᶜAbbās, which states: 'The disbelievers were two categories in the eyes of the Prophet and the Muslims. [The first category] was disbelievers of war who used to fight the Prophet, and the Prophet used to fight them. The [second] was the disbelievers of *ᶜahd*, covenant, who did not fight the Prophet and the Prophet did not fight them.'

Dār al-ḥarb

Dār al-ḥarb[3] is also sometimes referred to as *dār al-kufr, arḍ al-kufr*,[4] *dār al-shirk*[5] or *arḍ al-shirk*.[6] (*Dār al-Islam* is also sometimes known as *arḍ al-Islam*.) Ibn Taymiyya (Ḥanbali, 728 AH) (n.d., vol. 27, p. 47), also once referred to it as *arḍ al-Īmān* – the only scholar to do so.

The Ḥanafites, who are renowned for their fondness of thorough debates, have discussed this matter in more detail than other scholars. Al-Sarakhsī (Ḥanafī, 490 AH) had a criterion for defining a land as *dār al-Islam* or *dār al-kufr*. For him, the implementation of Islamic rules in the new land was a precondition for its classification as *dār al-Islam*: 'Conquering (the land) only without implementing the rules of Islam does not make it *dār al-Islam*' (al-Sarakhsī, n.d., vol. 10, p. 23).

Al-Kāsānī (Ḥanafī, 580 AH) summarized the opinion of the ḥanafite school on this issue saying: 'There is no dispute between our *aṣḥāb*[7] that *dār al-kufr* turns into *dār al-Islam* by the prevalence of the Islamic rules there' (al-Kāsānī, 1982, vol. 7, p. 130). However, there was disagreement on what factors turned *dār al-Islam* into *dār al-kufr*. Abu Ḥanīfa said (al-Kāsānī, 1982, vol. 7, p. 130) that 'It [*dār al-Islam*] does not become *dār al-kufr* unless three conditions are present: the first is the prevalence of the disbelief rulings, the second is the very closeness to *dār al-kufr* and the third is that no Muslim or *dhimmī* could be safe by the first security convention, i.e. the security convention of the Muslims.' Abu Yūsuf and Muḥammad, the companions of Abu Ḥanīfa, were, however, at variance with Abu Ḥanīfa and adopted the first condition only for *dār al-Islam* to change to *dār al-kufr* (al-Kāsānī, 1982, vol. 7, p. 130).

Al-Kāsānī comments on Abu Ḥanīfa's opinion as follows: 'If the Muslims were absolutely secure in that land and the non-believers were fearful all the time, then it is *dār al-Islam* and if the non-believers were absolutely secure and the Muslims were fearful all the time then it is *dār al-kufr*. The judgements are based on the security and fear, and not on Islam and disbelief' (al-Kāsānī, 1982, vol. 7, p. 130).

Al-Kāsānī here stresses the issue of security, which should be available at all times to Muslims, *dhimmīs* and those tied to the Muslims by other conventions such as *jiwār*, *ḥilf* or other contracts. This was apparent in the saying of Abu Ḥanīfa that the first *amān* is the *amān* that springs from the soul of Islam and is guaranteed by the head of the state to the Muslims, *dhimmīs* and other covenant people alike.[8] The non-believers al-Kāsānī mentioned are those who are at war with the Muslims; they do not include all non-believers.

The issue of security emerges here as another condition that defines *dār al-Islam* or *dār al-kufr*. Al-Sīwāsī (Ḥanafī, 681 AH) asserts this, saying: '*dār al-ḥarb* becomes *dār al-Islam* by implementing the [Islamic] rules and by guaranteeing security to the Muslims living there' (al-Sīwāsī, n.d., vol. 5, p. 480).

Al-Asbījānī (Ḥanafī, 700 AH) goes further in defining *dār al-Islam* and its features. Speaking about the Muslim lands invaded by Mongols in the eighth century AH, he states that the observance of rituals of worship such as *adhān*, congregational prayers, Friday prayers, etc., keeps the country *dār al-Islam* (Zaydān, 1982, p. 21). Al-Asbījānī is clearly keen to retain the attribute of *dār al-Islam* for the Muslim countries despite the fact that they were invaded by Tatars, the rulings of Islam were not implemented and the Muslims had no sovereignty over the land. Thus, the Islamic doctrine is reduced to the very basic principles such as prayer.

The insistence on continuing to classify the land as *dār al-Islam* despite all that had taken place could be explained by his hope that this invasion and occupation was only temporary. Another factor in al-Asbījānī's approach might be that to define these countries as *dār al-kufr* would mean that no land on Earth could any longer be considered *dār al-Islam*. The Tatars had invaded the symbol and the capital of the Muslim world, Baghdad, and other important Muslim lands.

In accordance with the Hanbalites' strict approach regarding the implementation of Islamic rules, Ibn Qayyim al-Jawziyya (Ḥanbali, 751 AH) defined *dār al-Islam*: 'It is the land that the Muslims conquered and the rules of Islam have been applied to it. If the rules of Islam have not been implemented, then it is not *dār al-Islam*' (Ibn Qayyim, 1997, vol. 2, p. 728). Therefore, the decisive factor became the rule of Islam and the implementation of its commands there. Ibn Qayyim al-Jawziyya does not accept the implementation of the rituals only, but requires the implementation of the main Islamic rules.

Al-Asbījānī and Ibn Qayyim al-Jawziyya differed significantly in their views on this issue, despite living in the same period. This demonstrates the enormous impact the nature of the *madhhab* has on scholars and their views.

Although Ibn Taymiyya (Ḥanbali, 728 AH) does not clearly state the implementation of the Islamic rules as a condition, it is certainly implied. He states that: 'A place could be *dār al-kufr* if its people are non-believers then it becomes *dār al-Islam* should its people convert to Islam' (Ibn Taymiyya, n.d., vol. 27, p. 143). By the nature of things converting to Islam means adhering to its commands and implementing its rules.

An interesting opinion was expressed by al-Ḥaṣkafī (Ḥanafī, 1088 AH) in the eleventh century. When commenting on the three conditions of Abu Ḥanīfa regarding *dār al-Islam* and *dār al-kufr*, he says: '*Dār al-ḥarb* becomes *dār al-Islam* by implementing the rules of Islam like the Friday and *ᶜīd* prayers, although some disbelievers may stay there and despite the fact that it is not connected to *dār al-Islam*' (al-Ḥaṣkafī, 1966, vol. 4, p. 176). This opinion is interesting in the sense that al-Ḥaṣkafī, like al-Asbījānī, was satisfied with prayers as evidence of the implementation of Islamic rules, despite the fact that the implementation of Islamic rules goes beyond the apparent rituals. In this context, most lands would today be considered *dār al-Islam* in the sense that even western secular states respect individual religious needs including the congregational prayers like Friday and *ᶜīd* prayers, and many other rituals in addition to political, religious, economic and social freedoms.

To add strength to this understanding, we find some scholars in the Shāfiᶜī school,[9] such as al-Bujayramī (Shāfiᶜī- 1155 AH) in the twelfth century AH, supporting this approach: 'If the non-believers conquered a country where Muslims live, like Ṭarsūs it would not become *dār al-ḥarb*' (al-Bujayramī, n.d., vol. 3, p. 189). He says these countries are originally Muslim countries, either built by Muslims like Baghdad and Basra, or converted to Islam like Medina and Yemen, or conquered by force like

Egypt and Iraq. In all these cases, these countries remain Islamic regardless of what happens afterwards.

Al-Dusūqī (Mālikī, 1230 AH) affirms this in the thirteenth century AH: 'The Muslim countries do not become *dār al-kufr* by conquering of disbelievers, as long as the rituals of Islam are still performed' (Al-Dusūqī, n.d., vol. 2, p. 188). Again we find more scholars from different schools at different times lay emphasis on the rituals as a sign of the implementation of Islam.

Ibn ᶜĀbdīn (Ḥanafī, 1307 AH) goes further and quotes from some earlier scholars who said that if the three conditions Abu Ḥanīfa set up for turning *dār al-Islam* to *dār al-ḥarb*, were evident and a Muslim judge was appointed to implement the Islamic ruling, then *dār al-ḥarb* becomes *dār al-Islam* (Ibn ᶜĀbdīn, 2000, vol. 4, p. 175). Apparently, the Islamic ruling in the environment of an occupied country does not mean rulings concerning governing, political affairs, home or foreign affairs, but rulings on personal affairs such as marriage, death, inheritance and so on.

Perhaps the most extreme opinion was that of al-Shaybānī (Ḥanafī, 189 AH). He exceeds all the boundaries when he says: 'The fact that one of us Muslims remains in a country whose people have become apostates prevents it from turning into *dār al-ḥarb*' (al-Shaybānī, n.d., vol. 8, p. 168). This opinion implies that a single Muslim performing Islamic rituals such as prayers, fasting, etc. would ensure that the title of *dār al-Islam* was retained in that place.

To sum up, it is apparent that while many scholars make the implementation of Islamic rules a pre-requisite for *dār al-Islam* or *dār al-kufr*, there are different opinions as to the meaning and signs of implementation. It is also significant that scholars such as al-Shaybānī, Ibn ᶜĀbdīn, Al-Dusūqī, al-Bujayramī and others who were keen to retain the attribute of *dār al-Islam* for lands once considered Muslim, all defined a land as Muslim regardless of whether it was originally Muslim or whether its people converted to Islam. In other words, they were quick to define a land as *dār al-Islam* but reluctant to withdraw this characteristic despite the apostasy and occupation that may occur, as long as the basic Islamic rituals such as Friday and *ᶜĪd* prayers were performed.

Dār al-ᶜAhd

Al-Shāfiᶜī (204 AH) was perhaps the only scholar to refer to *dār al-ᶜahd* as *dār al-amān*. He (1973, vol. 7, p. 350) says that this *dār* should be protected like *dār al-Islam*: 'It is prohibited to launch an attack on [a place] if it is *dār al-Islam* or *dār amān* [which becomes so] by a covenant that is struck by the Muslims, and nobody should be allowed to attack it.' So, it is not only that Muslims are not allowed to attack; they also have a duty to protect it since they made the deal with its people. He also mentions *dār al-ᶜahd* in the context of what the Muslims are allowed to do in each land they conquer (al-Shāfiᶜī, 1973, vol. 4, p. 257).

Literally, *ᶜahd* means *amān*, 'security', as al-Rāzī (1994, vol. 1, p. 192) says. Conventionally, it means the land Muslims conquer without force and with whose people they agree that the land remains theirs, provided they pay the tax, *kharāj*, as al-Mirdāwī (Ḥanbalī- 450 AH) states. While explaining the status of lands conquered by pacification, he defines *dār al-ᶜahd:* 'The second [choice] is to reach an agreement with them that the land is theirs and a duty, *kharāj*, [is] to be paid. This *kharāj* is equivalent to *jizya* and when they convert to Islam it will be abolished. Their land does not become *dār al-Islam* but *dār al-ᶜahd*. They also have the right to sell or mortgage it (al-Mirdāwī, n.d., vol. 1, p. 157).

This meaning was reaffirmed by Ibn Mufliḥ (Ḥanbali, 884 AH) in the ninth century AH.[10] Al-Buhūtī (Ḥanbali, 1051 AH) supports Ibn Mufliḥ in this opinion and adds that this 'land is theirs and they are free to do anything with it' (al-Buhūtī, 1996, vol. 1, p. 648). They can even build a church or another place of worship on it.[11] Al-Suyūṭī (Ḥanbalī- 1243 AH) used exactly the same wording to assert the same meaning regarding *dār al-ᶜahd*.[12]

From these discussions it is obvious that scholars have differed in their definitions of *dār al-Islam* and *dār al-ḥarb*. Some made the full implementation of Islamic rules an essential characteristic of *dār al-Islam*, while others were satisfied with the practice of the congregational prayers to consider that place *dār al-Islam*. The scholars were generally influenced by the environment they lived in, and shaped their definition accordingly. It could be concluded that the definition of *dār al-Islam* in modern times could differ from the earlier ones and should be based on implementation of the main Islamic principles and on the rights Muslims enjoy concerning their freedom to practise their religion and express their beliefs and opinions.

Nonetheless, categorizing the world into two or three *dārs* requires further scholarly discussion, especially given that the Prophet did not categorize the world as such, nor did the Qurʾān. Additionally, the world at the time of the Prophet differed significantly from the world today. Today, the world is dominated by national states with recognized borders, with international laws and universal conventions which, theoretically at least, govern the relations between states.

The definition of the term *mustajīr*

The term *mustajīr*, as explained in Chapter 1, was used by Arabs in the *jāhiliyya* to describe the person who flees his land seeking protection and welfare, regardless of the reasons that might drive him to do so. After the establishment of the Islamic state in Medina the custom of *jiwār* continued to exist, covering the non-Muslim who seeks protection with the Muslims, for example when Um Hāniʾ gave protection to two brothers-in-law and Zaynab, daughter of the Prophet, gave *jiwār* to her husband al-ᶜĀṣ Ibn al-Rabī.[13]

However, it should be noted that Muslims might also seek *jiwār* from other Muslims, particularly when they had committed a crime and fled in fear of punishment.[14] In view of this, it could be concluded that the term *mustajīr* was used for Muslims and non-Muslims.

The definition of the term *muhājīr*

The word *hijra* in Arabic is derived from the verb *hājara* which, according to al-Fayrūzabādī (n.d., vol. 1, p. 637) originally meant: 'To leave a land to [another] land'. Ibn Manẓūr (1956, vol. 5, p. 251) defines it as: 'The nomad or the citizen who departs his country to live in another country like the Arab tribes who migrated from Yemen to Mecca, Medina and Syria following the destruction of the Maʾrib Dam' (Ibn Kathīr, n.d., vol. 2, p. 159).

In the Islamic tradition, the term *hijra* has been used to describe the emigration of Muslims from Mecca to different places such as Abyssinia; however, they used it 'most commonly to refer to emigration from Mecca to Medina in the time of the Prophet' (Crone, 1994, p. 352). Later on, and particularly in the post-conquest period, a non-classical usage was developed, according to Welhausen: '*Hijra* no longer meant flight, but emigration (with wife and children) to a military and political centre in order to serve there' (Crone, 1994, p. 352).

Yet the term *hijra* has other subtle and important meanings associated with it. It means, as Ibn Manẓūr (1956, vol. 5, p. 251) states: 'To abandon something completely and neglect it'. This meaning of the term is supported by some traditions, as al-Nasāʾī reports (1991, vol. 5, p. 214) that the Prophet said: 'The *muhājir* is the one who abandons what God has forbidden.'

So, *hijra* is at once physical and psychological. It is physical because it involves moving from one place to another, and psychological in the sense that the *muhājīr* leaves not only his tribe, relatives and kinsmen but also their customs, tenets and rites.

It could also be said that *hijra* from a metaphoric perspective means the opposite of *hijra* in a literal sense. *Hijra* literally means leaving one's own place for a foreign place, while metaphorically it means leaving a foreign place to travel to one's own place. It is leaving disbelief, which is against the instinct, according to the tradition narrated by Muslim (al-Nawawī, 1972, vol. 16, p. 207).[15]

Thus disbelief, according to the Islamic understanding, is something foreign to man, and migrating to the absolute truth, the Creator who gives life, sustenance, satisfaction and security, is the original and right place for man to be in.

Regarding the Qurʾanic usage of this term, a search of the Qurʾān reveals that the term *hijra* and all its derivatives are mentioned 31 times in 27 verses in 17 *suras*.[16] Interestingly, in all these verses the term *hijra* or its derivatives came in a context where Muslims are the main focus, except in two verses (23:67, 25:30), which speak about disbelievers.

On the whole, it is difficult to divide these verses into completely separate topics without repetition, since many verses speak about multiple issues at the same time. However, in terms of the subject and the context in which they are mentioned, it seems the vast majority of these verses refer positively to those who emigrated for the cause of God and His Prophet. The emigration from Mecca to Medina was a focal point in many of these verses in terms of praising, honouring and promising rewards to the *Muhājirūn* and the *Anṣār* and also calling upon those who had not yet emigrated to do so.[17]

In these verses God's generosity to those emigrants and the rewards awaiting them in this life and the next are apparent. The rewards of this life included victory over their enemies (16:41, 9:20), entitlement to public money (24:22) and assurance of God's satisfaction and gratification (9:100). In the hereafter, the rewards would be even greater: forgiveness of sins (9:117), God having mercy upon them (2:218, 16:110), providing them with sustenance in Paradise (22:58), putting them in a higher hierarchy over the rest of people (9:20), rewarding them for their good deeds however small (3:195) and granting them a permanent living in the eternal pleasure of Paradise (9:21).

In addition, the Qurʾān urges Muslims to migrate under certain conditions, and imposes an obligation on them to do so. In this category, the Qurʾān motivates Muslims to emigrate in order to find comfort and affluence (4:100). Moreover, the Qurʾān goes further, making the emigration a condition for the loyalty *muwālā* of Muslims and the membership in their society (4:89, 8:72, 8:75, 33:6). More importantly, putting up with oppression by not migrating would be a cause for punishment (4:97). The Qurʾān praises those who welcomed and gave hospitality to the emigrants. In verse 59:9 God describes the *Anṣār* in a very positive way because they did not welcome the *Muhājīrūn* as a duty, but out of affection, warmth and love for those who had emigrated. Furthermore, in verse 8:74 God gives the *Anṣār* a great honour by stipulating that they are the true believers, thus they deserve forgiveness and great sustenance in the hereafter. In addition, God urges the Muslims to be generous towards the *Muhājirūn* and sets rights for them (60:10).

The fourth category of sources on the subject is the use of the term *hijra* to give the metaphorical and physical meaning of abandonment and rejection; for example the verses 4:34, 19:46, 73:10, and 74:5. In verse 4:34 we find the word اهجروهن في المضاجع means abandon the disobedient wives in bed as a kind of punishment. We find a similar meaning in verse 19:46, where the father of the prophet Ibrāhim angrily tells his son to go away if he does not follow his faith. In verse 73:10 God orders his Prophet Muḥammad to keep a psychological distance from the disbelievers but at the same time to be kind in this *hijra*. Casewit (1998, vol. 88, no. ii, p. 109) comments on this verse as follows:

> The Prophet is enjoined to patiently endure the abusive language of his oppressors and to dissociate himself from them in a dignified manner واهجرهم هجرا جميلا (Q.73:10). Here we find the imperative form of the verb *hajara* with its accompanying verbal noun *hijr* used with the conventional social implications of a deliberate, though not necessarily permanent, abjuration of social interaction and verbal communication with a particular person or party.[18]

In the same vein verses 23:67 and 25:30 speak about the psychological and physical abandonment of the disbelievers of the Qurʾān as a sign of rejection of the message of Islam. In the last verse in this category (73:10), God orders his Prophet to keep a physical distance away from the dirt and filth.

So, the term *hijra* goes beyond its apparent meaning to a much wider and more complicated context. It holds a philosophy that deals with the emigration from a new perspective and that combines heavenly and the earthly needs. It does not overlook the suffering and the hardship of the emigrants, caused by having to leave behind families, tribes, properties, businesses and homeland, but it does not regard emigration as catastrophic. Even more, Islam portrays the life of a human on this planet through many verses[19] and *ḥadīths*[20] as a journey or emigration from Paradise, where Adam and Ḥawwāʾ were created and lived, to earth as a temporary station. Then, the journey continues from earth to the hereafter. In other words, all humans on earth are just migrants waiting to return to their homes in the hereafter.

The Islamic tradition deals with the obstacles to emigration and tries to ease them in two ways. First, it tries to make the emigration a kind of worship and sacrifice in the cause of God. In return great rewards, in this life or in the hereafter, await those who emigrate. Secondly, God makes it obligatory on Muslims on the other side to welcome the emigrants and be generous in their hospitality towards them. This is what the *Anṣār* did in Medina, for which they deserved the praise and honour of God in this life and on Judgement Day.

While appreciating the torment with which emigration can be associated, this philosophy considers emigration as part of the religion and the sacrifice that should be made by its followers. It states bluntly that this was the way of the prophets and their followers in the past, and it is the way of Prophet Muḥammad and his followers as well.

Within this philosophy there is no sanctity associated with a particular place just because it is the place of one's birth. The most important thing is religion and the freedom to practise it. It even regards the rejection of emigration under certain circumstances as a cause for blame and punishment in the hereafter.

Finally, it should be noted here that the term *muhājīr* is used in the Qurʾān exclusively to describe the Muslim emigrants. In most cases it was associated with positive merits, while the term *mustajīr* was used for both the Muslims and non-Muslims alike.

The definition of the term *mustaʾmin*

The term *amān* literally means 'the opposite of fear' (Ibn Manẓūr, 1956, vol. 13, p. 26). The Islamic encyclopaedia defines it as 'safety, protection, safe conduct [and] *mustaʾmin* [is] the person who has received an *amān*' (Bearman et al., 2000, p. 429).

In the sixth century, al-Kāsānī made the earliest known attempt to define this term: 'The *mustaʾmin* is one of the people of *dār al-ḥarb*, he enters *dār al-Islam* not to stay there permanently, but [enters] for a temporary need which he satisfies and then goes back to his original country' (al-Kāsānī, 1982, vol. 7, p. 236). In this definition, al-Kāsānī considers the *mustaʾmin* a disbeliever and does not determine the reason for his asking *amān*.

In the seventh century al-Nawawī (Shāfiʿī, 676 AH) also gives a rather restricted definition. He states that: 'The *mustaʾmin* is the fighting disbeliever who enters *dār al-Islam* with *amān* (contract)' (al-Nawawī, 1987, vol. 1, p. 325). Al-Sīwāsī, (Ḥanafī, 681 AH), a contemporary of al-Nawawī, also gives very little detail in his definition. He states that: 'The *mustaʾmin* is the one who leaves *dār al-ḥarb* and enters *dār al-Islam*' (al-Nawawī, n.d., vol. 6, p. 109). However, both consider the *mustaʾmin* a disbeliever and do not discuss his reason for entering *dār al-Islam*.

In the eighth century Ibn Kathīr (774 AH) counts the cases where the non-believer should be considered a *mustaʾmin*. He says: 'Whoever comes from *dār al-ḥarb* to *dār al-Islam* for delivering a message, trading, asking peaceful settlement or truce, carrying *jizya* or something like that, and asked the *Imām* or his deputy *amān* he should be given it (Ibn Kathīr, 1980, vol. 2, p. 338). Thus the term *mustaʾmin* applies to several categories of people according to their circumstances and is not confined to those who come to *dār al-Islam* to learn about Islam, as verse 9:6 stipulates.

Moving to the ninth century we find that Mulla Khusru (Ḥanafī, 885 AH) gives a general definition of the *mustaʾmin* and applies this term to Muslim and non-Muslim alike. He says: 'The *mustaʾmin* is the one who enters another country with a (contract) of *amān* whether he was a Muslim or a disbeliever fighter.' By this definition Mulla Khusru becomes the first scholar to consider the *mustaʾmin* to be a Muslim in all likelihood.

Nonetheless, in the tenth century al-Qawnawī (Ḥanafī, 987 AH) follows Mulla Khusru in this consideration. He defines the *mustaʾmin* in general terms saying: 'The *mustaʾmin* is [derived] from asking *amān* and it is asking *amān* from the enemy whether he is a Muslim or a non-Muslim fighter' (al-Qawnawī, 1985, vol. 1, p. 185). In this century also we find al-Shirbīnī (Shāfiʿī, 977 AH) defining *ʿaqd al-amān* as 'a contract of safety between the Muslims and the non-Muslims to stop the killing and fighting' (n.d., vol. 4, p. 236). Al-Shirbīnī adds a new communal dimension to this contract. In his understanding it is not an individual contract but rather a contact between the Muslims and the non-Muslims as a whole.

This meaning was also affirmed by another Ḥanafite scholar in the eleventh century, Shaykhizāda (1078 AH), who states: 'The *mustaʾmin* is the one who enters another country with a (contract) of *amān*, and this includes the Muslim when he enters their country with *amān* and the disbeliever who enters our country with *amān*' (Shaykhizāda, n.d., vol. 4, p. 333).

However, it should be noted that this term is generally applied to the non-Muslims who enter *dār al-Islam* for a short period, as the Muslim by the virtue of being Muslim or the disbeliever by conversion to Islam enjoys *amān*. This is well founded in the *ḥadīth* narrated by al-Bukhārī (1986, vol. 2, p. 507): 'I was ordered to fight people until they say no deity is worthy of worship except Allah, and whoever says it then he will protect his money and soul save the rightful reasons and God will hold him accountable.'

Other *ḥadīths* show that the Muslim's soul, money and honour should always be saved and secure. Al-Bayhaqī (1994, vol. 8, p. 249) reports on the authority of Abu Hurayra that the Prophet said: 'The Muslim is forbidden to harm another Muslim in anything; his blood, money and honour.'

Additionally, the *sīra* of the Prophet deals with a number of incidents where the Prophet offered *amān* to certain tribes should they accept Islam.

One of the relevant examples is the account of Mālik Ibn Aḥmar, who came to the Prophet after converting and asked him to write a letter to his people to invite them to Islam. The Prophet agreed and the letter read, according to al-Ṭabarānī (1994, vol. 7, p. 50):

> In the name of God the most Gracious the most Merciful. This is a letter from Muḥammad the messenger of God to Mālik Ibn Aḥmar and whoever follows him from the Muslims. This is *amān* to them as long as they perform the prayers, give *zakāt*, follow the Muslims,

> avoid the disbelievers and give the one fifth of the war gains, the share of *al-Ghānimīn*, etc. [Should they do that] they will be secure by the *amān* of God and the *amān* of his Prophet.

Al-ʿQaylī (1983, vol. 3, p. 201) reports another account on the authority of ʿUthmān Ibn Abu Rāshid al-Azdī that he went with his brother to the Prophet and converted. Then the Prophet sent a letter with him to his people, Banī Azd. It reads as follows: 'From Muḥammad the messenger of God to whoever listens to my message; Whoever bear the witness that no God but Allah and Muḥammad is his messenger and perform the prayers then he will have the *amān* of God and the *amān* of his messenger.'

The Prophet sent similar letters to other tribes. Ibn Saʿd (n.d., vol. 1, pp. 258–91) reviewed most of these letters and mentioned the *amān* contracts the Prophet made with Arab Christian tribes. In these letters the Prophet offers his *amān* in exchange for *jizya*. An example of this is the case of the Dawma, Ayla and Taymāʾ tribes, who came to the Prophet headed by Yaḥna Ibn Rawba, the king of Ayla accompanied by the people of Syria, the people of Yemen and the people of Bahrain. The Prophet wrote them a letter saying: 'This is *amān* from God and Muḥammad, the Prophet and the messenger of God to Yaḥna Ibn Rawba and the people of Ayla and their ships and caravans in the land and sea. They and the people of Syria, Yemen and Bahrain will have the custody of God and Muḥammad His Prophet' (Ibn Saʿd, n.d., vol. 1, p. 289). The letter goes on to state the terms and the conditions of this contract.

To sum up we can say that the term *mustaʾmin* refers generally to the non-believer who comes to *dār al-Islam* seeking protection, regardless of the reasons that might drive him to do so. He could be a trader who needs to enter *dār al-Islam* to sell his products, or a messenger, or a person fleeing *dār al-ḥarb* out of fear or any other unfortunate circumstances. Thus, the term *mustaʾmin* encompasses all the aliens in *dār al-Islam* including refugees and asylum seekers. If someone comes to *dār al-Islam* he should be protected but his stay is temporary to fulfil his need. However, the contract of *amān* could be for individuals and groups also. It could be obtained by converting to Islam or paying *jizya*.

Dhimmīs in the Islamic tradition

The issue of *dhimma* is one that has taxed the minds of modern writers, scholars and researchers, be they Muslims or non-Muslims. Its significance has varied according to the motives and intentions of each writer. Some have used this subject to defend the Islamic position, as a theory and a historical practice, such as Al-Qaraḍāwī in his book entitled *Non-Muslims in the Islamic Society* (1977). In this he seeks to clarify 'the legal position, the rights and duties of the *Dhimmīs* in the Islamic society as well as to refute the accusations of the others who falsified the historical events and intentionally misinterpreted the legal texts in order to distort the unprecedented tolerance of Islam' (Qaraḍāwī, 1977, p. 4). Also, Mawdūdī, who was 'under the influence of the events that led to [the division of] India between the Muslims and the Hindus' (Zakī, 2006, p. 115) wrote a lengthy article about the subject entitled 'Rights of Non-Muslims in the Islamic State' (1982) to clarify the position of minorities in Pakistan, from an Islamic point of view, after its independence.[21]

Other writers who have focused on this issue have done so in order to criticise the Islamic tradition and its treatment of the *dhimmīs*, like Bat Yeᵓor who wrote a number of books on this topic: *Dhimmī Peoples, Oppressed Nations* (1984) and *Islam and Dhimmitude: Where Civilizations Collide* (2002) and *The Dhimmī: Jews and Christianity under Islam* in which she states: 'A truly scholarly, "objective" study becomes extremely difficult … though personally I do not believe in objectivity in the humanities … and yet, precisely, as has been said, passion is involved' (Yeᵓor, 1985, p. 31). Also in this regard we find a book called *The Myth of Islamic Tolerance: How Islamic Law Treats Non-Muslims* (2005) by Robert Spencer.

Other scholars have dealt with this topic from an academic perspective without any obvious agenda to defend or attack the Islamic tradition, for instance Hoyland (ed.) in *Muslims and Others in Early Islamic Society* (2004).

In discussing the term *dhimmī* in greater detail I will begin with the early scholars to see how they defined the *dhimmī* and what rights and duties they allocated to them. It will then be appropriate to see how contemporary scholars viewed this issue and whether there is a difference between the early and modern Muslim scholars in dealing with this matter.

The definition of the term *dhimmī*

Starting with the lexical definition, Ibn Manẓūr (1956, vol. 5, p. 251) says: *Al-dhimma* is *al-ᶜahd* الذمة العهد and 'the *dhimmī* is a man who has *ᶜahd* i.e., agreement' الذمي: رجل له عهد and 'the people of *dhimma* are people of covenant' أهل الذمة قوم معاهدون. Also, al-Rāzī (1994, vol. 1, p. 94) defines *al-dhimma* to be *al-amān*.

Conventionally, al-Ghazālī (1996, vol. 7, p. 55) and ᶜUlaysh (1988, vol. 3, p. 213) define the contract of *dhimma* as: 'Granting them [the non-Muslims] a permission to stay in our *dār*, protecting and securing them [on condition that] they pay *jizya*[22] and submit [to Muslims]'

Ibn Mufliḥ (1979, vol. 3, p. 404) and al-Baᶜlī (2002, vol. 1, p. 351) also define it to be: 'Permitting some disbelievers to remain in their disbelief provided they pay *jizya* and adhere to the rulings of the nation [the Muslims].'

Agreeing with this definition, al-Buhūtī (1970, vol. 2, p. 15) states that *dhimma* literally means: 'Promise, protection and security' and the legal evidence is verse 9:29: 'Till they [agree to] pay the exemption tax with a willing hand, after having been humbled [in war]'.

It is hence a contract between the Muslims and non-Muslims to allow the latter to stay in *dār al-Islam* keeping their faith and enjoying the protection of the Muslims providing they commit themselves to pay *jizya* and accept the general rulings of Muslims. More importantly, it is a contract that cannot be concluded without consent from both sides. Ibn Qudāma (n.d., vol. 9, p. 252) and Ibn Mufliḥ (1979, vol. 3, p. 404) describe it as 'a reciprocity contract that cannot be affirmed without mutual agreement'.

The term 'non-Muslims' in this context is also defined by scholars. Ibn Qudāma (n.d., vol. 4, p. 346) states that those who are eligible to have the contract of *dhimma* are 'the people of the book and the magians'. Al-Mirdāwī (n.d., vol. 4, p. 217) illustrates the meaning of 'the people of the book' by saying that they are: 'Jews, Christians and those who agree with them in believing in the Torah and the Gospel like the Samirites and Romans'. However, al-Fayrūzabādī (1982, vol. 1, p. 236) clearly affirms that this contract cannot be concluded with: 'Those who do not have a [heavenly] book or what could be a book, like the pagans'. Yet, al-ᶜAbdarī (1977, vol. 3, p. 380) reports that Mālik [Ibn Anas] ruled that *jizya* 'could be taken from those who worship the idols and fire'. Paying *jizya* means that they have the right to agree a *dhimma* contract with the Muslims.

Regarding the period of this contract there is apparent consensus between the scholars that this contract is perpetual and not temporary. Ibn Qudāma (1984, vol. 9, p. 240) and al-Suyūṭī (1961, vol. 2, p. 590) assert that it is 'a lifelong contract'. To leave no doubt about its permanent nature, al-Nawawī (1984, vol. 10, p. 297) stipulates that 'it is not permissible to conclude the contract of *dhimma* temporarily'. Additionally Ibn Mufliḥ (1997, vol. 6, p. 244) states that even 'the *Imām* has no right to change this contract' or to cancel it, as al-Mirdāwī (n.d., vol. 4, p. 220) stresses.

Due to the permanent nature of this contract on one hand, and 'its impact on the public interests of the Muslims' (Ibn Qudāma, n.d., vol. 4, p. 346) on the other, nobody was allowed to conclude this contract with the *dhimmīs* except the *Imām* or his deputy, as al-Baᶜlī (2002, vol. 1, p. 351) affirms. Al-Fayrūzabādī (1982, vol. 1, p. 236) agrees with this opinion but allows the *Imām* to delegate this right to anybody he deems suitable. Moreover, al-Mirdāwī (n.d., vol. 4, p. 217) states that there are other opinions about this issue within the Ḥanbalī school, yet the majority opinion is that it is the *Imām* and his deputy only who are entitled to conclude this contract. However, Ibn ᶜAbd al-Wahhāb (1985, vol. 1, p. 401), who is also from the Ḥanbalī school stresses that: 'It is not permissible [to conclude the contract] except by the *Imām* or his deputy [and] we do not know any disagreement about it.'

Owing to the sensitive nature of this issue and its relationship to the public interest, the scholars tended to stipulate certain conditions on *Dhimmīs* to ensure their contract would not have detrimental effects on Muslim society as a whole.

Al-Fayrūzabādī (1982, vol. 1, p. 237) emphasizes that 'the contract of *dhimma* cannot be struck without two conditions: adhering to the rulings of the nation and paying *jizya*'. Ibn Qudāma (n.d., vol. 4, p. 357) concurs with these conditions but elaborates on the rulings which they have to adhere to, such as rulings regarding the rights of other people in contracts and [financial] dealings. After reiterating these two conditions, al-Ḥusaynī (1994, vol. 1, p. 511) details that the contract of *dhimma* includes four obligations on the *dhimmīs*: 'To pay *jizya,* to apply the rulings of Islam on them, only to speak well about Islam and not to do anything that harms the Muslims.' These very same obligations are repeated by al-Shirbīnī (1994, vol. 2, p. 573) and Ibn Yūsuf (1969, vol. 1, p. 104).

Conversely, the Islamic state has certain obligations towards these people according to the *dhimma* contract. The first obligation is protection and security. Al-Shīrāzī (n.d., vol. 2, p. 257) affirms that 'the sole purpose of the *dhimma* contract is the security from both sides'. This means the *dhimmī* has the right to be safe and secure in the Islamic state while the Muslims have to be confident that the *dhimmī* will not act as spy for their enemies.

Al-Nawawī (1984, vol. 10, p. 303) asserts, however, that 'the *dhimma* contract gives the disbeliever the security for his person, his possessions and his slaves'. Speaking about conquered peoples, Ibn Sālim (n.d., vol. 1, p. 100) stresses that 'once they pay what is obligatory on them it is compulsory [on the Muslims] to accept it and it is [then] forbidden to fight them'.

Nonetheless, al-Ḥusaynī (1994, vol. 1, p. 511) elaborates further on these rights: 'What we are obliged to are two things: the first is to stop harming them either in their persons or their possessions and anyone who does so, has to compensate them, because they paid *jizya* to protect their blood and money. The second thing is that the *Imām* has to defend them against anyone who intends [to harm them] from the people of *dār al-ḥarb*.'

The same opinion is also given by Ibn Yūsuf (1969, vol. 1, p. 104), who says: 'It is prohibited to kill the people of *dhimma* or take their moneys and it is obligatory on the *Imām* to protect them and stop anyone from harming them.'

Hence, the *dhimma* contract in essence is a safety contract where the *Dhimmīs* reside in the Islamic state securely, provided that they keep the general order and pay *jizya*.

Concerning their rights in terms of work, finance and welfare, for example, the scholars stipulated a general rule. This rule was deduced from a *ḥadīth* in which the Prophet said: 'If they accept the contract of *dhimma*, then let them know that they have the same rights of the Muslims and they are committed to the same obligations'[23] (al-Kāsānī, 1982, vol. 2, p. 37).

Affirming their liberty in matters related to their beliefs, al-Zaylaᶜī (1895, vol. 2, p. 159) and al-Mirghinānī (n.d., vol. 1, p. 214) lay down another rule that says: 'We are ordered to leave them with what they believe in.' However, he exempts adultery and usury from the things that they are allowed to do, as the first matter is 'prohibited in all religions' and usury is prohibited by the *ḥadīth*: 'Except [who deals with] usury, there is no covenant between us'[24] (al-Zaylaᶜī, 1938, vol. 3, p. 203).

Yet, behaviour that was inconsistent with these rulings did not necessarily involve the abolition of their contract. The scholars generally were very reluctant to expand on the circumstances in which the *dhimma* contract could be cancelled, because of its permanent nature, as mentioned above. Al-Ghamrāwī (n.d., vol. 1, p. 555), al-Ramlī (1983, vol. 8, p. 109) and al-Nawawī (1984, vol. 10, p. 338) state clearly that 'the *dhimma* contract cannot be terminated by [mere] accusation'. Moreover, Ibn Nujaym (n.d., vol. 5, p. 125) affirms that 'the *dhimma* contract is cancelled by action not by words'. So, there must be an action and irrefutable evidence against the *dhimmī* for the *Imām* to be able to terminate his contract. Al-Shīrāzī (n.d., vol. 2, p. 257) rules that 'if he fights against the Muslims, his contract is nullified, whether this condition [not fighting the Muslims] was stipulated in the contract or not, as the requisite of the *dhimma* contract is security from both sides, and fighting [against the Muslims] negates that, so it nullifies the contract'.

A similar situation under which the contract could be terminated is if the *dhimmī* returns to *dār al-ḥarb* 'to live there permanently without returning to *dār al-Islam*' (Ibn ᶜĀbdīn, 2000, vol. 4, p. 171). Al-Rāzī (1996, vol. 1, p. 191) asserts that 'the contract cannot be terminated unless the *dhimmī* joins *dār al-ḥarb* or they take control over a place and fight us'. Al-Mirghinānī (n.d., vol. 2, p. 163) mentions the same scenario of joining *dār al-ḥarb* and justifies the termination by the fact that 'they become our enemies and that strips the contract of any advantage, i.e. preventing the evils of war'.

Other valid reasons for terminating the contract are refusing to pay *jizya* and disobedience to the rulings of the Muslims, as al-Fayrūzabādī (1982, vol. 1, p. 239) rules. Al-Shīrāzī (n.d., vol. 2, p. 257) provides an explanation of this ruling: 'The *dhimma* contract is not concluded without them [paying *jiyza* and adhering to the Muslim rulings], so it will not stay still without them'. Al-Ramlī (1983, vol. 8, p. 104), still puts a reservation on terminating the contract in this case. He states that the refusal to pay *jizya* should be without a valid reason to do so; otherwise, it should not be terminated.

However, if the *dhimmī* commits crimes other than those mentioned above, such as committing adultery with a Muslim woman, helping someone spy on behalf of the disbelievers, showing the weak points of the Muslims, forcing a Muslim to convert to another religion, or killing a Muslim, al-Fayrūzabādī (1982, vol. 1, p. 239) states that if these crimes were stipulated in the contract not to be committed, then his contract will be terminated otherwise it will not.

Committing these crimes will obviously be met with punishment, but it will not invalidate his contract. In practice, this means that the *dhimmī* enjoys the right of a permanent stay in the Islamic state and he is not dealt with as an alien, but as a member of society who could be punished for the crimes and the wrong deeds he commits.

Lastly, during particular periods in Islamic history we find some scholars stipulating other conditions on the *dhimmīs* in relation to their behaviour, worship, outward appearance, dress code, what to ride, where to reside, the height of their buildings and so on[25] (al-Fayrūzabādī, 1982, vol. 1, pp. 236–8). These conditions were later known as *al-shurūṭ al-ᶜUmariyya*, 'Umar ordinances' (Ibn Qayyim al-Jawziyya, 1961, vol. 1, p. 735). Furthermore, some scholars added that even paying *jizya* should be done in a certain humiliating manner, thinking that this is called for in verse 9:29. Ibn Sālīm (n.d., vol. 1, p. 100), for instance, says: 'They should be humiliated when paying [*jizya*] and they should be made to wait for a long time and be dragged from their hands.' Al-Ḥusaynī (1994, vol. 1, p. 511) mentions other forms of humiliation that should accompany the process of taking *jizya*, like making the *dhimmī* stand while the Muslim [the taxman] sits and to order him to take his hands out of his pocket, bend his back and bow his head whilst pouring what he has in the balance'. Yet, after mentioning these practices al-Ḥusaynī concludes that they are rejected and false. The claim that these conditions are recommended or obligatory is even more false, as nobody transmitted these forms from the Prophet or any one of his successors.[26]

Noth (Hoyland, 2004, p. 104) comments on these conditions, saying that they 'mainly deal with the sensitivities of the Muslims, not the victimization of religious minorities. These sensitivities only exist because the Muslims, as the victorious adherents of a different religion, had not demanded the conversion of the vanquished, but permitted them the concrete cultic manifestation of their faith.'

Despite agreeing to the above conditions, however, Ibn Qayyim al-Jawziyya (1961, p. 30) states that: 'They were not ordered to have a dress code, *al-ghayār*, in the Prophet's era, but it was following "ᶜUmar's ordinance'. So, there is no sound *ḥadīth* or verse of the Qurʾān that legalizes these regulations.

Modern Muslim scholars and the issue of *dhimma*

After the establishment of national states and the advent of the new Islamic movements that aim at reviving the Islamic tradition and advancing a better understanding of Islam, the issue of *dhimma* in Islamic society was revisited by many Muslim writers, researchers and thinkers.

In their various studies they tried to identify the meaning of the term 'citizen' and develop it to include all non-Muslims in Muslim countries. El-Affendī (Nafiᶜ, 2003, pp. 61–73) summarizes the position of many of the modern scholars, including Fatḥī ᶜUthmān, Fahmī Huwaydī, Ṭāriq al-Bishrī, Salīm al-ᶜAwwā, Aḥmad Kamāl, Rāshid al-Ghannūshī and others, on this issue. In doing so he makes the following observations:

- ᶜUthmān discusses this issue and calls upon the Muslim to go beyond the old classifications and categorizations and to accept the non-Muslims as full citizens who have as full rights as the others.
- Huwaydī, after defending the old styles of dealing with the non-Muslims by saying that they fit the old times, indicates that the new developments and the rise of the concept of equal citizenship have superseded the old styles. He also points out that the old styles were customary treatment and not necessarily based on the Qurʾān and the *Sunna*.
- Al-ᶜAwwā developed a new theory based on what he calls 'the legality of conquest' and 'the legality of liberation'. He says that the traditional Islamic authorities dealt with non-Muslims as a conquered people, while the new Muslim states came into existence following a liberation struggle that involved Muslims and non-Muslims alike. Thus, the latter deserve the rights of full citizenship and the old styles are not applicable in the contemporary world.
- Al-Ghanūshī, however, argues that citizenship in Islamic political life depends on two things: religious affiliation and residence. The non-resident Muslims and the non-Muslim residents are not full citizens and they do not have the right to occupy sensitive positions in the state, such as the head of the state and leader of the army.
- Based on the position of al-Māwardı, who differentiates between 'the minister of authorization' and 'the minister of execution' وزير تنفيذ and allows the non-Muslims to occupy the latter position, al-Bishrī comments that ministerial positions in democratic states, including the position of head of state, are executive and there is no absolute

authority. Hence all positions should be open to all citizens including non-Muslims.

El-Affendī lastly concludes that Islamic attempts to redefine the faith to encompass the modern demands of equal citizenship are going in the right direction; however, they do not go far enough.

From this discussion it is clear that the contract of *dhimma* is a security contract in essence, but it is a permanent contract. The scholars gave it more strength when they stressed its perpetuity and did not authorize the head of state to terminate it unless there was irrefutable evidence against the *dhimmī* that invalidated his contract.

The general rules the scholars stipulate to govern the rights and duties of non-Muslims in Islamic society show that to a large extent the *dhimmī* is considered a member of the Muslim society and not an alien.

The *jizya* was a tax paid by the *dhimmī* who enjoyed, in return, the protection of the Islamic state without participating in war or serving in the Muslim army (ᶜAmāra, 2003, p. 15). Once these non-Muslims serve in the army they do not have to pay *jizya*, as al-Qaraḍāwī (1977, p. 57) states.

There is a clear gap between the early Islamic tradition and contemporary Muslim scholars regarding the issue of *dhimma*. While some early scholars in certain periods deal with the *dhimmīs* as 'second class citizens', deprived of the right to occupy sensitive positions in the state due to the fact that they are conquered people, modern scholars have tried to identify a concept of citizenship in order to give non-Muslims equal rights with Muslims in the Islamic states.

The vagueness and sometimes confusion of some modern scholars around the issue of *dhimma* in terms of equalizing them with the Muslim citizens is due to their attempt to accommodate and apply the concepts of the Caliphate rulings regarding the *dhimmīs* to non-Muslims resident in modern national states. Although Mawdūdī makes the same mistake by implementing the ruling of the Caliphate to the national state, he (Mawdūdī, 1961, I) says: 'It should be clearly borne in mind that an Islamic State is essentially an Ideological state, and is thus radically different from a national state. This difference in the very nature of these two types of states has important bearing on the problem under discussion.'

It is important to note that many of the historical circumstances and concepts have changed and modern scholars should revisit the concept of *dhimma* to scrutinize it in the light of the new developments regarding the principle of equal citizenship in modern national states.

The interpretation of verse 9:6 and its relation to *amān*

The revelation of this verse was in the ninth year of the *hijra* in Medina, as al-Rāzī (2000, vol. 15, p. 176) says. Most scholars from different schools, when writing about *ᶜaqd al-amān*, cite this verse as the basis for its legalization. They started their arguments with this phrase: 'The basis of the *amān* is the verse (And if any of those who ascribe divinity to aught beside God seeks thy protection, grant him protection, so that he might [be able to] hear the word of God).'[27]

Thus, due to its great importance in this regard 54 books of exegesis[28] written by different scholars from the Sunnī, the Shīᶜites, Ibāḍī[29] and Zaydī[30] schools have been examined chronologically to spot any changes that have occurred during the course of time. Then, the research aims to establish whether contemporary scholars differ from earlier scholars in looking at this verse and how the passage of time has added to the meaning of the verse, if at all. In addition, I will try to analyze the impact of the environment and the *madhhab* of the scholars in terms of their understanding of this verse and its implications.

However, in order to understand the full significance of the verse it is necessary to be acquainted with the context, the historical background and the environment this verse was revealed in.

In short, the first five verses of this *sūra* are ordering the Muslims to sever relations and declare war against the disbelievers who continuously fight the Muslims and violate treaties with them.[31] However, the verses exempt those who respected their treaties with the Muslims (al-Ṭabarī, 1984, vol. 10, p. 62). Hence, none of the disbelievers is allowed to enter the holy mosque in Mecca, *al-Bayt al-Ḥarām*, in particular or Muslim land in general. Should any one of them do so he will be putting himself at risk and could be killed. Then verse six comes to exclude those who come to the Muslims asking for *amān*.

Taking into consideration this historical and ideological background, the majority of scholars tend to interpret the reason for *amān* as the hearing of God's word.

However, in the first two centuries AH we find three commentaries, the first *Tafsīr Ibn ᶜAbbās*[32] (68 AH), the second *Tafsīr Mujāhid* (104 AH) and the third *Tafsīr Muqātil* (150 AH).

These commentaries interpret the verse only briefly, saying that if a *mushrik* comes to the Muslims asking for *amān*, they should give him *amān* until he hears the word of God. Then he should be safe to return to his land. Yet, there is a slight difference in their interpretations regarding the 'word of God'. Ibn ᶜAbbās interprets it as: 'Your recitation of the Qurʾān', while Mujāhid (1976, vol. 1, p. 273) interprets it as 'to hear what you say and what has been revealed upon you', and Muqātil interprets it to be the Qurʾān.

This could be interpreted to mean that Ibn ᶜAbbās would like to shorten the period *al-mushrik* could stay in the Muslim land, as he deems the recitation itself would be enough for the disbeliever to convert, while the other two scholars want it to be longer to give the disbeliever the chance to hear and contemplate upon the whole Qurʾan and the Prophet's *ḥadīṭhs.*

In the third century AH three commentaries could found: *Aḥkām al-Qurʾān* by al-Shāfiʾı (204 AH), *Tafsīr al-Kitāb al-ᶜAzīz* by al-Hawwārī (third century AH), who is from the Ibāḍī school, and *Tafsīr Furāt al-Kūfī* by Furāt al-Kūfī, who is from the Zaydī school. The general understanding of the verse remains close to that of previous scholars. However, al-Shāfiᶜī affirms this meaning and stresses 'the word of God' by saying that: 'Whoever comes from the disbelievers wanting [to know] about Islam, then it is obligatory upon the *Imām* to protect him until he [the *Imām*] recites before him the Book of God and preaches to him in a way that he hopes God will make him accept Islam' (1979, vol. 2, p. 64). So it is not simply a matter of making him hear the Qurʾān, but using every possible means to convince him.

Al-Hawwārī, like al-Kūfī, affirms the general meaning and quotes al-Ḥasan saying that this verse is decisive and not abrogated. However, he reports a significant story about the implementation of *ᶜaqd al-amān* in the period of the Prophet. He narrates on the authority of al-Kalbī that a group of disbelievers, who did not have any treaty with the Prophet and did not attend the pilgrimage season, heard that the Prophet had ordered his people to fight the disbelievers who had no treaty with him after the month of *Muḥarram*. They therefore came to him in Medina to make a treaty. The Prophet declined and invited them instead to convert, but they refused. So the Prophet let them go and they reached a place of safety. The story goes on to tell us something noteworthy: 'They were Christians from Banī Qays Ibn Thaᶜlaba. They went to Yamāma until the people converted. Some of them converted and some of them adhered to their Christianity.' This account may lend itself to prove that the term 'disbeliever' mentioned in the verse is not confined to pagans and atheists only but includes Christians and all non-Muslims. This is quite important in this context, since it widens the range of people who are entitled to ask for *amān* in Muslim lands.

The scholars in the fourth century AH generally do not go far beyond the general meaning of the verse, except in small details, such as the period that the *mustaʾmin* could stay and his legal status after he enters *dār al-Islam*. In this period we find five commentaries: *Jāmiᶜ al-Bayān fī Tafsīr al-Qurʾān* by al-Ṭabarī (310 AH), *Maᶜānī al-Qurʾān* by al-Naḥḥās (338 AH), *Aḥkām al-Qurʾān* by al-Jaṣṣāṣ (370 AH) *Tafsīr Baḥr al-Ulūm* by al-Samarqandī (373 AH) and the first Shiᶜite *tafsīr* known as *Tafsīr al-Qurʾān* by al-Qummī (fourth century AH).

Al-Ṭabarī reports an account narrated on the authority of Saᶜīd that in one battle the Muslims caught a disbeliever and were about to kill him when he said: 'Take your weapons off me and let me hear the word of God.' After they had told him the main principles of Islam he converted (al-Ṭabarī, 1984, vol. 10, p. 80).

Significantly, this account emphasizes the practical side of *al-amān* and shows that it was not simply a theoretical and intellectual concept but also a practical one.

This meaning is also reaffirmed by al-Naḥḥās (338 AH), who says: 'If he [the disbeliever] asked to save him from killing to hear the word of God, then [you have to] give him *amān*' (al-Naḥḥās , 1984, vol. 3, p. 185).

In his commentary, al-Jaṣṣāṣ also concentrates on this issue. He elaborates on the duty of the Muslims to spread the message of Islam in a way that makes the non-Muslims understand it clearly, by providing all the necessary proofs and logic. He also states that the period the *mustajīr* is allowed to stay in the Muslim land is subject to fulfilling his needs, and then the *Imām* should order him to leave. 'Should he exceed a year, after the *Imām* ordered him to leave, he becomes a *dhimmī* and *kharāj* will be imposed upon him' (al-Jaṣṣāṣ, 1984, vol. 4, p. 273). This opinion is obviously important as it is related to the legal status of the *mustaʾmin* and how he acquires the right to stay permanently in *dār al-Islam* by becoming a *dhimmī*.

Al-Samarqandī and al-Qummī do not add any new meaning to the verse but briefly repeat the general meaning.

Moving to the fifth century AH we find six commentaries without any significant addition to the meaning of the verse, but with different approaches to its interpretation. The first is concerned with the abrogation and is contained in *al-Nāsikh wa al-Mansūkh* by al-Muqrī (410 AH). The second is *al-Nukat wa al-ᶜUyūn* by al-Māwardı (450 AH). The third is Shīᶜite *tafsīr* called *Tafsīr al-Tibyān al-Jāmiᶜ li-ᶜUlūm al-Qurᵓān* by al-Ṭūsī (460 AH, Shīᶜite) who concentrates mainly on the linguistics and the grammar in the verse. The fourth is completely different from the others discussed so far as it takes the *sūfı*, mystic, approach. It is named *Laṭāᵓf al-Ishārāt* by al-Qushayrī (465 AH). Then we find *Tafsīr al-Wajīz* by al-Wāḥidī (468 AH) which is really *wajīz*, brief. The last one is *Tafsīr al-Samānī* by al-Samānī (489 AH), who takes the conventional approach and is concise.

Due to the fact that al-Muqrī is concerned mainly with the abrogation side of the verse I will defer it to the last section specified for abrogation. Al-Māwardī comments on the 'word of God' by saying that this could mean either the whole Qurᵓān or *Sūrat* Barāᵓa[33] only. Being the first scholar to specify this *sūra* as an obligation on the *mustaᵓmin* to learn in order to 'know what it contains of the rulings regarding the *muᶜāhid*, [the *mustaᵓmin*], the rulings concerning those who breach their covenant, besides the fate of the disbelievers and the difference between them and the hypocrites'.[34]

After elaborating thoroughly on the linguistics and grammar in the verse, al-Ṭūsī (1960, vol. 5, p. 205) explains the meaning of the phrase أبلغه مأمنه 'make him attain his place of safety' and says that 'attaining [literally] is making [something] proceed to the ultimate end':

الإبلاغ التصيير إلى منتهى الحد

In other words he wants to say that the Muslims should do their best to protect the *mustaᵓmin* till he reaches his safe place regardless of whatever it may cost.

Al-Qushayrī, the *sufı*, brilliantly articulates his argument that God orders us to give *amān* to the disbeliever who does not know anything about Him. God also obliges us not to turn him away without letting him listen to His word. All this is out of His Compassion and Mercy. Al-Qushayrī continues to wonder how then would His treatment be of those who asked Him the *amān* considering that they worshipped

Him during their entire lives and knew how great and exalted is He. Al-Qushayrī[35] supports his view by the verse of poetry:

ومتى نُضَيِّعُ مَنْ يَنِيخُ بِبَابِنَا   والمُعْرِضون لهم نعيمٌ وافِرُ؟!

And how would we neglect those who lean at our door
while [We give] those who turn away abundant luxury.

Here he is saying that God, out of His infinite generosity and mercy, gives plenty of sustenance to those who turn away from his path and do not follow his orders. So how much more generously would He treat those who love him and come to knock on His door for mercy and forgiveness.

Al-Wāḥidī and al-Samʾānī reaffirm that the Prophet and the Muslims were ordered to fight the disbelievers; however, this verse makes an exemption for those who ask *amān* to listen to the word of God.

In the sixth century AH the five scholars who interpret this verse agree unanimously that if the *mustajīr* asks for *amān* in order to listen to the word of God, the Muslims should give him this opportunity. Apparently, they reiterate the general meaning of listening. However, some variation remains between them. Some of them make the listening brief, while others make it a slow process that requires an extended time to accomplish.

Starting with al-Baghawī (510 AH), he states that: 'If the disbeliever asked for *amān* after the end of the *Ḥarām* months to listen to the word of God, then secure him and make him safe until he acquaints his rights, duties as well as the reward and punishment' (al-Baghawī, n.d., vol. 2, p. 270).

Al-Zamakhsharī reads the same meaning: 'If he asked for *amān* to listen to what you preach about monotheism and the Qurʾān, and to verify what you had been sent for, then give him *amān* so as to listen and contemplate the word of God and reflect on the true nature of the matter' (al-Zamakhsharī, n.d., vol. 2, p. 236).

It is noticeable that al-Zamakhsharī in this phrase interprets the listening to be a lengthy process of discovering the truth. This means, by default, an extended period to finish this process and not confined to any restriction other than knowing the truth.

Another interesting matter al-Zamakhsharī adds in this context is the account of ʿAlī Ibn Abī Ṭālib with the disbeliever who asked: 'If a man of us [the disbelievers] wants to come to Muḥammad, after the end of this date, [the *Ḥarām* months][36] to listen to the word of God or for a need, would he be killed?' ᶜAlī said: 'No, because God exalted is He says: "If one of the disbelievers sought your *jiwār* grant it to him"'.

The importance of this account in this context is that it states clearly that a disbeliever may come to *dār al-Islam* to ask for something other than listening to the word of God, and ᶜAlī, whose position is known in Islam, affirms this and supports it by quoting the verse.

However, Ibn ᶜAṭiyya (542 AH) interprets this verse to mean that the *mustaᵓmin* comes to *dār al-Islam* 'to listen to the Qurᵓān and see the state of Islam'.[37] Hence, it is more than listening. It is listening and wandering about in the Muslim lands to see the social, economical, political aspects of Muslim daily life. To do this, he needs lots of time and the liberty to move around in the Islamic state.[38]

Al-Ṭabarsī (548 AH, Shīᶜa) does not go far beyond this meaning. He (al-Ṭabarsī, 1980, vol. 3, p. 17) affirms that: 'If the *mustaᵓmin* comes to listen to your preaching and argument from the Qurᵓān, give him *amān*, explain to him what he wants and give him enough time to listen and ponder upon the word of God'.[39] Again, the matter is not just a question and answer, but a process where the *mustaᵓmin* needs unrestricted time to listen, contemplate and reflect upon Islam.

Although Ibn al-Jawzī (597 AH) is brief in interpreting this verse, he makes it clear that 'if [the *mustaᵓmin*] asked for your *amān* to listen to the Qurᵓān and look into what he is commanded to do and prohibited from doing, give him *amān*' (Ibn al-Jawzī, 1983, vol. 3, p. 399).

The scholars of this period generally affirm the *mustaᵓmin*'s right to be given the full opportunity to learn about Islam, without making time an obstacle.

Moving to the seventh century we find four commentaries: the first is *al-Tafsīr al-Kabīr* by al-Rāzī (604 AH), the second is *al-Jāmiᶜ li-Aḥkām al-Qurᵓān* by al-Qurṭubī (642 AH), the third is *Tafṣīr al-Qurᵓān* by Ibn ᶜAbd al-Salām (660 AH) and the fourth is *Tafsīr Anwār al-Tanzīl wa Asrār al-Taᵓwīl* by al-Bayḍāwī (685 AH). The scholars in this period vary in regard to the length of their comments on the verse. Whereas al-Rāzī and al-Qurṭubī elaborate extensively on the verse and the rules it sets, Ibn ᶜAbd al-Salām and al-Bayḍāwī comment in a few words about the direct meaning of the verse.

After stating the aforementioned account of ᶜAlī Ibn Abī Ṭālib with the disbeliever, al-Rāzī takes the historical approach to put the verse in its context. He links it directly to the previous verses to show that the flow of events leads to the legislation of this verse which exempts the *mustaʾmin* from killing, as the previous verses stipulate. He then stresses several points in this verse.

One of them is the arrangement of wording in the verse, especially the phrase 'if one of the disbelievers asked your protection' وإن أحد من المشركين استجارك . Grammatically, he says, the verb 'asked your protection' استجارك should be mentioned before 'one of the disbelievers' أحد من المشركين and repeated after it. So the verse would be إن استجارك أحد من المشرآين استجارك فأجره. However, the Qurʾān did not repeat the verb and put it before the subject, the disbeliever, because God wanted to focus attention on the *mustaʾmin* himself. Al-Rāzī supports this opinion by quoting Sībawayh, the famous linguist, who says: 'They [the Arabs] bring forward the most important thing which they want to highlight' (al-Rāzī, 2000, vol. 15, p. 181). Then al-Rāzī comments that 'the apparent meaning in the previous verses (verses 1–5) was killing the disbeliever, so the Qurʾān puts forward the disbeliever in this verse to give him more attention in terms of saving and protection' (al-Rāzī, 2000, vol. 15, p. 181). This interpretation is appropriate considering the difficult and desperate situation the *mustaʾmin* must be in when he flees asking for protection and security.

The other issue al-Rāzī concentrates on is the period the *mustaʾmin* should be allowed to spend in *dār al-Islam*. He says:

> There is no evidence in the verse that shows the limits of the period; however, it may only be known by customary practice. When the marks of him being a seeker for the truth and a searcher for the proofs are evident then he should be given time and permitted to stay, while when it appears that he rejects the truth and wants to gain time by lies, then take no account of him [and end his *amān*] (al-Rāzī, 2000, vol. 2, p. 182).

Al-Rāzī is the first scholar who states this directly, while previous scholars, as in the sixth century, touched upon the issue and reiterated the same meaning in various phrases without relating it so clearly.

In addition, al-Rāzī points to some jurisprudential rules about the *mustaʾmin* and who is entitled to give *amān* in *dār al-Islam*.

In his role as a jurisprudent as well as a commentator, al-Qurṭubī focuses on the rulings in the verse. After giving the general meaning of the verse he discusses different aspects from a jurisprudential angle; for example who is qualified to give *amān*, and the differences among the scholars on this. He also argues whether the verse is abrogated or not. Yet, he raises quite an important point regarding the kinds of people who may ask for *amān* in *dār al-Islam*. He states: 'The apparent meaning of the verse is [specified] to who wants to listen to the Qur^ʾān and reflect upon Islam, however giving *jiwār* for another reasons is subject to the interests of the Muslims and what could be of benefit to them' (al-Qurṭubī, 1986, vol. 8, p. 75). Hence, asking for *amān* for reasons other than learning about Islam is principally acceptable if it does not harm the Muslims and may bring them benefits.

Al-Qurṭubī is the first of the exegetes to widen the reason for granting *amān*. This could be due to the fact that he was living in Cordoba, a powerful, civilized and settled city in the golden era of the Muslims in Spain. So he was not worried by the idea of foreigners entering *dār al-Islam* or the state of Muslims, which was great enough to convince many people to convert, or at least to be impressed.

In regard to the other two commentaries, Ibn ᶜAbd al-Salām (660 AH) and al-Bayḍāwī (685 AH) interpret the verse in brief and do not go beyond the general meaning. Nevertheless, al-Bayḍāwī emphasizes listening and reflecting and the importance of acquainting the *mustaʾmin* with the truth of Islam (al-Bayḍāwī, n.d., vol. 3, p. 130).

The eighth century AH witnessed the highest number of exegetes so far. They are, chronologically: *Tafsīr Madārik al-Tanzīl wa Ḥaqāʾiq al-Taʾwīl* by al-Nasafī (710 AH), *Nāsiḥ al-Qurʾān wa Mansūkḥih* by Ibn al-Bāzarī (738 AH), *al-Tashīl li-ᶜUlūm al-Tanzīl* by al-Kalbī (741 AH), *Tafsīr Lubāb al-Taʾwīl fī Maānī al-Tanzīl* by al-Khāzin (741 AH), *Tafsīr al-Baḥr al-Muḥīṭ* by Abu Ḥayyān (745 AH), *Tafsīr al-Qurān al-Karīm* by Ibn Kathīr (774 AH) and *al-Burhān fī ᶜUlūm al-Qurān* by al-Zarkashī (794 AH).

None of these books except *Tafsīr al-Baḥr al-Muḥıṭ* by Abu Ḥayyān (745 AH) and *Tafsīr al-Qurān al-Karīm* by Ibn Kathīr, add any new or significant meaning to the verse. However, Ibn al-Bāzarī, who is mainly concerned with the abrogation issue, will be considered in the next part of this section.

Abu Ḥayyān (745 AH) approaches his interpretation of this verse from different perspectives. He mentions the issue of abrogation and argues against the opponents who say it is abrogated. He also takes the jurisprudential approach and discusses some details in this regard, like the *amān* of the *Imām*, the slave, the woman and the boy and mentions the variations between the scholars about these issues.

The interesting thing in Abu Ḥayyān's interpretation is his use of the same wording as al-Rāzī in regard to the lessons formulated from this verse, especially the issue of reflection upon monotheism and considering it the highest hierarchy in Islam, without referring to al-Rāzī.

However, Abu Ḥayyān's comments on the word *ḥatta* حتى 'until' are significant here. He says: '*Ḥatta* could mean the time, i.e. until he hears [the word of God], or it could be for justification [the reason for giving *amān*]. In both cases it is linked with [the verb] أجره give him *amān*' حتى يصح أن تكون للغاية أي: إلى أن يسمع ويصح أن تكون للتعليل، وهي متعلقة في الحالين بأجره (Abu Ḥayyān, 1983, vol. 5, p. 11). So, in the first interpretation the period of *amān* should be restricted to the limit and the time of listening. Once the listening is over his *amān* should be terminated. Yet in the second interpretation the word *ḥatta* gives the meaning of purpose, i.e. give him *amān* so that he may hear the word of God, and thus he will be given the opportunity to learn about Islam. In these two scenarios the verse has nothing to do with the purpose of asking *amān* by the *mustaʾmin*, since it deals only with the duration of *amān* in the first scenario or the purpose of granting *amān* in the second one.

Nonetheless, Abu Ḥayyān also mentions that some linguistic scholars could accept that 'until' *ḥatta* is linked with the verb 'sought your protection' استجارك. In this case the verse would be: 'If one of the disbelievers sought your *amān* to listen to the word of God give it to him' وإن أحد من المشركين استجارك حتى يسمع كلام الله فأجره. So, the verse would mean that the disbeliever comes to *dār al-Islam* for the purpose of listening to the word of God, and thus the Muslims should grant him *amān* for that reason.

However, the majority of scholars, as Abu Ḥayyān (1983, vol. 5, p. 11) says, reject the association of the word 'until' *ḥatta* with the verb 'sought your protection' استجارك because in this case we should repeat the phrase 'until he hears the word of God' حتى يسمع كلام الله twice. The first phrase should be put after the verb 'sought your protection' استجارك since it is associated with it, according to this understanding, while the second one should be put after the verb 'give him *amān*' أجره. So, the verse would be read: 'If one of the disbelievers sought your protection "to hear the word of God" grant him protection "until he hears the word of God'" وإن أحد من المشركين استجارك حتى يسمع كلام الله فأجره حتى يسمع كلام الله

In this scenario, however, the first phrase 'to hear the word of God' حتى يسمع كلام الله is used to show the purpose of asking *amān,* and that is to listen to the word of God only, whereas the second phrase 'until he hears the word of God' حتى يسمع كلام الله is used to show the time and the limit, i.e. grant him *amān* until he hears the word of God, and once that is done the *amān* will be terminated. Nonetheless, there is a problem with this scenario, according to Abu Ḥayyān (1983, vol. 5, p. 11). The repetition of the phrase 'until he hears the word of God' حتى يسمع كلام الله is not acceptable grammatically, therefore the second repeated phrase should be replaced with a pronoun attached to the word *ḥatta,* instead. Hence the verse should be: 'If one of the disbelievers sought your protection to hear the word of God grant it to him until he hears it' وإن أحد من المشركين استجارك حتى يسمع كلام الله فأجره حتاه . Although in English it sounds right grammatically, in terms of Arabic grammar, there is a problem since the pronoun هـ cannot be attached to the word *ḥatta* حتى as is the case here حتاه.

Having said that, the word *ḥatta* cannot grammatically refer to the verb 'sought your protection' استجارك حتى i.e. 'sought your protection to hear the word of God'. The significance of this approach is that the verse does not state the reasons for seeking protection, whether it is hearing the word of God or anything else. The verse practically lifts any restrictions on the disbeliever to ask for protection, so whenever he feels that there is a need to ask for protection in *dār al-Islam* he should be able to do so. This would also mean that scholars who confine the reason for asking protection to listening to the word of God are wrong, simply because it is against the Arabic grammatical and linguistic rules.

According to this conclusion the word *ḥatta* should not be interpreted to mean the limitation and duration of the *amān*, as many classical scholars claimed. That is because this interpretation was based on the assumption that the disbeliever seeks *amān* in *dār al-Islam* to hear the word of God and thus once he hears it his *amān* should be terminated. However, since we have proved that this assumption is in contradiction with the grammar of the Arabic language, the meaning of the word *ḥatta* should be changed to mean 'so that' instead of 'until'.

Briefly, in light of this discussion the verse should be interpreted as follows: 'If one of the disbelievers, [regardless of his purposes], sought your protection, grant it to him [without limitation of time] so that he may hear the word of God.'

Adhering to his own method, Ibn Kathīr (774 AH) tries to bring in everything related to the topic from different perspectives. He interprets the verse in general and quotes from various sources to support his opinion. Yet, most of what he says here is not new. The significance of his comments becomes apparent when he mentions part of the account of *sulḥ al-Ḥudaybiya* related to the subject here, and the account of the messenger of Musaylama al-Kadhhāb to the Prophet. He does so to conclude that: 'Whoever comes from *dār al-ḥarb* to *dār al-Islam* for delivering a message, trading, asking peaceful settlement or truce, carrying *jizya* or something similar to that and asked for *amān* from the *Imām* or his deputy, he should be given the *amān* as far as he stays in *dār al-Islam* until he returns to his safe place and his homeland' (Ibn Kathīr, 1980, vol. 2, p. 338).

What is noteworthy in this quotation is that Ibn Kathīr does not restrict the *amān* for these categories only but makes it open to similar cases, which could include cases of refuge in modern times.

In the ninth century we could find four commentaries: *Tafsīr Gharāʾib al-Qurʾān wa Raghāʾib al-Furqān* by al-Qummī (850 AH), *Tafsīr al-Lubāb fī ʿUlūm al-Kitāb* by Ibn ʿĀdil (880 AH), *Tafsīr Naẓm al-Durar fī Tanāsub al-ʾĀyāt wa al-Suwar* by al-Biqāʿī (885 AH), *Tafsīr al-Aqʿam* by al-Aqʿam (ninth century AH, Zaydī).

As he states in his introduction, al-Qummī gathers material from his predecessors including al-Zamakhsharī, al-Rāzī and others. So it is no wonder that we find in some cases the same wording as al-Rāzī, especially when he mentions the hierarchy of contemplation in Islam and that the verse does not have any specific limitation to the stay of the *mustaʾmin*, and so on. However, al-Qummī reaffirms the last point by saying: 'As for the time of stay for contemplation, there is nothing in the verse that shows it. [Deciding the limit] could be up to the judgement of the *Imām*.'[40]

Nevertheless, al-Qummī also discusses the juristic side of the verse in regard to who is entitled to give *amān* and so on. In addition, he supports his ideas by mentioning the account of Um Hāniʾ, who gave *jiwār* to two disbelievers. He then argues about the abrogation of the verse.

Like al-Qummī, Ibn ʿĀdil (880 AH) quotes from the predecessors, yet without stating this. He almost copies what Abu Ḥayyan said about the word *ḥatta* and its relationship to the verb 'grant him protection' أجره

and the grammatical and linguistic justification for that. However, he adds more examples to support his position. In addition, he touches upon the abrogation argument between the scholars concerning this verse.

The other two scholars, al-Biqāᶜī and al-Aqᶜam , who is from the Zaydī school, do not contribute any important addition to the meaning of the verse. They reiterate the general meaning and al-Aqᶜam affirms that ᶜAlī Ibn Abī Ṭālib said that the verse is abrogated.

Moving to the tenth AH century we find three commentaries. The first is called *al-Durr al-Manthūr fī al-Tafsīr bi al-Maᵓthūr* by al-Suyūṭī (911 AH), the second *al-Jawāhir al-Ḥisān fī Tafsīr al-Qurᵓān* by al-Thaᶜālibī (928 AH) and the third *Irshād al-ᶜAql al-Salīm ilā Mazāyā al-Kitāb al-Karīm* by Abu al-Suᶜūd (951 AH).

In addition to the general meaning of the verse, al-Suyūṭī discusses the issue of abrogation of the verse. However, he narrates on the authority of al-Ḍaḥḥāk that the Muslims were not only ordered to protect disbelievers who wanted to listen to the word of God but also 'were ordered to take care of them financially as long as they are there'.

This account adds a new dimension to the issue of *amān* in which responsibility for the disbelievers lies on the shoulders of Muslims. They have to take care of them in terms of welfare, protection and everything else they may need as long as they stay in the *dār al-Islam*.

With regard to al-Thaᶜālibī, he comments on the verse briefly and stays within the general meaning cited by the other scholars.

Like the others, Abu al-Suᶜūd repeats the general meaning of the verse, but he also affirms what Abu Ḥayyān and al-Qummī said about the word *ḥatta* and its reference to the verb 'grant him protection' أجره rather than the verb استجارك. He justifies that by saying: '*Ḥatta*, whether it is to show limitation or rationalization, is referred to what is after it [the verb "grant him protection"] and not to the verb "sought your protection". [If it refers to "sought your protection"] this will lead to the use of *ḥatta* with the pronoun and that is what should not happen except by poetic license' (Abu al-Suᶜūd, n.d., vol. 4, p. 44).

Moreover, he goes on to comment on 'the need' mentioned in the account of ᶜAlī Ibn Abī Ṭālib with the disbeliever. He then interprets 'the need' by saying: 'It is the need related to religion and not the general need or the earthly needs' (Abu al-Suᶜūd, n.d., vol. 4, p. 44). In this comment, Abu al-Suᶜūd becomes the first scholar to explicitly restrict the reason for requesting *amān* to religious needs and bluntly exclude any other need.

While other scholars mentioned the religious need, they did not exclude other needs so categorically.

In the eleventh century, there is one commentary called *al-Ṣāfī fī Tafsīr Kalām Allah al-Wāfī* by al-Fayḍ al-Kāshānī (1090 AH, Shīᶜa). The author of this work does not add any different meaning and sticks to the general meaning stated by earlier scholars (al-Kāshānī, 1985, vol. 8, p. 921).

Like the century before it, in the twelfth century there is one book called *Rūḥ al-Bayān fī Tafsīr al-Qurʾān* by Ḥaqqī (1127 AH). This does add new meaning rather than simply affirming the previous understandings, especially in relation to the word *ḥatta*, which could mean 'until' or 'so that'.[41]

The thirteenth century AH witnessed the production of three commentaries. The first is *Fatḥ al-Qadīr* by al-Shawkānī (1259 AH), the second is *al-Baḥr al-Madīd fī Tafsīr al-Qurʾān al-Mjīd* by Ibn ᶜAjība (1266 AH) and the third is *Rūḥ al-Maᶜānī fī Tafsīr al-Qurʾān al-Aẓīm wa al-Sabᶜ al-Mathānī* by al-Alūsī (1270 AH). After examining these books, we find that the first two authors remain in broad agreement with the majority of scholars. However, al-Shawkānī adds a new meaning to the word 'his place of safety' مأمنه and says: 'It is the place he is safe in' (al-Shawkānī, n.d., vol. 2, p. 338). In other words, when returning the disbeliever it is not necessarily to his country of origin if it is not safe. Instead, the Muslims are obliged to send him to a safe place regardless of whether it is his home country or somewhere else. This point is quite important, as we shall see when discussing the concept of *non-refoulement* in Chapter 4.

However, Ibn ᶜAjība aligns himself with those who interpret the word *ḥatta* to mean 'so that'. He says: 'It is obligatory to give them *jiwār* so that they may listen and contemplate and that becomes a reason for their conversion.'[42] Then he applies this verse to the hierarchical system of Sufism. He makes it obligatory on the higher Sufis to give *jiwār* to the beginners in Sufism should they ask for it, especially when the latter enter 'the land of truths'.

Nonetheless, Al-Alūsī (n.d., vol. 10, p. 53) concentrates primarily on interpreting the word *ḥatta* and its implications. He argues strongly that *ḥatta* is for justification and thus related to the verb 'grant him protection'. He quotes al-Fāḍil Ibn ᶜĀdil saying that the majority of scholars refuse to consider *ḥatta* to be related to the verb 'sought your protection'. He then continues to refute his opponents' evidence. Lastly, he counters what Abu al-Suᶜūd said about the account of ᶜAlī and the word 'need' mentioned there.

In the fourteenth century AH we find four commentaries: *Hamyān al-Zād ilā Dār al-Maᶜād* and *Taysīr al-Tafsīr* both by Muḥammad Aṭfiyyash (1332 AH, Ibāḍī), *Tafsīr al-Taḥrīr wa al-Tanwīr* by Ibn ᶜĀshūr (1393 AH) and *Bayān al-Saᶜāda fī Maqāmāt al-ᶜIbāda* by al-Janābadhī (14th century, Shīᶜa). All these works agree that the disbeliever could come to the Muslim land and ask for *amān* not only for religious reasons but also because of an earthly need.

Aṭfiyyash interprets the verse in his second *tafsīr* at greater length than the first one, but the meaning remains relatively unchanged. In *Taysīr al-Tafsīr* he asserts that the disbeliever could ask for *amān* from the Muslims either for hearing the Qurʾān or for an earthly matter. He also emphasizes the word *ḥatta* and says that it is for justification and relates to the verb 'grant him protection'. He reaffirms that clearly, saying: 'He asked for *amān* generally, without the restriction of hearing'[43] استجارك مطلقا، لا بقيد السماع. He also comments on the phrase 'make him attain his place of safety' ثم أبلغه مأمنه and states that his safe place could be his homeland or anywhere else where he feels he will be safe.

Ibn ᶜĀshūr (2000, vol. 10, p. 26) states bluntly that the verse does not explain the reason behind asking for *jiwār*, because the reasons for that are different and nobody asks for *amān* without a valid reason. He also draws attention to the word 'then' ثم and says that it gives the meaning of slow motion. This means here that Muslims should not hurry the disbeliever to his safe place, but should allow him to stay as long as is necessary.

Lastly, in this century the Shīᶜa al-Janābadhī confirms that the disbeliever could come to Muslim lands for an earthly need rather than religious needs.[44]

Among the modern commentaries are several books: *Fī Ẓilāl al-Qurʾān* by Sayyid Quṭb (1387 AH), *al-Mīzān fī Tafsīr al-Qurʾān* by al-Ṭabāṭabāʾı (1402 AH, Shīᶜa), *al-Wasīṭ fī Tafsīr al-Qurʾān* by Ṭanṭāwī, *Taysīr al-Tafsīr* by al-Qaṭān and *Aysar al-Tafāsīr* by Asʾad Ḥawmid.

Generally speaking the above mentioned scholars do not go far beyond what the classical scholars stated, and in some cases they depend on their work. However, they sometimes add new meanings or put more emphasis on particular issues.

The controversial *Fī Ẓilāl al-Qurʾān*, whose author was hanged in Egypt in 1966 for his contentious and revolutionary views, comments comprehensively on this verse and the previous verses, and approaches them from a different perspective. He first goes through the historical background to put this verse in context. After piecing the verses together he concludes that this particular verse is a landmark of the greatness of Islam since it allows disbelievers to enter *dār al-Islam* with guaranteed security so that they can listen to and understand the core meaning of the religion (Quṭb, 1967, vol. 4, p. 142).

Al-Ṭabāṭbāʾī also gives a lengthy interpretation of the verse and touches upon various matters covered by the earlier scholars. Yet there are some variations, for example in relation to the word *ḥatta*. He says that it is 'the purpose of asking for *jiwār* and giving *jiwār*'[45] غاية للاستجارة والاجارة. Later on he restricts giving *amān* to those who ask for it to learn about Islam and not for anything else. He (al-Ṭabāṭbāʾī, 1971 vol. 9, p. 154) says: 'Then asking for *amān* was only for listening to the word of God and to querying of what the Prophet has of the matters related to his message.' Moreover, he emphasizes this in another place (al-Ṭabāṭbāʾī, 1971 vol. 9, p. 155) by saying: 'The verse only obligates giving *jiwār* to the *mustajīr* if he asked for it for a religious matter that is likely to be of good benefit to the religion. But the general *istijāra* [asking for *amān*] for non-religious reason and with no good of it to religion is not originally supported by this verse.' By saying this al-Ṭabāṭbāʾī becomes the second scholar after Abu al-Suᶜūd to restrict *asking for jiwār* to religious need, to the exclusion of all other needs.

After commenting on the verse extensively from different perspectives and reiterating what earlier scholars have said about it, Ṭanṭāwī affirms an important issue concerning the length of stay for the *mustajīr*. He says: 'It is obligatory on the *Imām* or whoever replaces him to give the *mustaʾmin* the period he deems would be enough for him to understand the truths of Islam.' He then quotes al-Rāzī to support his opinion.

Finally, he praises Islam for giving this opportunity to disbelievers and quotes Quṭb, without mentioning him, saying that the *amān* is the pinnacle of Islam and an indication that Islam is 'a system of guidance not a system of annihilation' since it not only gives unbelievers the opportunity to stay in the land, but also protects them and accompanies them until they reach a safe place should they refuse to convert.

Regarding al-Qaṭṭān and Ḥawmid, they interpret the verse briefly and stay within the general framework of earlier scholars.

The issue of abrogation[46]

Twenty out of the 54 scholars address the issue of abrogation. An examination of these commentaries makes it apparent that the main debate concerning this issue is based on two opinions. The first is that 'the verse is decisive' الآية محكمة and that is al-Ḥasan's opinion. The second is that the verse is abrogated by verse 9:5 or verse 9:36; this is what al-Ḍaḥḥāk, al-Siddī and Saᶜīd Ibn Abu Urūba claim.

However, the majority, 17 out of 20 scholars,[47] state in different phrases that the verse is decisive. Some of them go even further to say that 'the verse is not applicable for abrogation till the Judgement Day'.[48] However, others mention the two opinions on the verse without clarifying their views, like al-Ṭabarī (310 AH), Ibn ᶜAṭiyya (542 AH) and al-Kalbī (741 AH).

It is apparent that verse 9:6 forms the clearest Qurᵓanic evidence for legalizing *amān*. Interpretation of the verse has changed over the course of time and the understanding of scholars. Some scholars were satisfied with the apparent meaning in their interpretation whereas others were more questioning and went deeper in defining the *mustaᵓmin*.

From the meticulous discussions of the scholars about this verse, it is possible to conclude that the interpretation of verse 9:6 should be that if a non-Muslim, whether he is a follower of another religion or even without a religion, seeks the protection of the Muslims they should grant him their protection. The reasons that may drive such a person to seek protection in *dār al-Islam* are of no relevance in this context, since the verse itself does not specify any reason.

Based on the above discussion it could be said that the majority of scholars who based their interpretation on the assumption that the disbeliever comes to *dār al-Islam* to hear the word of God are not accurate, as this interpretation is in contradiction with the grammatical and linguistic rules of the Arabic language. The apparent meaning of the verse and the Arabic grammar supports my opinion.

The verse puts an obligation upon the Muslims to give *amān* to anyone who asks for it. On the other hand, Islamic society has a duty and a message of mercy towards other peoples, as stated in many verses of the Qurᵓān, and the greatest manifestation of this mercy is giving shelter and protection to those fleeing oppression and persecution.

More notably, the verse itself supports this meaning linguistically and grammatically. I agree with the scholars, including Abu Ḥayyān, Abu al-Suᵓūd and al-Qummī, who say the word *ḥatta* is referred to the verb 'grant him protection' فأجره and not the verb 'sought your protection' استجارك. However I disagree with them that the word *ḥatta* is for timing or to limit the duration of stay, since the *mustajīr* may not neccessarily ask for protection to listen to Islam. As mentioned above, he may ask for protection for any compelling reason. If the reason was to listen to the word of God, then limiting protection to the hearing would make sense; otherwise, it would not. However, if the disbeliever sought protection in the Islamic society out of fear, then limiting his stay to the hearing of the Qur'ān would be irrelevant to his case, because his protection could be ended while the reason that drove him to ask protection in the first place did not end. Thus, I believe that *ḥatta* is for rationalization of the whole process. Therefore, Muslims are obliged by this verse to grant their protection to whoever requests it so that they will have the opportunity to hear, learn and contemplate the Islamic principles. Thus, regardless of any reason, be it oppression, persecution, poverty, natural disaster or any other unfortunate circumstances, the Muslims should grant this *musta'min* the *amān* he asks for.

This understanding was also adopted by Ibn Kathīr, who discussed some cases from his time in which Muslims should grant *amān* to certain categories; eventually he left it open to accept similar cases in other times. Clearly, modern cases of refuge could be included.

We also have to bear in mind the examples mentioned above and especially the examples of al-Ṭabarī and Abu al-Suʿūd to assert that this matter was not theoretical but rather practical and relevant to their times. In addition, contemporary scholars such as Aṭfiyyash, Āshūr, al-Janābidhī and Sayyid Quṭb made it clear that the *musta'min* should be granted *amān* regardless of the reasons that drove him to seek it.

Another small, yet important, comment in the structure of the verse is the use of the letter ف in the word فأجره and letter ثم after the word أبلغه. According to the general Islamic belief every word and even every letter in the Qur'ān is placed intentionally and there is no randomness whatsoever in the Qur'ān. Even the apparent repetition in the Qur'ān is meant to give extra meanings.[49] Therefore, the two letters should be understood in this context. The Qur'ān uses the letter ف which is usually employed for coupling with the sense of speed associated with the verb 'grant him protection' أجره to tell the Muslims that they have to be swift in giving *amān* to those who seek it. This sense of speed in granting protection is crucially important in the case of destitute, distressed and fearful asylum seekers who flee their homes looking for a place of sanctuary.

When it comes to terminating the contract the Qurʾān uses the letter 'then' ثم which gives the sense of slow motion associated with the verb 'make him attain his place of safety' أبلغه مأمنه to order the Muslims to be slow in ending the contract of *amān* and give adequate time for the *mustaʾmin* before returning him to his place of safety.

This understanding of the verse harmonizes with the mercy the Prophet was sent to deliver to the worlds as in Qurʾanic verse 21:107: 'And we have not sent you but as a mercy to the worlds.'

Moreover, while the *mustaʾmin* stays in the Islamic state the Muslims should take care of him in terms of protection, welfare and finance, as al-Suyūṭī highlighted. Thus, it is a comprehensive responsibility given by God to all Muslims.

In addition, the phrase 'make him attain his place of safety' is vital in our discussion, especially when comparing the Islamic concept of refuge with the concept of *non-refoulement* stated in the Geneva Convention 1954 relating to refugees. This phrase puts an obligation on the shoulders of Muslims to protect the refugee until he reaches a safe place, without defining it or restricting it to the country of origin or the country where the refugee came from. The refugee's safety should not be jeopardized or compromised under any circumstances. If the refugee were to be expelled from a certain place, his or her safety should be secured by all means.

To sum up, in the Islamic tradition we find three terms used to identify the person who comes to the Islamic state seeking protection. They are: *mustajīr* – which applies to the Muslim and non-Muslim alike, *muhājīr* – a term used by the Qurʾān to describe Muslims only, and *mustaʾmin* – a loose term that includes all the foreigners who enter the Islamic state looking for protection, whether they are refugees or not, without specifying the reason for their visit. After entering *dār al-Islam* the status of each one would differ. The *muhājīr*, who is a Muslim, would enjoy permanent protection like the other citizens, while the *mustajīr* would enjoy temporary protection. The *mustaʾmin* would also enjoy temporary protection unless he became a *dhimmī*, in which case he would enjoy permanent protection like the Muslim. Figure 3.1 explains this situation.

However, in recent times and since the advent of national states, the situation has changed somewhat. All those who come seeking protection are called 'refugees' and their status is determined based on the laws of

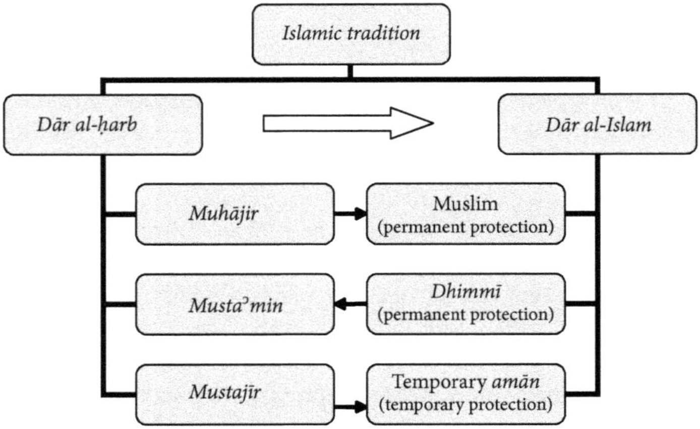

Figure 3.1 The position of the *mustajīr*, *musta'min* and *muhājir* in the Islamic tradition

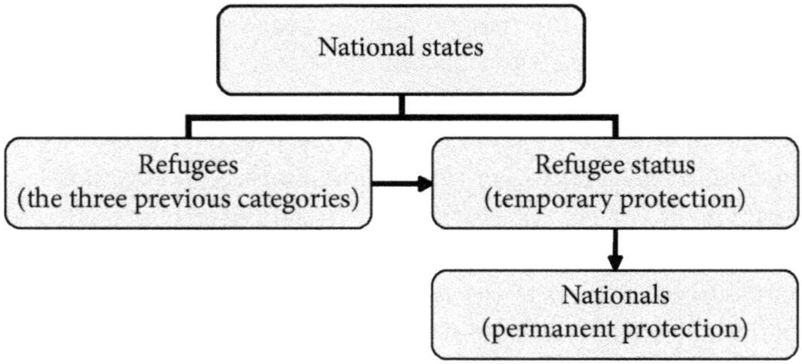

Figure 3.2 The modern position regarding refugees

the national state. Theoretically at least they enjoy temporary protection and if they stay longer then they are entitled to enjoy the nationality of the state. Figure 3.2 explains the situation.

An examination of the three terms indicates that the term closest in meaning to the modern term 'refugee' is '*mustaʾmin*', although the latter term encompasses other kinds of people. Hence from now on I will use it to mean a refugee.

Thus, based on the above discussion, the definition of the refugee in the Islamic tradition is 'the non-Muslim who enters the Islamic state looking for refuge, regardless of the reasons that drove him to do that, be it oppression, fear, natural disaster or any other unfortunate circumstances'. However, the authorities in the Islamic state have the right to organize the process according to the needs and the interests of Muslims without violating the right of others to seek refuge in the Islamic state.

The crucial point here is that the verse makes it obligatory on Muslims to give refuge to the seeker as an Islamic duty, while 'according to the modern refugee law, asylum is a right of the State and not of the individual' (Elmadmad, 1991, p. 473).

Finally, it could be rightly said here that the Islamic tradition provides a different system of protection than the modern system but the basic value of protection is embedded in both, and the traditional system could be implemented in a modern context. This justifies a closer examination of the type of protection granted by modern refugee status in comparison to the protection granted by *amān*; this will be done in the following chapter.

4

THE 1951 GENEVA CONVENTION RELATING TO THE STATUS OF REFUGEES IN THE LIGHT OF THE ISLAMIC TRADITION

This chapter studies the articles of the Geneva Convention from an Islamic perspective and examines the interface between the Convention and the Islamic tradition, with a view to identifying similarities and differences between the two. More importantly, it examines international refugee protection and protection granted by *amān* in the Islamic tradition.

The text of the relevant Articles of the Convention will be listed, along with the comments of legal experts where it is necessary to clarify it. The relevant articles will then be compared to the Islamic tradition to establish the evidence (if any) of endorsement, or otherwise.

This chapter follows the order of Articles in the UN Geneva Convention relating to the Status of Refugees adopted on 28 July 1951 by the United Nations Conference of Plenipotentiaries on the Status of Refugees and Stateless Persons convened under General Assembly resolution 429 (V) of 14 December 1950. The Articles under discussion are the following:

Article 1. Definition
Article 2. General obligations
Article 3. Non-Discrimination
Article 4. Religion
Article 12. Personal status
Article 13. Movable and immovable property

Article 15. Right of association
Article 16. Access to courts
Articles 17, 18 and 19. Gainful employment
Articles 20, 21, 22, 23 and 24. Welfare
Articles 26, 27, 28 and 29. Freedom of movement
Article 31. Refugees unlawfully in the country of refuge
Article 32. Expulsion
Article 33. Prohibition of expulsion or return 'refoulement'
Article 34. Naturalization

Some Articles have been omitted because they refer to administrative matters that are not relevant to the core of this study. Also, due to its particular importance, Article 33. 'Prohibition of expulsion or return "refoulement"' is not discussed in numerical order but immediately after the definition of 'refugee.' The discussion of Article 33 is followed up with a discussion of the 'safety of the refugee', which is not an Article in the Convention. This is due to its importance in the context of protection on one hand and to clarify the debate that took place between the Muslim scholars on this issue on the other. Lastly, I assume that if the Islamic tradition does not disagree with the main Articles of the Convention, then by default it will endorse them.

Definition of the term 'refugee' (Article 1)

The definition of the term 'refugee' is of critical importance, 'for it can mean the difference between life and death for an individual seeking asylum' (Chimni, 2000, p. 1).

It is evident that there are many definitions of the term 'refugee'. There is the definition of the 1951 Convention with the 1967 Protocol, the definition of the Organization of the African Unity (OAU) and the Cartagena Declaration, as well as the Asian-African Legal Consultative Committee definition.

Broadly speaking, these different definitions were to some extent influenced by the circumstances at the time of the legislation. This is evident from the 1951 Convention which names the categories of the people who are entitled to seek refuge, all of which relate to that particular historical period. Hathaway points out that 'there is no avoiding the Cold War origins of the 1951 Convention definition and its Eurocentric focus' (Chimni, 2000, p. 2). He adds that 'in addition to their desire for the refugee definition to serve strategic political objectives, the majority of states that drafted the Convention sought to create a rights regime conducive to the redistribution of the post-war refugee burden from European shoulders' (Hathaway, 1991, p. 8).

Moreover, the OAU definition, as Chimni (2000, p. 62) indicates, reflects more closely 'the realities of Africa during a period of violent struggle for self-determination and national development'. The Cartagena Declaration, Arboleda explains, 'broadened the definition still further recognising the special attention deserved by the Central American situation' (Chimni, 2000, p. 62).

The Islamic definition was also influenced by the environment in which it was formed. Earlier chapters have discussed the diversity of Muslim scholarly opinion over the course of time regarding the definition of the term 'refugee'.

The significance of the 1951 Convention and the 1967 Protocol

This Convention with the Protocol, as Goodwin-Gill (1996, p. 20) says: 'Remain the principal international instrument benefiting refugees and their definition has been expressly adopted in a variety of regional arrangements aimed at further improving the situation of recognized refugees. It forms the basis for article I of the 1969 OAU Convention on refugee Problems in Africa.' Even the Cartagena Declaration is based on the elements of the 1951 Convention and the Protocol that broadened it (Goodwin-Gill, 1996, p. 20).

However, it is appropriate to touch on these different definitions, before expanding on the 1951 Convention and the 1967 Protocol.

The OAU Convention and the Cartagena Declaration

The Convention and the Declaration came about because the definition of the refugee in the 1951 Convention, as Arboleda puts it, 'did not adequately respond to the variety of situations in the sixties and seventies; for the drafters of the early definitions neither considered nor anticipated the problems of the less developed world' (Chimni, 2000, p. 62).

The OAU Convention defines the term 'refugee' as:

> [E]very person who, owing to external aggression, occupation, foreign domination or events seriously disturbing public order in either part or the whole of his country of origin or nationality, is

> compelled to leave his place of habitual residence in order to seek refuge in another place outside his country of origin or nationality.

The important addition of this Convention was, as Arboleda (Chimni, 2000, p. 63) states, that 'for the first time, the legal term "refugee", albeit at regional level, was extended to individuals forced to leave their countries owing to aggression by another State and/or as a result of an invasion'. Arboleda goes on to say that the OAU Convention marked the beginning of a refugee protection system that directly addressed the causes of mass refugee influxes, by emphasizing conditions in the country of origin.

Although the Cartagena Declaration did not grow out of a regional organization, and is not a formally binding treaty, it 'represents endorsement by the States concerned of appropriate and applicable standards of protection and assistance' (Goodwin-Gill, 1996, p. 21).

In addition, the definition of this Declaration, according to Goodwin-Gill (1996, p. 21) includes 'persons who have fled their country, because their lives, safety or freedom have been threatened by generalized violence, foreign aggression, internal conflicts, massive violation of human rights or other circumstances seriously disturbing public order'.

With regard to the Cartagena Declaration, Arboleda (Chimni, 2000, p. 63) maintains that it 'was the first document in the Latin American context to establish guidelines for states faced with mass inflows of refugees. It was also the first instrumental declaration recognising that the victims of generalised violence, internal conflicts and massive human rights violations deserved refugee status.'

The 1951 Convention and the 1967 Protocol

The main object of this Convention is 'to endeavour to assure refugees the widest possible exercise of the fundamental rights and freedoms enshrined in the Charter of the United Nations and the Universal Declaration of Human Rights' (Nicholson *et al.*, 2003, p. 100).

This Convention and its Protocol have become so important that 'it is unlikely that the Convention drafters envisaged the extent to which it would become a standard feature of courtroom dispute or generate so prolific a body of work amongst legal academics' (Nicholson *et al.* 1999, p. 4). Notwithstanding this, the Convention has limitations and falls short of other conventions in terms of the definition of 'refugee'. Nonetheless, it still forms the most important convention relating to the status of refugees. That, according to Hathaway (1991, p. v) is owing to the fact that 'it has been subscribed to by more than one hundred nations in the only refugee accords of global scope. Many nations have also imported this standard into their domestic immigration legislation as the basis upon which asylum and other protection decisions are made.'

The 1951 Convention, according to Nicholson (Nicholson *et al.* 2003, p. 100), defined the term 'refugee' to apply, first, to any person who had been considered a refugee under the earlier arrangements or under the IRO Constitution, and secondly to any person who:

> As a result of events occurring before 1 January 1951 and owing to well-founded fear of being persecuted for reasons of race, religion, nationality, membership of a particular social group or political opinion, is outside the country of his nationality and is unable or, owing to such fear, is unwilling to avail himself of the protection of that country; or who, not having a nationality and being outside the country of his former habitual residence as a result of such events, is unable or, owing to such fear, is unwilling to return to it.

With regard to the 1967 Protocol it states that:

> For the purpose of the present Protocol, the term 'refugee' shall, except as regards the application of paragraph 3 of this article, mean any person within the definition of article I of the Convention as if the words 'As a result of events occurring before 1 January 1951 and …' and the words '… as a result of such events', in article 1 A (2) were omitted.
>
> The present Protocol shall be applied by the States Parties hereto without any geographic limitation, save that existing declarations made by States already Parties to the Convention in accordance with article I B (I) (a) of the Convention, shall, unless extended under article I B (2) thereof, apply also under the present Protocol.

The key feature of that Protocol was that it 'removed the temporal and geographical limitations in the 1951 Convention' (Chimni, 2000, p. 7). It achieved the formal, but not the substantive, univerzalisation of the Convention definition of refugee status.

Overall, the Convention as Hathaway (Chimni, 2000, pp. 14–15) explains:

> May be viewed as comprising five essential elements, each of which must be established before status is appropriately recognised …
>
> The first is persons who have left their country of nationality, or in the case of stateless persons, their country of habitual residence …
>
> Second, the refugee claimant must be *genuinely at risk*. It is not enough that she truly believe herself to be in jeopardy. Rather, there must be objective facts to provide a concrete foundation for the concern which induces her to seek protection in another state …
>
> Third, the claimant's flight must be motivated by prospect of 'persecution', that is *risk of serious harm* against which the state of origin is *unwilling or unable to offer protection* …
>
> Fourth, the risk faced by the refugee claimant must have some nexus to her race, religion, nationality, membership in a particular social group, or political opinion. The critical question is whether but for her *civil or political status* she could reasonably be said to be at risk of serious harm …
>
> Fifth and finally, there must be a genuine need for and legitimate claim to protection.

The Arab and Islamic Declarations and the issue of refuge

Regrettably, Muslim scholars in modern times have paid little attention to the issue of refuge, as far as their studies and debates are concerned. However, the Cairo Declaration on Human Rights in Islam, which was adopted by the 19th Islamic Conference of Foreign Ministers in 1990, made mention of this topic in Article 12:

> Every man [sic] shall have the right, within the framework of the *Sharīᶜah*, to free movement and to select his place of residence whether within or outside his country and if persecuted, is entitled to seek asylum in another country. The country of refuge shall be obliged to provide protection to the asylum-seeker until his safety has been attained, unless asylum is motivated by committing an act regarded by the *Sharīᶜah* as a crime.

The Arab Charter on Human Rights, adopted by the League of Arab States in 1997, also touches on the issue of refuge in Article 23:

> Every citizen shall have the right to seek political asylum in other countries in order to escape persecution. This right shall not be enjoyed by persons facing prosecution for an offence under the ordinary law. Political refugees shall not be extraditable.

In terms of the motives it appears the same as the Cairo Declaration, stating that the reason for seeking asylum should be persecution, without extending it to other reasons.

Lastly, like the Cairo Declaration it cites clearly that political refugee should not be extradited.

The definition of 'refugee' in the Islamic tradition and the Geneva Convention

As explained above, in the Islamic tradition there are three terms that come close to the meaning of the modern term 'refugee'. These are *mustajīr*, *muhājīr* and *mustaᵓmin*. The usage and context of these three terms has varied over time. Yet, the closest of them to the modern term 'refugee' is *mustaᵓmin*, as indicated earlier.[1]

For the purposes of comparison, however, I will consider the five elements employed by Hathaway as standards to see how far the Islamic definition I have reached of the term 'refugee' agrees or disagrees with the 1951 Convention.

With regard to the first point about leaving one's country, it seems that although the Muslim scholars did not state this formally, the fact of departure was implicit. When interpreting Qurᵓanic verse 9:6 or discussing *ᶜaqd al-amān* all scholars supposed that the disbeliever comes to the Islamic country asking for refuge. However, it should be noted here that the terms 'borders' and 'nationality' were not identified at the time of the early Islamic state as we identify them today.

Such terminology is relatively modern. Instead, the early Muslim scholars divided the world into three categories: *dār al-Islam*, *dār al-ḥarb* and *dār al-ᶜahd*, with some variations between them, as discussed in Chapter 2. Yet they agreed that the conversion of the *ḥarbī* to Islam allows him to enjoy all rights of Muslims in *dār al-Islam*.

The issue of nationality in the Muslim state will be discussed later in this chapter. However, at this point it is important to note that religion played a significant role in determining geographical limitations and borders in the early days of Islam.

The second element, about genuine risk, is quite specific in the Convention, but not so detailed in the Islamic tradition. Even though neither the Qurʾan nor the Prophet stipulated it, we still find that some scholars interpret verse 9:6 as permitting disbelievers to come to *dār al-Islam* for reasons other than listening to the word of God. Moreover, as discussed in Chapter 3, close scrutiny of the verse shows that it does not specify any particular reason for asking *amān* in *dār al-Islam*; thus, the feeling that one is at genuine risk should be one of the valid reasons for asking for protection in the Islamic state.

Based on this, it could be said that the Islamic thinking on this point is wider than the Convention. This might be due to the nature of Islam as a universal religion with a message of mercy that tries to spread far and wide, by allowing the vulnerable to seek protection in its land and to learn about Islam. This could explain why neither the Qurʾan nor the Prophet specified the reason for seeking refuge. Nevertheless, Muslim scholars did indicate that there should be some control over the granting of protection to refugees by saying that this protection should not go against the interests of Muslims as a whole. In theory, the borders of the Muslim state should be open to refugees regardless of why they are seeking refuge there. However, in practical terms, this should not be in conflict with the State's general interests, public security or even its capacity. Obviously, this matter is left to the authorities in the Islamic state to decide on.

The third, fourth and fifth elements are related to the previous element. From an Islamic perspective they are important despite the fact that Islamic jurisprudence has not formally detailed such cases. All cases of refuge that early Muslims experienced arose because of oppression and persecution. The Islamic tradition opened the door wide to refugees, but that is not to say that the Islamic state should not have certain regulations for controlling this process. On the contrary, as the scholars said, the head of state should ensure that regulations exist to manage the process effectively and to ensure a balance between the accessibility of the Muslim state for refugees and the national interest of the Muslims.

In brief, the differences between the Islamic definition I arrived at and the UN Convention definition is that in theory at least the Islamic tradition is wider than the UN's definition and does not specify particular reasons for seeking refuge. In fact, the Islamic tradition leaves it up to the authorities in the Islamic state to decide who deserves to be a refugee.

Exclusion clauses

Regarding the definition of the term 'refugee', international conventions specify particular criteria for those who are entitled to the right of asylum. Nevertheless, 'they also establish criteria by which individuals may be excluded from international protection' (Chimni, 2000, p. 57).

Over the years 'awareness of the background and past of certain asylum seekers has increased, inter alia as a result of the atrocities committed during the Yugoslav wars. Paying increased attention to the issue of the application of the exclusion clause was apt and timely' (Van Krieken and Asser, 1999, p. 1).

Even before the UN Convention saw the light of day, the drafters of the Universal Declaration of Human Rights (UDHR) in 1948, as Van Krieken and Asser (1999, p. 1) state, 'not only laid down the right to seek and enjoy asylum from persecution (Article 14.1) but they also added that certain categories of persons were excluded from seeking, not to mention enjoying, asylum'.

The exclusion clauses were stipulated in the Geneva Convention in Article 1. F. After defining the term at length the 1951 Convention excludes certain people from this definition:

> F. The provisions of this Convention shall not apply to any person with respect to whom there are serious reasons for considering that:
>
> (a) He has committed a crime against peace, a war crime, or a crime against humanity, as defined in the international instruments drawn up to make provision in respect of such crimes;
> (b) He has committed a serious non-political crime outside the country of refuge prior to his admission to that country as a refugee;
> (c) He has been guilty of acts contrary to the purposes and principles of the United Nations.

The crimes listed above have been subject to debate and analysis by legal experts such as Goodwin-Gill (1996, pp. 95–114) and Van Krieken and Asser (1999).

Obviously, as Chimni (2000, p. 57), states:

> the primary purposes of these exclusion clauses are to deprive the perpetrators of heinous acts and serious common crimes of such protection, and to safeguard the receiving country from criminals who present a danger to the country's security. If the protection provided by refugee law were permitted to afford protection to perpetrators of grave offence, the practice of international protection would be in direct conflict with national and international law, and would contradict the humanitarian and peaceful nature of the concept of asylum. From this perspective, exclusion clauses help to preserve the integrity of the asylum concept.

An examination of the Islamic heritage will determine to what extent the Islamic tradition agrees or disagrees with this principle.

But before that, it is appropriate to point out that the Arabs in the *jāhiliyya* also exempted some people from enjoying their *jiwār*.

As explained in Chapter 1, *jiwār* was applied extensively in the *jāhiliyya*, and occupied a significant place in the social life of the Arabs at that time, for a number of reasons. Yet there are some examples where people were refused *jiwār*. A major reason for this was that the party being asked for protection was too weak to defend the *mustajīr* against powerful enemies.

One example of this was the incident of al-Ḥārith Ibn Ẓālim al-Mirrī, who killed the son of al-Nuᶜmān Ibn al-Mundhir and then fled, asking many tribes to give him *jiwār*. They refused, saying: 'who will give you *jiwār* against Hawāzin, the tribe, and al-Nuᶜmān after you killed his son?' (al-Shaybānī, 1994, vol. 1, p. 447). The question was purely rhetorical, because nobody would have given him *jiwār* after committing such a crime. No tribe had the power to stand up to the mighty Hawāzin, the tribe he had offended against.

This excuse of weakness or moral responsibility, in some cases, continued in the Islamic state, where the custom of *jiwār* was maintained, apart from *ᶜaqd al-amān*. The literature includes a number of examples where certain elite and powerful personalities in the Islamic community refused to grant *jiwār* to various people because of the nature of their crimes. As recorded in Ibn al-Jawzī's *History of Baghdad* (1939, vol. 12, p. 22)[2] in 249 AH al-Mustaᶜīn Billāh, the caliph, refused to grant *jiwār* to his minister Atāmish, when the public revolted against him as a consequence of his crimes against them.

We also can find examples where prominent personalities refused to give *jiwār* to others to avoid angering the ruler or the chief of the province they lived in. When Yūsuf Ibn Abī ᶜAyyād was defeated by the Sultan's forces in Morocco, he sought *jiwār* of Makhlūf Ibn ᶜAbbū, but the latter refused lest he upset the Sultan (Ibn Khaldūn, 1984, vol. 7, p. 311).[3] In addition, when Yazid Ibn Rabīᶜa clashed with ᶜUbayd Allah Ibn Ziyād, the ruler of al-Basra during the Umayyad period, and fled to Syria, al-Aḥnaf Ibn Qays and Khālid Ibn Usayd refused to give him *jiwār* so as not to anger the ruler (al-Ḥamawī, 1993, vol. 5, p. 639).

Concerning the issue of exclusion in the Islamic tradition, there is no concrete evidence or a direct ruling in the Qur'ān that stipulates a judgement on this issue. However, the concept of exclusion is mentioned in the Qur'ān in reference to the weighing of people's sins on the Day of Judgement. Some Qur'anic verses stipulate clearly that particular sins will not be forgiven and those who are guilty of them will be excluded from God's forgiveness and mercy and will not enter Paradise. The greatest sin of all is apostasy and associating other beings with God. The Qur'ān (4:48) stipulates: 'Verily, God does not forgive the ascribing of divinity to aught beside Him, although He forgives any lesser sin unto whomever He wills: for he who ascribes divinity to aught beside God has indeed contrived an awesome sin.' This means all sinners may be forgiven except those who do not believe in God or associate others with Him in their worship. So, the association of others with God is the biggest sin in the Islamic creed and in the hereafter God will exclude those who associate others with him from his forgiveness and from Paradise.

This exclusion is also stressed clearly in Qur'anic verse 5:72, where God forbids Paradise for the disbelievers.

Islam is a monotheistic faith and requires belief in God as the sole Creator and the only one worthy of worship. Disbelief or association in this context contradicts the very foundations of the Islamic faith and this may explain why it cannot be forgiven and why anyone commiting these acts will be excluded from mercy in the hereafter, while other sins could be forgiven.

With regard to the exclusion in this life concerning refugees, the *sīra* holds some relevant examples. One account is narrated by al-Ṣuyūṭī (1993, vol. 4, p. 351) on the authority of Saᶜd Ibn Abī Waqqāṣ: 'On the day of Mecca conquest, the Prophet, peace be upon him, gave *amān* to all people except four men and two women, and said: Kill them even if you find them hanging to the cloths of the Kaᶜba. [They are]: ᶜIkrima Ibn

Abī Jahl, ᶜAbdullah Ibn Khaṭal, Maqīs Ibn Ḍabāba[4] and ᶜAbdullah Ibn Abī Sarḥ'.[5]

From the strong wording of this *ḥadīṭh* we can guess at the nature of the crimes. The Kaᶜba is the most sacred place and it gives security to anyone around it. The Qur'ān states this clearly in verse 3:97: 'Whoever enters it attains security.' Hanging on to its cloth was the strongest form of sanctuary one could aspire to. Despite that, some would not benefit from the sacredness of this place and nothing on earth could save them from punishment.

Regarding the two women, the narrations vary in identifying them. Some suggest that they were the slaves of Ibn Khaṭal, who used to satirize the Prophet (al-Bayhaqī, 1989, vol. 8, p. 205). Other narrations identify them as Um Sārah, 'a slave singer of Banī Hāshim who used to curse the Prophet every day and night' (al-Fākihī, 1993, vol. 5, p. 220) and Bunāna, of whom Abī Barza narrated that he heard the Prophet saying: 'All people are safe except ᶜAbdullah Ibn Khaṭal and the immoral Bunāna' (Ibn Saᶜd, n.d., vol. 4, p. 299).

Studying the different narrations carefully informs our understanding of the grounds on which the Prophet excluded these six people from the general *amān* extended to the people of Mecca, and facilitates the extraction of general rules and regulations with regard to exclusion.

Starting with the first man named in the previous *ḥadīth*, ᶜIkrima Ibn Abī Jahl, the literature includes at least 294 accounts of him, scattered throughout the *sīra*, *ḥadith*, *fiqh* and *tafsīr*. Unfortunately, none of these state clearly why the Prophet excluded him from the *amān*. Many describe him positively after his conversion to Islam, while other accounts refer to his strong enmity towards the Muslims before converting.

When he came to the Prophet apparently repentant and willing to convert, he admitted, according to the account narrated by al-Naysābūrī (1990, vol. 3, p. 270) that he was still hostile towards the Prophet and had been plotting aggressively against the Muslims.

Another account highlights some of the terrible acts that may have driven the Prophet to exclude him from the *amān*. al-Ṣuyūṭī (1993, vol. 1, p. 571) reports on the authority of Abu Isḥāq that ᶜIkrima was one of those who enticed and encouraged the people of Quraysh to kill Khubayb Ibn ᶜAdyy.

The story of Khubayb as narrated by Ibn Ḥibbān (1993, vol. 15, p. 512) was that the Prophet sent a group of Muslims to bring him news of

Quraysh.[6] On their way to Mecca they were intercepted by the tribe of Banī Laḥyān. After a fierce fight they were all killed, with the exception of Khubayb Ibn ᶜAdyy and Zayd Ibn al-Dithna who were sold as slaves to Quraysh. Eventually, Quraysh killed the captives, encouraged by ᶜIkrima.

The role of ᶜIkrima in Khubayb's death, in addition to his heinous acts, may be the reason behind his exclusion from the general *amān* enjoyed by the people of Mecca at the time.

Despite this exclusion, the Muslims did not kill ᶜIkrima. According to the account narrated by al-Bazzār (1988, vol. 3, p. 350) ᶜIkrima tried to flee by sea. When the storm was about to tear his boat apart he vowed that he would return to the Prophet and become a Muslim.[7] The Prophet accepted his repentance and forgave him.[8]

Concerning ᶜAbdullah Ibn Khaṭal, there are 112 narrations that provide reports about him. Most of these accounts concentrate on the manner in which he was killed, but few explain why he was excluded.

The way he was killed is narrated by many scholars.[9] The narrations all agree that: 'As for ᶜAbdullah Ibn Khaṭal [he] was caught hanging on to the cloths of the Kaᶜba. [When they saw him] Saᶜīd Ibn Ḥurayth and ᶜAmmār Ibn Yāsir competed to get him. Saᶜīd outran ᶜAmmār as he was the younger of the two and killed him [i.e. Ibn Khaṭal]' (Abu Yaᵓlā, 1984, vol. 2, p. 100).

Several reasons are offered for his exclusion from the general *amān*. Ibn ᶜAbd al-Barr (1967, vol. 6, p. 170) and Ibn Ḥajar state that:

> He ordered the killing of Ibn Khaṭal because he was a Muslim and the Prophet sent him as a messenger (to some people). The Prophet sent with him a man from the *Anṣār* and a slave to serve him, and he was a Muslim. In their way they stopped over, and Ibn Khaṭal ordered the slave to slaughter a goat and make food for him. The slave slept and woke up without making anything for him. So he [Ibn Khaṭal] attacked him and killed him. Then he reverted to disbelief. He also had two slave singers who used to ridicule the Prophet (Ibn Ḥajar, n.d., vol. 4, p. 61).

Not only, then, did he kill a Muslim without a valid reason, but he also reverted to disbelief and allowed his slaves to vilify the Prophet. His crimes were an explicit challenge to the Prophet that clearly could not be tolerated or forgiven.

Nevertheless, al-Suyūṭī (1993, vol. 8, p. 517) gives a different reason for the exclusion. He reports on the authority of Saᶜīd Ibn Jubayr that ᶜAbdullah Ibn Khaṭal [after his conversion] came to the Prophet and asked to be one of those who wrote down the Qurʾān. The Prophet agreed and started to tell him what to write. Ibn Khaṭal purposely changed the order of the wording. Instead of writing 'the most Knowledgeable, the Wise', as told by the Prophet, Ibn Khaṭal would change the order, putting forward 'the Wise, the most Knowledgeable'. He then read back to the Prophet what he had written in an attempt to confuse him. Eventually, Ibn Khaṭal went to Quraysh, the enemy of the Muslims, and told them that 'his message is nonsense'. Thus Ibn Jubayr concludes: 'So he became one of the four whom the Prophet did not give *amān* to' (al-Suyūṭī, 1993, vol. 8, p. 517).

Concerning the third person, Maqīs Ibn Ḍabāba, I found no fewer than 80 reports about him in different books.[10] The majority concentrate on how he was killed, but some also make mention of why he was killed.

Al-ᶜAynı (n.d., vol. 18, p. 182) reports the story at length. When Maqīs discovered that his brother Hishām had been killed by Banī al-Najjār, he told the Prophet. The Prophet sent with him a messenger to Banī al-Najjār and ordered them to hand over the killer, if they knew who he was. Banī al-Najjār swore that they did not know the killer and showed their willingness to pay the blood money. After they had paid Maqīs 100 camels, he killed the messenger of the Prophet who was with him. Then he reverted to disbelief and returned to Mecca. When the Muslims conquered Mecca, they killed him in the market.[11]

Al-Haythamī (1986, vol. 6, p. 168) offers a more graphic account. While al-Fahrī [the Muslim from the tribe of Banī Fahr] slept Maqīs got up, took a big stone and smashed his head. Then he said these verses:

شفى النفس من قد مات بالقاع مسندا   يضرج ثوبيه دماء الاجادع

وكانت هموم النفس من قبل قتله   تهيج فتنسيني وطاة المضاجع

حللت به ثأري وأدركت ثورتي   وكنت الى الاوثان أول راجع

He has cured the soul the one who has died and stretched in the Qāᶜ[12]
With the blood [of his nose and head] covering his cloths
The stress, before getting him killed used to attack.

me to the extent I that I could not sleep
I have taken revenge and attained my desire
And I am the first to revert to the idols.

His crimes were unforgivable. Acceptance of blood money meant the negation of the right to revenge. But Maqīs, after taking the blood money, deceived the innocent messenger who accompanied him and killed him. He then reverted to disbelief and went back to Mecca.

With regard to ᶜAbdullah Ibn Abī Sarḥ, al-Ṭabarī and al-Suyūṭī agree that he was the person mentioned in Qurʾanic verse 6:93:

> And who could be more wicked than he who invents a lie about God, or says, 'This has been revealed unto me', while nothing has been revealed to him? – or he who says, 'I, too, can bestow from on high the like of what God has bestowed'? If thou couldst but see [how it will be] when these evildoers find themselves in the agonies of death, and the angels stretch forth their hands [and call]: 'Give up your souls! Today you shall be requited with the suffering of humiliation for having attributed to God something that is not true, and for having persistently scorned His messages in your arrogance!'

Al-Ṭabarī (1984, vol. 7, p. 272) explains that he used to write down the Qurʾān as recited by the Prophet. He started to change the ends of verses and doubt crept into his heart. He reverted to disbelief and went back to Quraysh. Afterwards he would say: 'If Muḥammad is the recipient of revelations, then so am I. And if God brings down the Qurʾān, well I have brought down the same. Muḥammad says: The All-Hearing, the All-knowing and I say: the All-knowing, the Wise.'

Moreover, he committed another crime by revealing the secret about the conversion of ᶜAmmār and Jubayr to Banī ᶜAbd al-Dār who took them, cut off ᶜAmmār's ear and tortured them till they reverted to disbelief (al-Ṭabarī, 1984, vol. 7, p. 272).

It could be that the Prophet ordered his death because of these crimes. However, after the conquest of Mecca ᶜUthmān Ibn ᶜAffān pledged to the Prophet to give him *amān*. The Prophet, as al-Nasāʾī (1991, vol. 2, p. 302) reports, refused to give him *amān* three times but then, reluctantly, agreed to do so. The Prophet's comment after giving him the pardon is self-explanatory. He turned to his companions and said: 'Was not there a reasonable man amongst you who is ready to go to this man and kill him when he saw that I withheld my hand so as not to accept his allegiance?' (al-Suyūṭī, 1993, vol. 4, p. 351).

Regarding the two women, one was a slave singer who used to deride the Prophet while the other was Um Sārah, who was involved in spying against the Muslims, as al-Ṭabarānī (1994, vol. 6, p. 343), al-Suyūṭī (1993, vol. 8, p. 127), and al-Hindī (1998, vol. 10, p. 234) report.

According to these reports Um Sārah was the messenger who carried a letter to Quraysh telling them that the Prophet was preparing to attack them. When the angel Jibrīl revealed this to the Prophet, he sent ʾUmar and ʾAlī to capture her. At first she refused to give them the letter, but under threat of death she untied her hair and surrendered it (al-Ṭabarānī, 1994, vol. 6, p. 343).

This type of crime could be classified by the Muslims, or indeed by any nation nowadays, as one of the most dangerous crimes, since it threatens the security of the whole country and makes it vulnerable to enemies.

To sum up, after studying these incidents in detail a common factor emerges. As Ibn Taymiyya (1984, vol. 3, p. 773) concludes: 'In the year of conquest, the Prophet gave *amān* to all fighters except those who had committed a special crime that necessitated his killing.'

In all cases the crimes were serious and many had resulted in the death of innocent people. Ibn Khaṭal killed the Muslim who was accompanying him. Maqīs killed the man from Banī Fahr after taking blood money from his tribe.

Killing a Muslim, from the Islamic perspective, is greater than the destruction of the whole world, as the Prophet said in the *ḥadīṯh* reported by al-Jīrāḥī (1984, vol. 2, p. 119): 'Surely, the demolishing of the earthly life, in the eyes of God, is lesser than killing a believer without a rightful reason.' In the Qurʾān God gives killing a single human being a universal dimension. Verse 5:32 reads:

> Because of this did We ordain unto the children of Israel that if anyone slays a human being unless it be [in punishment] for murder or for spreading corruption on earth – it shall be as though he had slain all mankind; whereas, if anyone saves a life, it shall be as though he had saved the lives of all mankind. And, indeed, there came unto them Our apostles with all evidence of the truth: yet,

> behold, notwithstanding all this, many of them go on committing all manner of excesses on earth.

As far as Ibn Abī Sarḥ is concerned, the accounts mentioned earlier indicate that he may have been killed because he cheated the Prophet, reverted to disbelief and started to mock the Prophet after the Prophet had trusted him to the extent that he allowed him to help write down the Qurʾān.

Lastly, the crimes of the two women could be explained. Um Sārah was involved in spying against the Muslims and was caught carrying a message to enemies of the Prophet revealing the secrets of the Muslims, while the other woman was involved in cursing the Prophet and vilifying the message of Islam, according to the previous accounts.

What is more, the arguments of the scholars in regard to the punishment of those who commit severe crimes offer more evidence to strengthen the previous opinions.

They argued about the interpretation of the verses (5:33/34):

> It is but a just recompense for those who make war on God and His apostle, and endeavour to spread corruption on earth, that they are being slain, or crucified, or have their hands and feet cut off from opposite sides, or are being [entirely] banished from [the face of] the earth: such is their ignominy in this world. But in the life to come [yet more] awesome suffering awaits them (34) save for such [of them] as repent ere you [O believers] become more powerful than they: for you must know that God is much-forgiving, a dispenser of grace.

Al-Ṭabarī mentions disagreements between scholars about the interpretation of these verses and quotes those who said that even if the *Imām* gave the criminal *amān* this does not mean the people he harmed would lose their right to retribution or compensation. He must return what he had taken (al-Ṭabarī, 1984, vol. 6, p. 221). Al-Ṭabarī then reinforces his argument by quoting Mālik, who affirms that the rights of other people will not be abolished by the *amān* that he might get from the *Imām*.

Furthermore, al-Ṭabarī cites scholars who made granting *amān* conditional on the size of the crime, concluding that 'his crime should not be big' (al-Ṭabarī, 1984, vol. 6, p. 223). He goes on to narrate on the authority of Sa^c^ıd Ibn Jubayr that he said: 'If he [the one who committed a crime] came repentant and did not commit a robbery nor killed anybody then he will be left [given *amān*]. This is what God said: "Except for those who repent before they fall into your power". He means those who did not kill nor commit any robbery.'

Al-Ṭabarī also narrates on the authority of ^c^Urwa Ibn al-Zubayr that: 'He [the one who committed a crime and fled and then came back asking *amān*] should be punished for the crimes he committed and nobody is allowed to give him *amān*.' Finally, al-Ṭabarī quotes a scholar, Abu ^c^Amr, saying that: 'If he [the criminal] fled in *dār al-Islam* and the *Imām* gave him *amān*, then this *amān* is not valid.'

Al-Qārī (2001, vol. 5, p. 616) states unambiguously that even Mecca will not give sanctuary to criminals like those who rebel against the Caliph.

From all these narrations it is apparent that certain crimes could not be tolerated or forgiven, and that those who committed such crimes were not entitled to refuge or asylum in the Islamic state.

These examples illustrated the types of crime that demanded the withdrawal of the right to seek asylum in the Islamic state. The nature of the crime may vary from time to time and there is no clear text from the Prophet to determine these crimes. However, these examples from the Prophetic custom and the opinion of scholars give a clear indication to contemporary scholars of the kinds of crimes that demanded such a punishment.

Comparison

After examining the Islamic tradition in regard to the exclusion clause we can now compare the Convention exclusion clause to the Islamic tradition.

There is in fact a great deal of agreement between the two. Both agree in principle that some people should be excluded from asylum on account of their crimes. They also agree that these crimes are so serious that they cannot be tolerated under any circumstances.

Regarding the definition of these crimes, the Convention has defined the categories, while in Islam there is no such clear classification. That could be due to the universal nature of Islam and its validity in different places and times, as the Muslim scholars claim. In other words, Islam provides the general principles, while the scholars in each generation must shape the rulings in accordance with these general principles to suit their time and place.

Nonetheless, the Islamic tradition can and should adopt the categories outlined in the Convention. The Prophet considered the killing of a single person to be grounds for exclusion from the right to seek refuge, so it goes without saying that crimes on a larger scale, such as crimes against peace, war crimes, or crimes against humanity, should be included. Some examples mentioned above could fall under the category of war crimes, as defined by Goodwin-Gill (1996, p. 98), which includes the killing of hostages. Moreover, the attacks against the Prophet and the attempts to destroy the core of his message could be of a universal nature from the Islamic point of view, especially when the Qurʾān states clearly that the Prophet was sent as a mercy to all mankind.

In regard to the second category in Article 1 F (c), 'a serious non-political crime outside the country of refuge prior to his admission to that country as a refugee', also applies in the Islamic tradition. Most of the previous examples fall under this category, such as the incident of Maqīs Ibn Ḍabāba, who killed a Muslim, and the others who committed different crimes prior to conquering Mecca.

Even the third category in Article 1 F (c): 'acts contrary to the purposes and principles of the United Nations' is generally endorsed by the Islamic tradition. The objective of these principles, as stated by Goodwin-Gill (1996, p. 109), is 'to prevent war, to reaffirm faith in fundamental human rights, to establish the condition under which justice and respect for obligations can be maintained, and to promote social progression and better standards of life in larger freedom'. These humane principles do not, on the whole, contradict Islamic principles. On the contrary, they coincide broadly with Islamic teachings.

In terms of preventing war, we find in the *ḥadīth* narrated by al-Bukhārī (1986, vol. 6, p. 2644) that the Prophet tells his followers: 'Do not wish to fight the enemy and ask God for safety.' In other words the Prophet tells them that if you can stop war from happening, do so, and pray to God that war will not break out.

Concerning human rights, generally speaking many *ḥadīths* and verses of the Qurʾān made people equal in their humanity. The Prophet pointed out that all people are the same: 'People are like the teeth of the comb' (al-Quḍāʿī, 1986, vol. 1, p. 145). The Prophet also said (Ibn al-Mubārak, 1986, vol. 1, p. 147) 'O people, your God is one and your father is one.

Surely, no superiority for the Arabs over the non-Arabs, nor for the non-Arabs over the Arabs, nor for the black over the red and nor the red over the black save the piety of God.'

Furthermore, the importance of justice and mercy to all human kind is emphasized throughout the Qurʾān, for example in 21:107: 'And [thus, O Prophet,] We have sent thee as [an evidence of Our] grace towards all the worlds.' There is a great deal of material in the Islamic tradition to support social justice, freedom from all kinds of oppression and noble morals. The *ḥadīth* narrated by al-Bayhaqī (1989, vol. 10, p. 191) on the authority of Abu Hurayra that the Prophet said: 'I was only sent to make the moral qualities perfect' fits into this context. Moreover, al-Haythamī (1986, vol. 8, p. 167) reports on the authority of Anas Ibn Mālik that the Prophet said: 'He is not a believer in me who sleeps with full stomach while his neighbour next to him sleeps hungry, and he knows about him.' In addition, Ibn Ḥibbān (1993, vol. 11, p. 571) narrates that the Prophet said: 'Support your brother if he is the oppressed or the oppressor. The companions said "O the Prophet [we] support him if he is oppressed, but how can we support him if he is an oppressor?" The Prophet said: "Prevent him from continuing his oppression".'

These narrations show that the Islamic tradition in principle does not contradict the UN principles, but supports them for the good of all mankind.

In brief, the Islamic tradition has legislated the exclusion clauses in practice but not in clearly stated principles. Moreover, the Islamic tradition leaves the door open for scholars to construct judgements that are appropriate for their time with regard to the crimes that exempt the criminal from the right to seek asylum in the Islamic state.

Prohibition of expulsion or return: '*refoulement*' (Article 33)

The term '*non-refoulement* derives from the French *refouler*, which means to drive back or to repel, as in an enemy who fails to breach one's defences' (Goodwin-Gill, 1996, p. 117). To summarize the concept of *non-refoulement* in relation to refugees, it is 'a concept which prohibits States from returning a refugee or asylum seeker to territories where there is a risk that his or her life or freedom would be threatened on account of race, religion, nationality, membership of a particular social group or political opinion' (Feller *et al.* 2003, p. 89). This principle is 'distinguished from expulsion or deportation, the more formal process whereby a lawfully resident alien may be required to leave a State, or be forcibly removed' (Goodwin-Gill, 1996, p. 117).

This concept is enshrined in Article 33 of the 1951 Convention relating to refugees. It stipulates that:

> 1. No Contracting State shall expel or return '*refouler*' a refugee in any manner whatsoever to the frontiers of territories where his life or freedom would be threatened on account of his race, religion, nationality, membership of a particular social group or political opinion.
>
> 2. The benefit of the present provision may not, however, be claimed by a refugee whom there are reasonable grounds for regarding as a danger to the security of the country in which he is, or who, having been convicted by a final judgement of a particularly serious crime, constitutes a danger to the community of that country.

According to Feller (*et al.* 2003, p. 91), the principle has also appeared in various instruments, such as:

(a) The 1966 Principle Concerning Treatment of Refugees, adopted by the Asian-African Legal Consultative Committee, Article III(3).
(b) The 1967 Declaration on Territorial Asylum adopted unanimously by the United Nations General Assembly (UNGA) as Resolution 2132 (XXII), 14 December 1967, Article 3.
(c) The 1969 Organization of African Unity (OAU) Convention Governing the Specific Aspects of Refugee Problems in Africa, Article II(3).
(d) The 1969 American Convention on Human Rights, Article 22(8).
(e) The 1984 Cartagena Declaration, section III, paragraph 5.

This principle has been adopted by many countries. 'State practice, individuals and within international organisations, has contributed to further progressive development of the law. By and large, States in their practice and in their record views, have recognized that *non-refoulement* applies to the moment at which asylum seekers present themselves for entry … the concept now encompasses both non-return and non-rejection' (Goodwin-Gill, 1996, p. 124).

Nevertheless, this issue was mentioned in the Cairo Declaration on Human Rights in Islam at the 19th Islamic Conference of Foreign Ministers in 1993. In Article 12 it indicates that: 'The country of refuge shall be obliged to provide protection to the asylum-seeker until his safety has been attained.' Moreover, the Arab Charter on Human Rights, adopted by the League of Arab States in 1997, stated in Article 23 that 'political refugees shall not be extraditable'.

Non-refoulement in the Islamic tradition

A search of the books of the Islamic tradition for incidents in the Prophet's life that relate to the modern principle of *non-refoulement* throws up a few relevant passages in the account of *ṣulḥ*, the truce agreement of *al-Ḥudaybiya*, and other accounts.

Ṣulḥ al-Ḥudaybiya is the agreement signed between the Prophet and the delegate of Quraysh in 6 AH. This agreement is reported in detail throughout the histories and *sīra*. The details are not relevant here, but some incidents are worthy of mention.

The first is about a group of slaves who fled Mecca to join the Muslims. Most scholars[13] report this incident with almost identical wording:

> On the day of *al-ḥudaybiya* prior [to signing] the agreement, some slaves fled to the Prophet. Their masters wrote to the Prophet and said: O Muḥammad, by God they did not flee to you out of love for your religion, but they ran away fleeing slavery. Some people [of the companions] said: O the messenger of God they are right, hand them [the slaves] back to them [Quraysh]. The Prophet got angry and said: I do not see you will stop, O the people of Quraysh, until God sends you [someone] who will cut your necks for this.[14] He refused to hand them back and said they were God's freed men.

The other three narrations[15] cite the account with almost the same wording but add that these slaves converted to Islam.

This account is significant here as it appears to be a typical form of seeking refuge, as we witness in modern times. All the factors appropriate to the principle of *non-refoulement* are apparent. This group fled their place of residence because of the treatment they faced at the hands of Quraysh. They sought refuge with other people, the Muslims. When their masters asked for them to be handed back, the Prophet refused to allow it, despite the fact that they had not taken refuge with the Muslims out of fondness for their religion, as some of the companions affirmed, but in search of safety.

What is important here is that this incident occurred before the signing of the agreement that included a condition that 'anyone comes to you, even if he follows your religion, has to be sent back to us or you let us free to take him' (al-Bukhārī, 1986, vol. 2, p. 967). On the other hand if a Muslim comes back to Quraysh, they are not obliged to send him back to Medina as stated in this agreement: 'And whoever comes to you from us, [you have] to hand him back to us' (Muslim, n.d., vol. 3, p. 1409).

When the bewildered Muslims asked the Prophet about these conditions he said: 'Whoever from us go to them, then God has distanced him from us, and who comes from them, God will make a way and exit for him' (Ibn Abī Shayba, 1988, vol. 7, p. 385).

Immediately after signing the *ṣulḥ* the Prophet was tested on his adherence to the last condition in particular. Abu Jandal, the son of Suhayl Ibn ᶜAmr, the Qurayshi negotiator, fled to the Muslims asking for refuge. As al-Ṭabarī (1984, vol. 26, p. 100) reports, he 'threw himself amongst the Muslims'. When Suhayl saw that, he said: 'O Muḥammad, this is the first I will judge you with. [You have] to return him to us.' The Prophet asked Suhayl twice to give Abu Jandal *jiwār*, but he refused. Then his companion named Mukriz told the Prophet that he would give him *jiwār*. Eventually, the Prophet returned Abu Jandal to Quraysh. At that moment the shocked Abu Jandal shouted amongst the astounded Muslims: 'O Muslims, [are you going] to return me to the disbelievers while I came to you as a Muslim? Do not you see what I have been through?' None of the Muslims was, however, able to do anything once the Prophet had decided to return him to Quraysh, in fulfilment of his promise.

To assert his adherence to the contract, the Prophet also returned Abu Basīr when he fled to Medina from Mecca. Al-Bukhārī (1986, vol. 2, p. 979) reports the incident and says that when Quraysh learned about his escape they sent two men to the Prophet to get him back. They came to the Prophet and said: '[we ask you to fulfil] the Promise you made to us'. The Prophet then handed Abu Basīr to them. On their way back to Mecca the men stopped at a place called dhu al-Ḥulayfa to eat dates. While there, Abu Basīr started to praise the sharpness of one of the men's swords and asked to see it. Unwisely, that man gave the sword to Abu Basīr, who killed him. The narration goes on to tell that the other man escaped to tell the Prophet what had happened. When Abu Basīr returned to Medina he gave the Prophet his account of what had happened. Fearing that the Prophet would hand him over again to Quraysh he left Medina and began to form a militia with others who had fled Mecca but could not go to Medina.[16] Eventually, after the trade caravans of Quraysh came under attack from this group, Quraysh pledged to the Prophet to abolish this condition from the *ṣulḥ*, which the Prophet gladly did.

Others came to the Prophet seeking refuge but the Prophet returned them all to Mecca as al-Bayhaqī (1989, vol. 9, p. 229) says: 'All the men who came to him in that period were returned even though they were Muslims'.

In these incidents it is quite apparent that the Prophet gave the *ṣulḥ* priority, and did not allow anything, even the maltreatment and the torture of his followers, to justify breaking his agreement.

Nevertheless, when it came to women the case was different. The exemption of women from this agreement was made by God. The first woman who migrated from Mecca to Medina after *ṣulḥ al-Ḥudaybia* was Um Kulthūm Bint ᶜUqba, as Ibn Saᶜd (n.d., vol. 8, p. 230) states: 'We do not know any woman from Quraysh who converted to Islam and left her parents migrating to God and His messenger, except Um Kulthūm Bint ᶜUqba. She left Mecca on her own and then accompanied a man from Khuzāᶜa until she arrived to Medina.'

Upon her arrival in Medına her two brothers, al-Walīd and ᶜAmāra, according to the narration of Ibn Saᶜd (n.d., vol. 8, p. 230), followed her. They went to the Prophet asking him to hand her over to them, providing that this was one of the terms of *ṣulḥ al-Ḥudaybiya*. Um Kulthūm then said to the Prophet: 'I am a woman and status of women is weak as you know. If you return me to the disbelievers they will examine my faith, and I do not have patience.'

Just then, the Qurʾanic verse 60:10 was revealed to the Prophet:[17]

> O you who have attained to faith! Whenever believing women come unto you, forsaking the domain of evil, examine them, [although only] God is fully aware of their faith; and if you have thus ascertained that they are believers, do not send them back to the deniers of the truth, [since] they are [no longer] lawful to their erstwhile husbands, and these are [no longer] lawful to them. Nonetheless, you shall return to them whatever they have spent [on their wives

> by way of dower]; and [then, O believers,] you will be committing no sin if you marry them after giving them their dowers. On the other hand, hold not to the marriage-tie with women who [continue to] deny the truth, and ask but for [the return of] whatever you have spent [by way of dower] – just as they [whose wives have gone over to you] have the right to demand [the return of] whatever they have spent. Such is God's judgement: He judges between you [in equity] – for God is all-knowing, wise.

Obviously, after this revelation the Prophet refused to return the woman to Mecca. Then the Prophet examined her and all women after her by asking them to testify that: 'By God, nothing has driven you to migrate except the love of God, His Prophet and Islam and you have not migrated for the sake of husband or money.' She instantly replied positively, and the Prophet kept her in Medina.

The response of the Prophet towards this woman was totally different from his response to Abu Baṣīr. The difference could be due to the fact that the fleeing person in the first case was a woman who could not stand the persecution and examination. In the second case, the returned Muslim was not only a man, but also a defiant fighter, who could defend and take care of himself. What supports this analysis is the Prophet's comment when he heard that Abu Baṣīr had killed his captor and escaped. The Prophet said: 'He is capable of fuelling a war, if he had men.' This comment shows that Abu Baṣīr was not a weak person who could be oppressed and maltreated easily, and the Prophet was not worried for him.

The Prophet's expectations turned out to be true, when Abu Baṣīr formed a sort of militia and started to attack the trade caravans of Quraysh. Eventually, Quraysh sent a delegation to the Prophet requesting him to remove this term from *ṣulḥ al-Ḥudaybiya*, which the Prophet promptly did and Abu Baṣīr and his group returned to Medina.

The Qurʾanic verse specified women in this case, for non-return, because of their absolute need for protection and also for the certain danger and persecution they would face were they to be returned. However, in the case of men the level of risk was not comparable, especially when it came to 'honour and shame' in that tribal society.

Nevertheless, the examination of migrating women mentioned in verse 60:10 was meant to make sure that any migrating woman was genuinely migrating for the sake of Islam and not for anything else; in this case, the responsibility for protecting her life lay on the Muslims, particularly after verse 60:10 cut the ties between these women and their non-believer relatives: 'Neither are these [women] lawful for them, nor are those [men] lawful for them.'

It could be said that this verse sets a principle of inspection and legislates for the examination of the migrant to make sure he is genuine in his claims. In the case of the migrant woman the examination was to make sure she was truly a believer. Thus, the verse could be extended these days to include all migrants to the Islamic state to see whether they are genuine migrants or not. This is not to say it restricts access for refugees, since that contradicts the message of verse 9:6, but it permits examination to make sure that they are genuinely in need of refuge.[18]

However, the exclusion of men from this term continued for some period. Quraysh requested the abolishment of this exclusion after the actions of Abu Baṣīr and his brothers and the rule was applied to everybody, men and women, that no immigrant would be returned to his country.

Another account of *non-refoulement* is narrated by Ibn Sa^c^d (n.d., vol. 7, p. 15). In the year 8 AH during the conquest of al-Ṭā'if, Abu Bakra, a slave belonging to Thaqīf, fled to the Prophet while the Muslims were besieging al-Ṭā'if. When Thaqīf asked the Prophet to return him, the Prophet refused, saying 'He is the freeman of God and his Messenger'. However, al-Bayhaqī reports that it was a group of slaves who fled to the Prophet and converted to Islam. When Thaqīf came to the Prophet asking him to return the slaves he refused and said: 'They are the freemen of God' (al-Bayhaqī, 1989, vol. 9, p. 229).

This incident, which occurred after *ṣulḥ al-Ḥudaybiya*, shows that the general rule in such circumstances is to accept those who flee to Muslims and not to return them to where they were oppressed, while the condition of *ṣulḥ al-Ḥudaybiya* that stated otherwise for a short period of time, was an exception and should not be understood as the standard.

Another imperative issue in this verse is the phrase 'make him attain his place of safety'. This states that after providing him with protection and care, Muslims should not put the life of the refuge-seeker at risk when ending his *amān*. On the contrary, they must ensure he reaches a safe place.

The verse does not specify where the refugee is to be returned to, whether it is his home or anywhere else. The Qurʾān is not specific about this, simply because the destination itself is not central in this context. The most crucial point here is safety and wherever safety is available the refugee should be able to get there. The verse also obliges Muslims to protect the refugee and get him to where he feels safe. In other words, the refugee's safety should not be jeopardized or compromised and if he has been expelled from a place, his safety must be assured.

Remarkably, this understanding of the verse fits perfectly with what contemporary legal experts think about the place of return. As Nicholson states, the word 'territories' mentioned in the Article holds two important points:

> the first point is that this expression does not refer only to refugee or asylum seeker's country of origin (whether of nationality or former habitual residence), even though the fear of persecution in such territories may well be at the root of that person's claim to protection. The reference is to the frontiers of 'territories', in plural. The evident import of this is that *refoulement* is prohibited to the frontiers of any territory in which the person concerned will be at risk – regardless of whether those territories are the country of origin of the person concerned.

The second point is:

> the word used is 'territories' as opposed to 'countries' or 'States'. The implication of this is that the legal status of the place to which the individual may be sent is not material. The relevant issue will be whether it is a place where the person concerned will be at risk.
>
> Thirdly, they state clearly that Article 33(1) of the 1951 Convention cannot be read as precluding removal to a '" safe" third country', nevertheless, it should be interpreted to preclude 'removal to a place from which the refugee would be in danger of subsequent removal to a territory of risk' (Nicholson *et al.* 2003, pp. 122–3).

To sum up it could be said that the Islamic tradition has stipulated that the refugee should not be returned to his country or to any other place where his safety is threatened. When ending refugee status, verse 9:6

places responsibility on Muslims to ensure that the refugee reaches his place of safety. This means that the Islamic state should bear all the costs and take all necessary measures to secure his journey to the safe place. The Prophet also demonstrated in practice that this principle is Islamic and must be respected.

In light of this discussion, it could be concluded also that the Islamic tradition matches the spirit and the letter of Article 33 of the Geneva Convention about the principle of *non-refoulement*.

The safety of the *mustaʾmin*

The safety and the protection of the refugee are of course of fundamental importance. Protection from harm is the foremost right that should be guaranteed to him since in most cases he has fled the threat of physical or psychological injury.

As Hathaway (2005, p. 448) points out, however, '[E]ven though physical security is clearly fundamental to any notion of refugee protection, the Refugee Convention is silent on this issue'. The drafters failed to reach agreement on the wording and the proposal tabled for approval was rejected because it was too ambitious (Hathaway, 2005, p. 448). However, the Convention as a whole is based on giving safety to refugees. In addition, refugees could rely on other Articles in the Convention to claim protection. For instance, 'those who are threatened by armed conflict may invoke the protections of the Geneva Convictions on the Law of Armed Conflict and their Protocols, in particular Common Article 3' (Hathaway, 2005, p. 449).

The Islamic tradition, in turn, affirms the safety of the refugee and places particular responsibility on the Islamic state to guarantee the safety of the *mustaʾmin*, even after the cancellation of his *amān*, according to verse 9:6. Many scholars have affirmed the *mustaʾmin*'s right to good care, protection and welfare, like Ṭanṭāwī,[19] who says: 'The *mustaʾmin* is not to be harmed, on the contrary, the Muslims should protect him in his person, his money and his honour as long as he stays in *dār al-Islam*.' Furthermore, al-Shīrāzī (1982, vol. 1, p. 239), speaking about the rights of the *mustaʾmin*, says: 'The *Imām* has to protect all those who live in *dār al-Islam*, defend them against anyone who wanted to harm them as well as freeing those who are in captivity [by the enemy].'

However, there was a hypothetical debate between scholars about the value of the life of the *mustaʾmin* and whether it was equal to the *dhimmī* and the Muslim. This will be discussed below, but it is important here to explore the Islamic tradition with regard to harming the *mustaʾmin*.

The *ḥadīth*, narrated in several books with different phrasing, was clear on this point. In the account of Ibn Abī Shayba (1988, vol. 2, p. 356) and al-Qazwīnī (n.d., vol. 2, p. 896), the Prophet says: 'Whoever gives *amān* to a person and kills him, will be given the flag of treason in the hereafter.' In another narration the Prophet says: 'Whoever gives *amān* to a man and kills him, then I am disassociated from the killer even if the killed [person] was a disbeliever'[20] (al-Tabrīzī, 1985, vol. 2, p. 1146).

The point in this *ḥadīth*, 'and even if the killed person is a disbeliever', is significant in this context. It demonstrates that being a disbeliever does not diminish someone's value or humanity. More importantly, being a disbeliever does not excuse the treason or the act of killing. The significance of this *ḥadīth* will be more apparent in relation to the scholarly discussion regarding the punishment of a Muslim who kills a *mustaʾmin*.

Ibn Qayyim al-Jawziyyah states clearly: 'The *mustaʾmin* is protected and his blood-money is guaranteed.' However, if he was killed by a Muslim the scholars of Islamic jurisprudence differed over the punishment for that crime. Some maintained that the Muslim should only pay blood money, since the *mustaʾmin* was a fighting *ḥarbī* and his life was not equal to that of a Muslim. Others claimed that all lives were of equal value and that the killer should be treated as if he had killed a Muslim.

Remarkably, scholars of the first opinion were in a majority. Al-Shāfiʿī even claims that: 'There is no dispute [between all the scholars] that [the Muslim] should not be killed [for killing] the fighter *mustaʾmin*' (al-Jaṣṣāṣ, 1984, vol. 1, pp. 173–8). This opinion should be considered in light of the perception of the *mustaʾmin*. The *mustaʾmin* was defined as an enemy in the first place, who decided for some reason to come from *dār al-ḥarb* to *dār al-Islam* for a short period of time. His immunity from killing is therefore temporary. After this appointed time he would return behind the enemy lines and may later fight the Muslims. Al-Sarakhsī (n.d., vol. 26, p. 133) puts it bluntly: 'The dubiosity that allows the shedding of his blood is that of being a fighter and the ability to go back to *dār al-ḥarb*.' Moreover, Ibn ʿAbdīn (2000, vol. 4, p. 169) declares: 'No penalisation of the Muslim or the *dhimmī* for killing a *mustaʾmin*.' Ibn Nujaym (n.d., vol. 5, p. 154) concludes that all the killer has to do is pay the blood money. Moreover, al-Shāfiʿī (1973, vol. 7, p. 4) states that even if the killing of the *mustaʾmin* was deliberate, a Muslim should not be killed for that.

As mentioned above, the scholars' outlook was underpinned by their division of the world into two categories: *dār al-ḥarb* and *dār al-Islam*, and the state of war between them. Thus, the killing of the disbeliever from dār al-ḥārb is allowed, simply because their attempts to kill Muslims are ongoing. According to this understanding, the general rule is to kill the disbelieving fighters and the exception is to save them as long as they have *amān*. So, the *amān* is temporary and limited to an appointed time and that is the end of the contract.

On the other hand, scholars like Abu Yūsuf who held the second opinion justified it, claiming that: 'The dubiosity that allows the shedding of his blood is negated by the contract of *amān*' (al-Sarakhsī, n.d., vol. 26, p. 133). Thus, he adds: 'There is no doubt that the penalisation of killing must be applied upon the *mustaᵓmin*[21] and the Muslim alike.'

In fact, this opinion more closely matches the spirit of the Islamic principles and the aims behind legislation regarding the *amān* contract. Refuge is provided to save those fleeing death, oppression or humiliation in another place. Keeping the refugee alive and safe is an obligation from God on Muslims through verse 9:6, as we have seen previously.

However, this issue is related to a wider debate between the scholars regarding the equality of Muslims and *dhimmīs* in the Islamic state. This is relevant in view of the general rule in dealing with the *mustaᵓmin* as stated by many scholars[22] that: 'The *mustaᵓmin* in our *dār*, before becoming a *dhimmī* is treated like a *dhimmī*' (Ibn ᶜAbdīn, 2000, vol. 4, p. 169).

The scholars[23] who claim the superiority of the Muslim over the *dhimmī* rely primarily on narrations, combined with their understanding of belief and disbelief in general. The *ḥadīth* they draw on was narrated by al-Bukhārī (1986, vol. 3, p. 1110) and others,[24] on the authority of ᶜAlī Ibn Abī Ṭālib that the Prophet said: 'A Muslim should not be killed [for killing] a disbeliever.'

Others, according to al-Jaṣṣāṣ (1984, vol. 1, p. 177), support their opinion by the *ḥadīth* 'The Muslims are equal in their blood' and conclude that 'this makes the blood of the disbeliever unequal [to that of the Muslim]'.

In addition, Ibn Taymiyya (n.d., vol. 14, p. 85) justifies this opinion by saying that there is nothing in our religion that makes the blood of the Muslim equal to the blood of the disbeliever, since belief is the basis for hierarchy.

Those who say the Muslim and the *dhimmī* are equal in terms of the punishment strengthen their position with reference to other proofs.

Regarding the first *ḥadīth* 'a Muslim should not be killed [for killing] a disbeliever', al-Jaṣṣāṣ (1984, vol. 1, p. 175) rejects their interpretation, explaining that this *ḥadīth* belongs to certain circumstances and should not be generalized. He says that the Prophet mentioned this in his speech on the day of the Mecca conquest. A man from Khuzāᶜa tribe had killed a man from Hudhayl tribe in the *jāhiliyya* and it seems he wanted revenge for that killing. The Prophet said that *ḥadīth* to stop the killing of a Muslim because he had killed a man in the days of the *jāhiliyya*. In other words, the Prophet wanted to open a new chapter and to draw a line under all past killings and demands for vengeance between tribes before the advent of Islam. The Prophet acted as a leader who wanted to spread peace and harmony among his people.

To support this view, al-Jaṣṣāṣ (1984, vol. 1, p. 176) also cites the *ḥadīth* of the Prophet during the same speech: 'All blood spilt in the *jāhiliyya* is placed under my feet.' Thus, there is no revenge any more and a Muslim should not be killed for something he did in the *jāhiliyya*.

Concerning the second *ḥadīth* 'The Muslims are equal in their blood' al-Jaṣṣāṣ (1984, vol. 1, p. 177) maintains that this does not negate the equality of the blood of Muslims and non-Muslims. The benefit of this *ḥadīth*, he says, is to affirm the equality between Muslims themselves. In other words, the Prophet wants to confirm that all Muslims are equal, whether they are young, old, pious, non-pious, white or black and so on. But the *ḥadīth* did not state that non-Muslims are not equal to Muslims.

Responding to those who claim that disbelief is what made their blood susceptible, al-Kāsānī (1982, vol. 7, p. 237) says: 'The equality in religion is not a condition [for revenge from the killer]. Do not you see that if a *dhimmī* killed a *dhimmī* and then the killer converted to Islam, he will be killed for that [his previous crime before converting].' He continues: 'It is not acceptable to say that disbelief makes killing him permissible. What could make it permissible is the disbelief that motivates war and the disbelief of the *dhimmī* is not [motivating him to fight the Muslims], so he is immune.'

Furthermore, al-Kāsānī (1982, vol. 7, p. 237) supports his opinion by verses from the Qurʾān, such as 2:178:

> O you who have attained to faith! Just retribution is ordained for you in cases of killing: the free for the free, and the slave for the slave, and the woman for the woman. And if something [of his

> guilt] is remitted to a guilty person by his brother, this [remission] shall be adhered to with fairness, and restitution to his fellow-man shall be made in a goodly manner. This is alleviation from your Sustainer, and an act of His grace. And for him who, nonetheless, wilfully transgresses the bounds of what is right, there is grievous suffering in store.

He also cited the Qurʾanic verse 5:45:

> And We ordained for them in that [Torah]: A life for a life, and an eye for an eye, and a nose for a nose, and an ear for an ear, and a tooth for a tooth, and a [similar] retribution for wounds; but he who shall forgo it out of charity will atone thereby for some of his past sins. And they who do not judge in accordance with what God has revealed, they are the evildoers!

Also he employed verse 17:33:

> And do not take any human being's life – [the life] which God has willed to be sacred – otherwise than in [the pursuit of] justice. Hence, if anyone has been slain wrongfully, We have empowered the defender of his rights [to exact a just retribution] but even so, let him not exceed the bounds of equity in [retributive] killing. [And as for him who has been slain wrongfully] behold, he is indeed succoured [by God].

These verses, he claims, are general and 'do not differentiate between a killed [person] and another, or between a soul and another, or between an oppressed person and another. Whoever says that this is restricted to Muslims has to bring the evidence [for such restriction].'

Finally he cites verse 2:179: 'For, in [the law of] just retribution, O you who are endowed with insight, there is life for you, so that you might remain conscious of God!' and comments that: 'What is really meant by life [in this Qurʾanic verse] is more evident in relation to killing a Muslim for killing a *dhimmī* rather than killing a Muslim for killing a Muslim, because religious enmity drives him to kill especially when angry, so a deterrent is even more necessary' (al-Kāsānī,1982, vol. 7, p. 237).

In addition, those scholars who equalize between Muslim and *dhimmī*, like Abu Ḥanīfa, Abu Yūsuf, Muḥammad, Zufar, Ibn Abu Layla, ᶜUthmān al-Battī and al-Jaṣṣāṣ, used other *ḥadīths* to support their stance. Al-Jaṣṣāṣ states that the Prophet 'killed a Muslim because he killed a *dhimmī* and said: I am the first to fulfil my obligation [to grant protection]'.

This *ḥadīth* was narrated by some scholars with different wording in regard to the person who was killed initially. Al-Zaylaᶜī (1895, vol. 6, p. 103) and Abu Dāwūd (n.d., vol. 1, p. 207) narrate that the person who was killed was *dhimmī*, while Ibn Ḥajar (n.d., vol. 12, p. 262) adds significant detail. He says: 'The Prophet killed a Muslim for killing a disbeliever and said I am the first to fulfil his obligation.' This description is particularly significant since it shows clearly that the killed person was a non-Muslim without defining what his status was, which means he could be *mustaʾmin* or *dhimmī*. Lastly, al-Ṣanᶜānī (1959, vol. 3, p. 242) narrates this *ḥadīth* saying that: 'The Prophet killed a Muslim for killing a *muᶜāhid*[25] and said I am the first to fulfil his obligation'.

Additionally, al-Jaṣṣāṣ (1984, vol. 1, p. 175) states that it was narrated upon ᶜUmar, ᶜAlī and ᶜAbdullah that they killed a Muslim for killing a *dhimmī*. After allowing the relatives of the killed *dhimmī* the opportunity to apply the law of retaliation, ᶜAlī Ibn Abu Ṭālib commented: 'We gave them what we gave them to make their blood like ours and our blood-money like theirs.' This comment is relevant to this discussion. Although ᶜAlī was talking about the *dhimmī* it certainly applies to the *mustaʾmin* in the sense that both the *dhimmī* and the *mustaʾmin* had a covenant with the Muslims with a common factor between them, namely the *amān*. In essence the *amān* the Muslims gave to both of them was identical in regard to safety but different in terms of length: the *dhimmī* contract is permanent while the *mustaʾmin* contract is temporary. Therefore, there must be equality between the *dhimmī* and the *mustaʾmin* in terms of the value of their lives, at least during the period of *amān*.

Briefly, Muslim scholars in general affirm the need to give the *mustaʾmin* protection. The debate between scholars regarding equality between the Muslim and the *mustaʾmin* does not mean that the *mustaʾmin* was vulnerable and subject to harassment and attack by Muslims. On the contrary, even those who argued for inequality between the Muslim and the *mustaʾmin*, such as Abu Ḥanīfa and Ibn ᶜAbdīn, state categorically that Muslims should treat the *mustaʾmin* well in order to show him the value of Islam and induce him to convert. They also place a duty on the *Imām* to support the *mustaʾmin* (Shaykhī Zāda, 1998, vol. 2, p. 452).[26] Effectively, therefore, the discussion was theoretical rather than practical. Nevertheless, this research contends that the *mustaʾmin* is equal to the *dhimmī* and both of them are equal to the Muslim, as Abu Yusūf said. Once the Muslims give him the *amān* he is eligible for their full protection and care. The essence of the *amān* contract is safety and anything that diminishes this safety must be rejected.

Additionally, the Qurʾān does not differentiate between humans when it comes to killing, particularly verse 5:32. So, a soul is a soul whether it is the soul of a Muslim, a *dhimmī* or a *mustaʾmin* and it should not be slain without rightful reason.

One of these rightful reasons, according to the *ḥadīth* narrated by Ibn Kathīr (1980, vol. 1, p. 535), was 'a soul for soul', again, without differentiation between the souls.

Commenting on this verse, al-Buhūtī (1996, vol. 3, p. 328) and al-Ṣuyūṭī (1961, vol. 6, p. 146) say that it makes no difference whether the killed person was a *mustaʾmin* or a Muslim because both are humans.

This opinion is perfectly in tune with the message of mercy in Islam and the core aims of granting refuge. This message, as we've seen, welcomes the refugee and obliges the Muslim to take good care of him. Diminishing the value of their lives does not fit with this message.

General obligations (Article 2)

In Article 2 under the title 'General obligations' the Geneva Convention states that: 'Every refugee has duties to the country in which he finds himself, which require in particular that he conform to its laws and regulations as well as to measures taken for the maintenance of public order.'

When drafting this Article, 'a number of governments felt that such a provision was superfluous in view of the general duty of foreigners to obey the law of their country of residence' (Hathaway, 2005, p. 98). However, some governments argued that the obligation of the refugees should be stated clearly. 'Largely out of respect for the significant refugee protection contributions made by France, it was decided to include a specific reference in the Convention to the duties of the refugees' (Hathaway, 2005, p. 99).

If it goes without saying that refugees should comply with the laws of the country they are in, a problem arises in how to apply these laws without conflict with the basic human rights of the refugee in terms of freedom of expression. Refugees, as Johnson (Chimni, 2000, p. 208) explains, are

> persons whose fundamental rights have been violated. They seek refuge abroad precisely in order to be able to continue to enjoy their basic human rights, including the right to freedom of opinion and expression ... The repeated call by States that refugees have a duty not to engage in subversive activities, should not prohibit them from enjoying such rights. The only permissible limit would be when, for example, in the exercise of the right to freedom of opinion and expression, refugees incite violence or the use of force.

Another relevant question here is whether, if the refugee committed a crime or did not adhere to the law of the country he was seeking refuge in, would he be expelled or his rights forfeited?

According to Hathaway (2000, pp. 104–6), after a lengthy discussion between the contracting states

> the legal position is that Art. 2 does not authorise the withdrawal of refugee rights for even the most serious breaches of a refugee's duty to the host state. Because there is no reciprocity of rights and obligations under the refugee Convention, refugees must be dealt with in the same way as any other person who violates a generally applicable law, regulations, or public order measure.

The duties of the refugee from an Islamic perspective

Like the drafters of the Geneva Convention, Muslim scholars have dealt with this issue briefly and in general terms. Zaydān sums up the duties of the *mustaʾmin* by saying that he should refrain from 'what is demerit to the Muslims or disrespect to their religion' (Zaydān, 1982, p. 208).

Among the works of jurisprudence, al-Sarakhsī (n.d., vol. 9, p. 56) affirms this point and denies that *amān* may allow disrespect of the Muslim faith: 'We did not give him *amān* to deride the Muslims.' In practical terms that means he has to respect the Muslims, their faith, way of life and certainly the general order.

To be clear on this point, Ibn Taymiyya states that: 'His [the *mustaʾmin*'s] derision of the Prophet and his harm to God the Almighty and his messenger will not make it possible to grant him *amān* and covenant' (Ibn

Taymiyya, 1983, vol. 3, p. 768). In this context, he also relates the case of the two slave singers whom the Prophet allowed to be killed during the conquest of Mecca for abusing him, as a proof that the *amān* is not compatible with the abuse of the Muslim faith.

This particular point is important and will be dealt with at length when discussing the terms and conditions of cancelling the *amān* and expelling the *mustaʾmin*. However, it is clear that Ibn Taymiyya requires respect for Islam as a precondition for granting *amān* to the *mustaʾmin*. Respecting the faith necessarily involved respecting the way of life and rulings.

With regard to punishment for crimes committed and the question of nullification of the *amān*, it is interesting to note that the Muslim scholars engaged in a discussion very similar to that which took place among the drafters of the Geneva Convention over this Article.[27] Some of them, such as Ibn Taymiyya, held that certain crimes, like abusing the Muslim faith, invalidated the *amān*. Others went even further and made any crime a valid reason for cancelling the *amān*. Among them was Ibn Mufliḥ (1979, vol. 3, p. 394) who judged that: 'If [the *ḥarbī*] came to us with *amān* and then treated [someone] unfairly his *amān* will be nullified.'

Others still argued that committing a crime did not abolish the contract – although the perpetrator should be held to account for it. Abu Yūsuf and al-Shāfiʿī declare: 'He is subject to punishments like the *dhimmī*, and as long as he stays in our *dār* he should adhere to our rulings' (al-Sarakhsī, n.d., vol. 9, p. 56). They justify their opinion with reference to the fact that these rulings are applied in *dār al-Islam* to protect it. In this case, anyone who comes to it must adhere to the general order of that *dār*.

Elsewhere, al-Shāfiʿī is more specific about the *mustaʾmin* who kills a Muslim. He (al-Shāfiʿī, 1973, vol. 6, p. 46) says: 'If a *mustaʾmin* committed a crime the law of retaliation should be applied upon him.'

By making these general judgements, Abu Yūsuf and al-Shāfiʿī do not differentiate between the rulings that relate to crimes against God or rulings relating to crimes against people. They make it obligatory on the *mustaʾmin* to adhere to them. Abu Yūsuf validates his opinion as follows: 'When he [the *mustaʾmin*] enters *dār al-Islam*, he then commits himself to the rulings of Islam as long as he stays there, so he becomes like the *dhimmī*' (al-Kāsānī, 1982, vol. 7, p. 34). Nevertheless, Abu Yūsuf excludes the punishment for drinking alcohol, because it is not applicable to the *dhimmī* and should not therefore be applicable to the *mustaʾmin* (Ibn Nujaym, n.d., vol. 5, p. 19).

Other scholars do not agree with this trend. For instance, al-Sarakhsī differentiates between the crimes for which the *mustaʾmin* might be punished, making a distinction between crimes committed against people and those committed against God. Al-Sarakhsī concludes: 'The *mustaʾmin* is liable to be punished for [the crimes] concerning the rights of other people' (al-Sarakhsī, n.d., vol. 9, p. 109). This means that because he is a non-Muslim he is forgiven for other crimes concerning the faith, for which a Muslim would be punished. Abu Ḥanīfa and his student Muḥammad state clearly: 'The punishments which relate to crimes against God the Almighty do not apply to the *mustaʾmin*, even if it was proven evidently or by observation or by his confession' (al-Sarakhsī, n.d., vol. 18, p. 170). Al-ᶜAdawī (1991, vol. 2, p. 426) declares that: 'There is no *ḥadd*[28] applicable to the *ḥarbi*.'

Furthermore, Abu Ḥanīfa believes that 'there is no punishment applicable to the *mustaʾmin* or *mustaʾmina*[29] except the punishment for *qadhf*.'[30,31] He excludes this crime because it involves the rights of other people and when the *mustaʾmin* accepts *ᶜaqda al-amān* it means he commits himself not to harm Muslims (al-Kāsānī, 1982, vol. 7, p. 34). Abu Ḥanīfa defends his position: 'The application [of the punishments] is built on loyalty, and loyalty is built on adherence [willingly]. If we were to force him to adhere [to our rulings] without his commitment, this will drive him away from our dār, and God has ordered us to treat him in a way that leads him to enter our dār to see the beauties of Islam and convert' (al-Zaylaᶜī, 1895, vol. 3, p. 182).

It seems that Abu Ḥanīfa is affirming here that so long as the *mustaʾmin* is not a Muslim, he should not have to adhere to the same rulings and punishments applicable as those who have converted to and embraced the rulings of Islam. Yet, when it comes to the public order and the rights of other people, the *mustaʾmin* should adhere to public rulings. Abu Ḥanīfa states plainly:

> He by accepting *amān* had committed [himself to respect] people's rights … and to treat them justly as he is treated justly and do not harm them as he is not harmed, so he is committed to these things by his acceptance [the *amān*]. As to God's rights they are not applicable to him because he did not commit himself to [them by conversion] (al-Zaylaᶜī, 1895, vol. 3, p. 182).

Abu Ḥanīfa gives an example of the crimes that are not applicable to the *mustaʾmin*: 'If the *mustaʾmin* committed adultery with a female Muslim or female *dhimmī* or female *mustaʾmin*, there is no punishment for him or her [female *mustaʾmin*]' (al-Kāsānī, 1982, vol. 7, p. 34). Furthermore, if the *mustaʾmin* stole from a Muslim, the punishment of cutting his hand should not apply to him as it is *ḥadd*. This example appears confusing, because it involves the rights of others and, as we have seen above, the *mustaʾmin* is punished for the crimes he commits against other people. However, Abu Ḥanīfa says this *ḥadd*, i.e. cutting off his hand, is not applicable here because the *ḥudūd* are applicable only to Muslims. This *mustaʾmin*, however, could be punished with other penalties called *taᶜzīr*[32] which could be decided by the judge.

With regard to financial dealings with the *mustaʾmin*, the scholars imposed a tax called the *ᶜushr*[33] on those engaged in trading. Al-Ghazālī (1996, vol. 7, p. 76) reports that: 'ᶜUmar Ibn al-Khaṭṭāb imposed the *ᶜushr* on every *ḥarbī* who trades in our country.' Al-Ghazālī (1996, vol. 7, p. 76), and Ibn ᶜĀbdīn (2000, vol. 4, p. 169) affirm this.

Al-Shāfiᶜī, however, maintains that this condition should be imposed while granting the *amān* (Ibn ᶜAbd al-Barr, 2000, vol. 3, p. 165). Ibn ᶜAbd al-Barr gives a new dimension to this tax and makes it subject to the customary law between states. He says: 'The *ᶜushr* should be taken from the *ḥarbī* unless his people take less from us,[34] if so, it should be taken from them like what they take from us. If they do not take from us we should not take anything from them' (Ibn ᶜAbd al-Barr, 2000, vol. 3, p. 165).

Clearly, the similarities between the Geneva Convention and the rulings of Muslim scholars with regard to the duties of the refugee/*mustaʾmin* towards the host state are quite remarkable. Both assert the need to adhere to the general laws of the host state and the measures taken to ensure public safety.

In addition, Muslim scholars stress that refugees must respect the faith of the majority in the Islamic state and behave respectfully. At the same time, they exempt the non-Muslim refugee from certain rules due to his disbelief, particularly the rules relating to the Islamic faith and its obligations. So, he may retain his identity, customs, dress and even unashamed behaviours, such as drinking alcohol or eating pork, as far as this does not harm Muslims or disturb public order. This particular issue contrasts with the requirements of some modern democratic states such as France which require even their own Muslim citizens, for example, to remove their headscarves in order to attend school.

In terms of the punishment, the Convention does not give any exemptions in this regard. Yet it states that the crimes committed by the refugee should not invalidate his status. Muslim scholars, as we have seen, differentiate in regard to punishment and take into account the faith of the refugee. Generally speaking, they respect his faith and allow him to act accordingly despite the fact that, in some cases, it conflicts with the social and religious rules of Muslim society.

Finally, regarding taxation and other financial dealings, it is left to the officials to decide on according to the circumstances of the time. There is nothing permanent in this regard. It is, as Ibn ᶜAbd al-Barr said, subject to international law and what states can agree on.

Non-discrimination (Article 3)

The issue of non-discrimination in dealing with refugees is vital. The legislators and experts who framed the Geneva Convention gave it precedence, making it the first right to be granted to the refugee. Article 3 in the Convention states: 'The Contracting States shall apply the provisions of this Convention to refugees without discrimination as to race, religion or country of origin.'

In the Islamic tradition there is no text which stipulates this right with equal clarity. However, there are general principles in Islam which serve the same purpose of this Article.

The issue of race was addressed by the Qurʾān in different verses. It is clear that the Qurʾān and *ḥadīth* opposed those pre-Islamic Arab customs which discriminated against people on the basis of race. First, the Qurʾān declares all human beings are equal by virtue of the fact that all emanate from the same origin. The Qurʾanic verse 25:54 states: 'And He it is who out of this [very] water has created man and has endowed him with [the consciousness of] descent and marriage-tie thy Sustainer is ever infinite in His power.' Al-Ṣanᶜānī (1959, vol. 3, p. 128) comments on the verse: 'It is deduced from this verse the equality between the sons of Ādam.' In another verse (4:1) the Qurʾān reasserts this fact and clarifies that all peoples were created from one soul:

> O mankind! Be conscious of your Sustainer, who has created you out of one living entity, and out of it created its mate, and out of the two

> spread abroad a multitude of men and women. And remain conscious of God, in whose name you demand [your rights] from one another, and of these ties of kinship. Verily, God is ever watchful over you!

The Prophet affirmed this meaning: 'All people are the sons of Ādam and Ādam was created from soil'[35] الناس كلهم بنو آدم وآدم خلق من التراب (al-Suyūṭī, 1993, vol. 7, p. 580).

Furthermore, God states that He has honoured humans, all humans, and made them superior to many of His creatures in verse 17:70: 'Now indeed, We have conferred dignity on the children of Ādam, and borne them over land and sea, and provided for them sustenance out of the good things of life, and favoured them far above most of Our creation.'

Yet, Islamic principles establish a standard for superiority among humans, the criterion for which is piety and good conduct. In verse 49:13 God directs His speech to all humans, Muslims and non-Muslims, regardless of colour, telling them: 'O men! Behold, We have created you all out of a male and a female and have made you into nations and tribes, so that you might come to know one another. Verily, the noblest of you in the sight of God is the one who is most deeply conscious of Him. Behold, God is all-knowing, all-aware.' Al-Aṣfahānī (n.d., vol. 1, p. 429) comments on the nobleness mentioned here and says: 'It is the praised actions.'

This standard was repeated and rephrased by the Prophet in many *ḥadīths*, like that reported by Muslim (n.d., vol. 4, p. 1987) on the authority of Abu Hurayra: 'Verily, God does not look at your appearances and monies, but He looks at your hearts and deeds.'[36] The Prophet emphasized the significance of this principle, in his last pilgrimage: 'O people, verily your God is one. Verily, your father is one. Verily, no favour for the Arab over the non-Arab, there is no favour for the non-Arab over the Arab, there is no favour for the black over the red and there is no favour for the red over the black except by piety' (al-Suyūṭī, 1993, vol. 7, p. 579).

This piety, however, is not just a claim devoid of substance. On the contrary, it should be practical and people should feel its good effect. The Prophet was asked about the best Muslim and said: '[The best Muslim] is who people are safe from his hand and tongue'[37] (Ibn Ḥibbān, 1993, vol. 2, p. 76). In the narration of al-Nasāʾī (1991, vol. 6, p. 530) the Prophet added: 'And the true believer is the one to whom people entrust their blood and money.' So, it is the practice and the action that makes some people excel over others.

This question of who is the best was asked directly to the Prophet who replied: '[The best] is the one who lives longer and makes his deeds better'[38] (al-Naysābūrī, 1990, vol. 1, p. 489).

To enshrine this principle in the minds of Muslims required far more than a single *ḥadīth*. It was a long process that was particularly difficult for those Arabs who could recall the *jāhiliyya* and its customs. Pride in race and tribe was engrained in that society[39] and it was not easy to relinquish. Despite their sincere adherence to the teachings of the Prophet, some Muslims on occasion failed the test and unconsciously longed for the days of the *jāhiliyya*. In an incident reported by al-Ṭabarī (1984, vol. 4, p. 23), two men of al-Aws and al-Khazraj recalled the days of the *jāhiliyya* and recited its poems when the two tribes met each other in the famous battle of Buᶜāth. Then, each of them started to call on his people to fight in his line. When the Prophet heard about this he immediately went to them and scolded them for this *jāhiliyyī* act. His speech is well known: '[Do you fight each other] in the name of the *jāhiliyya* whilst I am still alive amongst you?' (al-Ṭabarī, 1984, vol. 4, p. 23).

In such cases, the Prophet would frequently deter Muslims from taking pride in their tribal lineage, regarding it as a sign of the *jāhiliyya*. On the authority of Salmān the Prophet said: 'Three things are from the *jāhiliyya*; the pride of the tribal line, the tarnishing of ancestry and lamentation [over the dead]'[40] (al-Ṭabarānī, 1983, vol. 6, p. 239).

On other occasions the Prophet thanked God publicly for stripping his companions of this negative trait. Ibn Ḥumayd (1988, vol. 1, p. 253) reports that the Prophet would say: 'All praise due to God who removed from you the stain of the *jāhiliyya* and its pride in the forefathers.'[41]

When the Prophet felt that his leniency was not having the desired impact, he threatened those who still exhibited *jāhiliyya* behaviour: 'If those who take pride in their forefathers do not stop, then God will make them lower than the *juᶜlān*'[42] (al-Suyūṭī, 1993, vol. 7, p. 582).

Discrimination based on colour was also reprimanded and associated with the *jāhiliyya*. Individuals who made such mistakes were admonished by the Prophet. Abu Dharr one day called a companion while quarrelling 'O the son of the black mother.' When the Prophet heard about it he summoned him and told him: 'You are a man with remains of the *jāhiliyya*' (al-Bukhārī, 1986, vol. 1, p. 20). Abu Dharr was contrite and asked that companion for forgiveness.[43]

With regard to the issue of religion, Qurʾanic verse 9:6 is considered the cornerstone in legislating the principle of refuge in the Islamic tradition and does not differentiate between refugees on the basis of colour or country of origin. The term used to describe the refugee is 'one of the disbelievers' without any specifications, descriptions or limitations. So, it is general and could encompass all non-Muslim refugees.

However, when it comes to Muslim refugees we find that the Islamic tradition dealt with them differently – as the *sīra* shows. When the Prophet and his companions fled Mecca for Medina they were treated no less favourably than the residents of Medina itself. The brethren contract the Prophet struck between the people of Medina made the *Muhājirūn* and the *Anṣār* equal in duties and responsibilities from the day the Meccan migrants arrived in Medina.[44] They not only became residents, but also rulers, and occupied high positions in Medinan society. The non-Muslim *mustaʾmin*, meanwhile, had to secure an *amān* contract to stay in the Islamic state for a short period which could be extended to a year, according to the most tolerant opinions of the early scholars.[45]

This is due to the fact that *amān* at the time was also obtained by converting to Islam. So, once the disbeliever converted, he had the full right to be protected in the Islamic state which was built on the basis of religion and not geography, borders or lineage.

The religious relationship was stronger than and superior to any other relationship, whether based on blood lineage, geography, marriage or any other tie. The concept of loyalty (to God, his Prophet and one's fellow Muslims) and dissociation (from the disbelievers, even if they were relatives) was manifest. On this relation Islamic society was built.

However, after migration to Medina and the establishment of the Islamic state there, the issue of migration emerged as another condition for participation in the Islamic state. Nonetheless, there was still some relationship between those who did not migrate and the Islamic state. This relationship was illustrated by verse 8:72:

> Behold, as for those who have attained to faith, and who have forsaken the domain of evil and are striving hard, with their possessions and their lives, in God's cause, as well as those who shelter and succour [them] – these are [truly] the friends and protectors of one another. But as for those who have come to believe without having migrated [to your country] – you are in no wise responsible for their

> protection until such a time as they migrate [to you]. Yet, if they ask you for succour against religious persecution, it is your duty to give [them] this succour – except against a people between whom and yourselves there is a covenant, for God sees all that you do.

So, non-resident Muslims could expect some rights from the Islamic state subject to its own capacity, like the right of support, as al-Ghanūshī (1993, p. 46) states.

This means that Muslim migrants had more rights than others in terms of obtaining permanent residence and becoming part of Islamic society.

Such rules applied to the Caliphate state which existed at different times in Islamic history. It is significant, however, that in the modern age of national states, the rules should be different, as al-Mawdūdī states. During a discussion on the status of *dhimmīs* in the Islamic state he claims: 'It should be clearly borne in mind that an Islamic State is essentially an Ideological state, and is thus radically different from a national state. This difference in the very nature of these two types of states has an important bearing on the problem under discussion' (Mawdūdī, 1961, I). Thus, this issue should be readdressed by Muslim scholars who must also detail the rulings and judgements concerning refugees to the modern national state separately from the rulings that governed the Caliphate state.

Thus, if we were to compare the Islamic teachings on this issue with the Convention we would say that the Islamic tradition in principle rejects any sort of discrimination based on race or colour and regards such discrimination as a sign of backwardness and of reverting to the *jāhiliyya*. One of the main principles in Islam is the equality of humanity. There is no superiority for one race over another. The measure of superiority is excellence in doing good and acting positively, regardless of race, lineage or colour. From these principles, which came without restriction or limitation, we can generalize for application to all refugees.

With regard to religion, the Islamic tradition afforded Muslim migrants priority over non-Muslims in terms of the speed of assimilation into and membership of Muslim society. This was due to the nature of the Caliphate state, which was established on religion and had different duties and responsibilities towards Muslims. However, the favourable treatment of Muslim migrants did not entail a rejection of non-Muslim refugees. In practice, it meant that Muslim refugees did not fall into the same category because of their faith and their theoretical relationship to the Caliphate state.

Nevertheless, with the disappearance of the central Caliphate state and after the advent of modern national states, the whole concept of support and loyalty had to be revised according to current realities.

Thus, with regard to Article 3 of the Convention, it could be concluded that the Islamic tradition provides sufficient grounds to match this Article, particularly in terms of non-discrimination based on colour or country of origin. Concerning religion, the Islamic tradition was not in full tune with this Article, based on the nature of the Caliphate state. Yet, in the modern national state, the favourable treatment of Muslim migrants should be dropped and there must be equality in the treatment of refugees, since all refugees generally share a common experience of suffering and a need of protection. It could be said that the Islamic tradition provides the basis for contemporary Muslim scholars to revise, rethink and detail the appropriate judgement from the tradition in light of current realities.

Religion (Article 4)

In its fourth Article entitled 'Religion' the Geneva Convention states: 'The Contracting States shall accord to refugees within their territories treatment at least as favourable as that accorded to their nationals with respect to freedom to practise their religion and freedom as regards the religious education of their children.'

According to Hathaway (2005, p. 570), the drafters did not feel a need for such an article at first. However, at the conference of Plenipotentiaries there was overwhelming support for codification of this right to impose a contractual obligation on states to respect the religious liberties of refugees. This vast support was partially due to the fact that lack of religious freedom was a frequent cause of refugee flight. Thus 'it would clearly be unacceptable if refugees forced to flee religious persecution were to be required to accept as "protection" conditions of life which denied them the very freedom which forced them abroad' (Hathaway, 2005, p. 572).

The place this Article occupied in the Convention demonstrates the importance the drafters attached to it. 'It is the only article in the Convention which comprises a principled obligation on states to take steps for the benefit of refugees beyond even what is done for their own citizens' (Hathaway, 2005, p. 572).

With regard to educating children, the Article 'ensures that refugee parents are free (if they have resources) to enrol their children in schools which provide their preferred form of religious instructions; and if they are not able to fund education of that kind, they enjoy the liberty to withdraw their children from any non-preferred form of religious instructions provided within the public school system' (Hathaway, 2005, p. 583).

Article 4 and the Islamic tradition

In their extensive debate about the rights and duties of the *mustaᵓmin*, Muslim scholars discussed the religious freedom of non-Muslims who seek *amān* in *dār al-Islam*. They also debated the religious freedom of the *dhimmī*, whose status was similar to that of the *mustaᵓmin*.[46]

According to Ibn Qudāma there was consensus among the scholars that forcing the *dhimmī* and *mustaᵓmin* to convert to Islam was prohibited. He states: 'The people of knowledge agree that so long as the *dhimmī* and the *mustaᵓmin* keep their contract, it is prohibited to abolish it or force them to do something that was not agreed on … like professing [that there is no God but Allah and Muḥammad is his Prophet]' (Ibn Qudāma, 1984, vol. 9, p. 29):

أجمع أهل العلم على أن الذمي إذا أقام على ما عوهد عليه والمستأمن
لا يجوز نقض عهده ولا إكراهه على ما لم يلتزمه ... الإقرار.

The scholars based their judgement on the Qurᵓanic verses that prohibit Muslims from coercing non-Muslims to convert, for example verse 2:256: 'There shall be no coercion in matters of faith. Distinct has now become the right way from [the way of] error: hence, he who rejects the powers of evil and believes in God has indeed taken hold of a support most unfailing, which shall never give way: for God is all-hearing, all-knowing.'

Al-Nasafı (n.d., vol. 1, p. 125) comments: 'There is no compulsion to follow the true religion, and that is the religion of Islam.' Ibn Kathīr (1980, vol. 1, p. 311), al-Saᶜdı (2000, vol. 1, p. 111) and al-Samarqandī (n.d., vol. 1, p. 195) affirm this meaning: 'Do not force anyone to convert to this religion because it is clear, obvious, its proofs are apparent and it does not need anyone to be forced to follow it.'

The contemporary commentator Sayyid Quṭb, who was imprisoned, tortured and eventually hanged for his beliefs, glorified this freedom and widened it to include the freedom to preach the faith. He said:

> religious freedom is the first right of the human with which he is rightly described 'a human'. He who dispossesses a human of his religious freedom actually dispossesses his humanity. Religious freedom should be accompanied by the freedom to preach the faith securely from any harm or inquisition. Otherwise, it is a freedom in name only, without any meaning in real life (Quṭb, 1967, vol. 1, p. 30).

These scholarly interpretations are strengthened by the actual reasons for the revelation of this verse. These reasons are immensely important in this perspective, as they give practical examples of how Muslims dealt with the issue of freedom to religion.

The scholars mentioned two reasons for the revelation. The first account was reported by al-Nasāʾī (1991, vol. 6, p. 304), Abu Dāwūd (n.d., vol. 3, p. 58) and Ibn Ḥibbān (1993, vol. 1, p. 352) on the authority of Ibn ᶜAbbās:

> If a woman happens to be barren she vows that if her baby lives she will convert him to Judaism. When Banū al-Naḍīr were evacuated from Medina, some of the *Anṣār*'s sons were with them. They [the *Anṣār*] said we will not let our children [go away with the evacuated tribe], so God the Almighty revealed 'There shall be no coercion in matters of faith', truly the right way has become clearly distinct from error.

In the narration of al-Ṭabarī the *Anṣār* asked the Prophet what to do and the Prophet said: 'Give them the choice, if they choose you, they belong to you and if they choose them [Banī al-Naḍīr] then they belong to them' (al-Ṭabarī, 1984 vol. 3, p. 15).

The other reason for the revelation, however, is similar to this and was also narrated on the authority of Ibn ᶜAbbās, who said: 'This verse was revealed because of a man from the tribe of Banī Sālim Ibn ᶜAwf from the *Anṣār* called al-Ḥuṣayn. He had two Christian sons and he was a Muslim. He asked the Prophet [permission] to force them to convert after they refused [to convert willingly] and stayed Christians, so God revealed this verse'[47] (al-Qurṭubī, 1986., vol. 3, p. 280).

These two incidents are the true embodiment of this principle. The Muslims could easily have forced their sons to convert to Islam, especially since at that time they were victorious, very close to the Prophet and had strong belief in him and his message. However, their enthusiasm for their religion did not make them exceed the limits established by God. God revealed this verse to establish a universal principle spelling out that freedom of religion should be protected in the Islamic state even though it may allow the existence of faiths and creeds that contradict the fundamentals of the Islamic faith.

Another explanation for the tolerance of those Muslims could be the fact that they themselves had been subject to harassment and torture at the hands of the disbelievers when they chose a different religion and way of life. So, they did not want to do the same with their sons and become their oppressors.

The religious freedom enshrined in this verse is general and should be valid for all ages and generations. It should not be restricted to any time or specific incident, since the general jurisprudential rule is: 'The point is in the general phrasing and not in the specific cause'[48] (al-Ghazālī, 1992, vol. 1, p. 236).

The other verse the scholars depended on in their verdict is verse 10:99: 'And if thy Lord willed, all who are in the earth would have believed together. Wouldst thou (Muḥammad) compel men until they are believers?'

Al-Kalbī (1983, vol. 2, p. 99) comments on this verse, maintaining that the meaning of the verse is: you, the Prophet cannot put faith in people's hearts to make them convert. Yet, al-Zamakhsharī (n.d., vol. 1, p. 331) explains more: 'God could have forced people to convert if He wished, but He did not do that and made conversion the subject of a personal choice.'

Al-Alūsī (n.d., vol. 11, p. 195) in turn asserts that the verse orders the Prophet 'not to force people to convert but to point them towards that which may bring them to it'. Ibn al-Jawzī (1994, vol. 1, p. 39) concludes unequivocally that 'faith is not proper by compulsion'.

These verses were taken to heart by the early Muslims, and the trend of religious tolerance and freedom continued to the following generations. Al-Aṣbahānī (1984, vol. 9, p. 34) reports that ᶜUmar the caliph, had a servant called Wasaq. ᶜUmar used to invite him to convert by making him offers: 'If you convert I will use you to help me in carrying my duties, as I am not allowed to use, in ruling the Muslims, someone who is not from them.' But Wasaq refused and then ᶜUmar said: 'There shall be no coercion in matters of faith.' When ᶜUmar was dying he freed Wasaq and told him to go wherever he wished.[49]

Although ᶜUmar surely had the power to force his servant to convert, he did not do so because conversion should be based only on absolute conviction and persuasion. ᶜUmar believed that conversion is not just a matter of a few words to be uttered, but a heartfelt belief, and no one can make that happen by force, as al-Nasafī (n.d., vol. 2, p. 143) said.

As a result, this tolerance and religious freedom was asserted by the scholars when they judged that forced conversion is not acceptable and no ruling may be built on that. Ibn Qudāma (n.d., vol. 4, p. 164) stresses: 'He who was forced wrongly to convert like the *dhimmī* and the *mustaᵓmin*, his conversion is not acceptable and no Islamic ruling should apply to him.' In another book he repeats this opinion and adds that this conversion will not be accepted until there is a proof after the removal of force that he still adheres to Islam, otherwise if he died he would not be considered a Muslim (Ibn Qudāma, 1984, vol. 9, p. 29).

Al-Nawawī (1997, vol. 9, p. 151) agrees, stating that if enforcement happened then it was wrong since the basic term of the contract was to leave him free to his religion.

Besides, many scholars in their debates concerning the rights of the *dhimmī* and the *mustaᵓmin* repeatedly used the phrase: 'We gave them *amān* subject to the condition that we leave them with what they believe in'[50] (al-Sarakhsī, n.d., vol. 9, p. 56). Al-Kāsānī (1982, vol. 2, p. 311) affirms this rule and adds: 'They should not be harmed in their worshipping other than God, although it is forbidden [for the Muslims].'

To fortify this principle and demonstrate sincerity in its application, the Muslim scholars granted the *mustaᵓmin* rights supplementary to the right of religious freedom. The scholars gave him freedom in personal affairs such as marriage, drawing up wills, food, dress, etc. according to his belief, with the exception of only a small number of areas which impacted on the wider community such as dealing in usury.[51]

Moreover, al-Zaylaᶜī reports that Abu Ḥanīfa also said they are allowed to drink and sell alcohol and pork in *dār al-Islam*, as 'we are ordered to leave them with what they believe in.'[52] Not only that but if a Muslim, out of anger or enthusiasm, decided to destroy forbidden goods, such as alcohol, he will be forced to compensate the owner (Shaykhī Zāda, 1998, vol. 4, p. 94).

Furthermore, the scholars argued about the right to places of worship. Some of them refused, stating that the Islamic state should be a place for worshipping God in the Islamic way only and thus no churches should be built there. Al-Subkī (n.d., vol. 2, p. 373) claims that: 'It is a consensus [between all the Muslim scholars] that building a church is prohibited.' To support his claim he mentions a few *ḥadīths* like: 'There is no church building in Islam and no refurbishment to the old ones' and 'There is no emasculation in Islam and there is no church building' and 'Demolish the churches and the abbeys'.

The irony in al-Subkī's position is that he himself judges that these *ḥadīths* are weak (al-Subkī n.d., vol. 2, p. 373). Therefore, we cannot consider them, let alone deduce a valid judgement from them on such an important issue. Moreover, the Qur'ān and the *ḥadīth* clearly show that non-Muslims could live in the Islamic state despite the fact that they are disbelievers. This by default means that they may practise their religion and certainly they would need a place to practise it.

Above all, the *sīra* of the Prophet and his companions show that they did not demolish any church or place of worship. On the contrary, we find the Prophet and his caliphs ordering their armies to avoid worshippers and the places where they worship. Ibn Ḥusām al-Dīn (1998, vol. 4, p. 203) reports an account that Abu Bakr instructed Yazīd Ibn Abu Sufyān, ᶜAmr Ibn al-ᶜĀṣ and Shuraḥbīl Ibn Ḥasana, the leaders of his army: 'Do not demolish an abbey'. In the narration of al-Bayhaqī (1989, vol. 9, p. 90) he told them: 'You will find people who have locked themselves in these abbeys [for worship], leave them with what they locked themselves for.'[53]

However, another opinion is that they are allowed to build and rebuild the demolished churches. This was the opinion of Abu Ḥanīfa (Shaykhī Zāda, 1998, vol. 4, p. 452) and some Shāfiᶜı scholars, according to al-Shīrāzī (n.d., vol. 2, p. 255). Contemporary scholars such as al-Ghanūshī (1993, p. 47) and Zaydān (1982, p. 99) also support this opinion.

This opinion seems the most logical and agrees with the spirit of the Qur'ān and the Prophetic teachings. It goes hand in hand with the fact that Islam not only allowed disbelievers to live among Muslims, but also left the door open for non-resident disbelievers to come in and see the beauty of its principles, as we have seen in the interpretation of verse 9:6.

This obviously places certain responsibilities upon the Islamic state, such as allowing those non-Muslims to worship and a place to worship in.

Finally, based on the above discussion it can be concluded that the Islamic tradition agrees with Article 4 of the Geneva Convention. Religious freedom is a firmly fixed principle in Islam and certainly applies to refugees in the Islamic state.

Personal status (Article 12)

In its 12th Article the Geneva Convention tackles the personal status of the refugee and formulates:

> 1. The personal status of a refugee shall be governed by the law of the country of his domicile or, if he has no domicile, by the law of the country of his residence.
>
> 2. Rights previously acquired by a refugee and dependent on personal status, more particularly rights attaching to marriage, shall be respected by a Contracting State, subject to compliance, if this be necessary, with the formalities required by the law of that State, provided that the right in question is one which would have been recognized by the law of that State had he not become a refugee.

Despite lengthy discussions about the definition of the term 'domicile', the contracting states failed to agree a definition and left it to 'the courts of the reception country to determine the domicile' (Hathaway, 2005, p. 216).

Still, the adoption of this Article is important in that it enables 'persons to move between countries without thereby jeopardizing basic entitlements' (Hathaway, 2005, p. 210).

Personal status in the Islamic tradition

The debate which took place between drafters during the coding of the Convention[54] is remarkably similar to the discussion that occurred between Muslim scholars concerning the *mustaʾmin* and his personal affairs, including the status of his marriage and will before entering *dār al-Islam*. Such discussions, and especially those relating to marriage, are of relevance in the current context, since the Convention gives special attention to the subject of marriage.

As is well known in Islamic jurisprudence, the groom has to give a dowry to his bride. In terms of the *ḥarbī* who is a non-Muslim, the Ḥanafites, as reported by al-Kāsānī (1982, vol. 2, p. 312) agree that: 'If a *ḥarbī* married a *ḥarbiyya*[55] in *dār al-ḥarb* without dowry, it would be accepted.' Obviously that is in contradiction with the Islamic tradition, but it is nonetheless acceptable and Muslims do not have the right to compel the *mustaʾmin* to do otherwise. The Ḥanafites agreed on the basis of this ruling and expressed it in different wording. Muḥammad and Zufar[56] justify it on the grounds that 'they are not obliged to adhere to our rulings', while Abu Ḥanīfa validates this on the basis that 'we are ordered to leave them with what they believe in'.[57]

This opinion is stressed again by al-Mirghinānī (n.d., vol. 1, p. 214), but more explicitly. He says that if a *mustaʾmin* got married and the dowry was a dead animal, it would be accepted. Obviously, this is a hypothetical case to demonstrate that whatever they agree on, it will not be rejected by the Muslims, notwithstanding the fact that it might contradict their rulings. In this particular example it is clear that such a marriage is not allowed for the Muslims, firstly because the dowry is a condition for the correctness of the marriage and secondly the dowry should not be something prohibited for the Muslims to eat or to deal with. What the scholars agreed was that in practical terms the personal status of the refugee prior entering the Islamic state is respected, regardless of whether or not it is in accord with Islamic rulings.

This opinion was straightforwardly endorsed by al-Jaṣṣāṣ (1984, vol. 5, p. 330): 'If the *ḥarbī* entered to us with *amān*, the divorce between him and his wife should not occur.' This is further confirmation from a well-known scholar to respect the personal status of the *mustaʾmin* when he is in the Islamic state.

Another issue of particular importance to the personal status of the *mustaʾmin* was not addressed by the Convention but was discussed in detail by the Muslim scholars. That is the issue of religion and conversion to Islam after entering *dār al-Islām*. The Muslim scholars placed certain rulings on the *mustaʾmin* when he converted. Al-Shaybānī (n.d., vol. 1, p. 189) presents ten different scenarios of the *mustaʾmin*'s marriage and the rulings after his conversion. Obviously, discussing these cases is beyond the terms of this book, but the point here is that conversion, by necessity, changed the rulings relating to the *mustaʾmin* and could affect his personal status.

Nonetheless, some of these rulings could be very serious in relation to the marital status of the *mustaʾmin* and might nullify it completely according to some scholars. Mālik, al-Ūzāʿı, al-Layth, al-Shāfiʿī and Abu Ḥanīfa say: 'If one of them converted while they were in *dār al-ḥarb* and then entered *dār al-Islam* their marriage will be void' (Ibn Qudāma, 1984, vol. 7, p. 120). On the other hand, al-Buhūtī argues that this is not necessarily the case, since Um Ḥakım converted in Mecca while her husband ʿIkrima fled to Yemen and later converted and their marriage remained valid despite 'the difference in the homestead and religion' (al-Buhūtī, 1996, vol. 2, p. 686).

Religion, therefore, plays a clear role in determining the personal status of the refugee in the Islamic tradition. Obviously, the focus of this research is not to show how it could be affected, but rather to demonstrate in principle that the conversion to Islam by the *mustaʾmin* might have some impact on his personal status.

Another issue discussed by the Muslim scholars concerning the personal status of the refugee was the will of the *mustaʾmin* in *dār al-Islam*. They argued over its validity and whether to execute it in the way he determined or in conformity with Islamic rulings.

Abu Ḥanīfa rules that the *mustaʾmin*'s will should be treated like the *dhimmī*'s: 'If a *dhimmī* bequeathed his house to be a church for unnamed people it will be correct like the will of the *mustaʾmin*' (Ibn Nujaym, n.d., vol. 8, p. 519). He defends his position by saying: 'This is a good deed in their belief and we are ordered to leave them with what they believe in, so it is allowed [to do that] according to their belief.' However, Muḥammad and Zufar disagree: 'The will is invalid because it is actual sin although it is a good deed in their belief. To determine a sin by a will is null and its execution is affirming the sin' (Ibn Nujaym, n.d., vol. 8, p. 519).

Al-Shāfiʿī in turn affirms the opinion of these two scholars and gives a clear example of a will that becomes void: 'If he determined by his will to use his money to buy alcohol and pigs and then donate them to the needy … we will invalidate his will' (al-Shāfiʿī, 1973, vol. 4, p. 213).

The Islamic law of inheritance is too detailed for a full discussion here. However, concerning the point above, while the *mustaʾmin* is allowed to determine a sin by his will, the Muslim is not, otherwise his will is nullified, according to al-Kāsānī (1982, vol. 7, p. 341). This shows that the Islamic tradition gives the *mustaʾmin* some rights which the

Muslim is not entitled to, simply because the the *musta'min* has a different religion which should be taken account of in the Islamic state.

From this discussion we may conclude that the Islamic tradition respects the personal status of the *musta'min* as governed by the laws of his domicile, including rights previously acquired. With regard to the status of marriage in particular, non-Muslim refugees have the right to adhere to their beliefs and Muslims must respect that.

Although the Islamic tradition provides the refugee with a great deal of liberty to conduct his personal matters, some rights in certain cases have to be in agreement with Islamic principles, otherwise they could be rejected. This understanding conforms to the condition put by the Convention on the nature of the personal issue and its legality in the host country. A clear and relevant example of this could be the issue of same-sex marriages. These marriages have been legalized in some countries, while in others they are not recognized and the subject is still considered an issue for debate. In the Islamic tradition this right is not recognized since it is prohibited by the Qur'ān and the Prophetic custom. Thus, the refugee may not enjoy this right as it is at odds with one of the fundamental principles of Islam concerning the family in Islamic society. This is simply an example and the scholars could impose other conditions to preserve the identity of the Islamic state, keep the public order and secure the national interests.

To sum up, the Islamic tradition of jurisprudence provides sufficient grounds to argue that the principles of Article 12 can be accepted subject to certain conditions. These conditions could be verified by the scholars of law according to their circumstances.

Movable and immovable property (Article 13)

Article 13 of the Geneva Convention states: 'The Contracting States shall accord to a refugee treatment as favourable as possible and, in any event, not less favourable than that accorded to aliens generally in the same circumstances, as regards the acquisition of movable and immovable property and other rights pertaining thereto, and to leases and other contracts relating to movable and immovable property.'

According to Hathaway (2005, p. 524), this Article 'not only protects the right to acquire all forms of property, but also guarantees non-discrimination in regard to "other rights pertaining thereto," specifically including related contractual interests'. However, Hathaway maintains that the article does not establish 'an absolute guarantee of property rights for refugees' (Hathaway, 2005, p. 524) because 'the drafters rejected pleas fully to enfranchise refugees in order to promote their speedy assimilation. Some states took the view that there was no good reason to privilege refugees relative to other non-citizens. Others simply wanted to be able to reserve some property rights for either their own citizens, or for citizens of states with which they were allied in an economic or political association' (Hathaway, 2005, pp. 525–6).

However, Hathaway (2005, p. 527) concludes that 'the benefits of Art. 13 can now be invoked by any refugee under a state's authority, including those not yet formally recognized as refugees'.

Property and the Islamic tradition

The amount of time and space devoted to this issue by scholars is quite remarkable. So, too, is their neutral and unbiased approach to the property rights of the *mustaʾmin* in *dār al-Islām*. They simply did not allow 'religious passion', as Zaydān (1982, p. 133) states, to restrict the rights the *mustaʾmin* was entitled to.

However, it is worth noting that the scholars generally thought of the *mustaʾmin* as a trader *mustaʾmin*. This is quite clear from the justification they give for their judgement.

Ibn Nujaym, for example, asserts that Muslims should permit the *mustaʾmin* to stay for a short period of time, because if we did not allow him to stay it 'will cause the cessation of importing provisions and closing the door for trading'. This opinion was also affirmed by al-Mirghinānī (n.d., vol. 2, p. 154), al-Zaylaʿī (1895, vol. 3, p. 268) and al-Sīwāsī (n.d., vol. 6, p. 22).

The protection of the mustaʾmin*'s property*

The Muslim scholars expressed the inviolability of the *mustaʾmin*'s possessions in different ways and stressed that his money was protected as much as his person. Ibn Qudāma (1984, vol. 9, p. 198) judged that: 'By his entrance to *dār al-Islam* with *amān*, the *amān* of his money is confirmed.' Al-Buhūtī (1996, vol. 1, p. 653) and al-Suyūṭī (1961, vol. 2, p. 579) extend his personal *amān* to include his relatives and his money: 'The *amān* fulminates into the *mustaʾmin*'s accompanying relatives and money unless it [the *amān*] is restricted to him only.'

Al-Sīwāsī (n.d., vol. 7, p. 39) in his turn affirms that: 'His money has become protected by the *amān*' Ibn ᶜAbd al-Barr (2000, vol. 3, p. 166) phrases it differently: 'The *amān* saves the blood and the money.' Al-Sarakhsī (n.d., vol. 7, p. 200) agrees with the other scholars: 'The property of the *mustaᵓmin* is respected by the *amān*.' He reaffirms this elsewhere (n.d., vol. 10, p. 52): 'It is prohibited to possess the money of the *mustaᵓmin* by force.'

Taking money from the *mustaᵓmin* without his consent is not allowed, as Ibn Ḍuwayyān (1984, vol. 1, p. 277) states: 'What is taken from the disbeliever by oppression like the money of the *mustaᵓmin* is not a spoil.' His money, according to al-Kāsānī (1982, vol. 7, p. 132), 'is protected against any damage'.

Moreover, in order to emphasize the inviolability of the *mustaᵓmin*'s money, the Muslim scholars consider the *amān* of his money absolute and separate from his personal *amān*. This means that if his personal *amān* is nullified for one reason or another, the *amān* of his money could remain unharmed. Ibn Qudāma (1984, vol. 9, p. 198) refutes the saying that: 'The *amān* of the money is secured by attachment [to the *mustaᵓmin*] and once it is invalidated in the followed [the *mustaᵓmin*] it is nullified in the follower.' He asserts that: 'The *amān* of the money is attained for itself since it got into [*dār al-Islam*] with him.' He adds: 'This requires the affirmation of the *amān* to the money even if it is not affirmed to the person.' He then supports his argument by saying: 'If the *mustaᵓmin* sends his money with a trader or an agent, the *amān* is affirmed to his money, while it is not affirmed to his person' (Ibn Qudāma, 1984, vol. 9, p. 198). Al-Shīrāzī (n.d., vol. 2, p. 264) supports this opinion using very similar wording: 'The *amān* is confirmed by originality as if he sent it with a trader or an agent.'

Establishing such protection for the possessions of the *ḥarbī* who comes from *dār al-ḥarb* is remarkable, especially given the state of war between *dār al-Islam* and *dār al-ḥarb* at the time.

In addition to this protection, the scholars gave the *mustaᵓmin* the absolute right to do whatever he chose with his money. Provided it was not used to harm the citizens or disturb public order, as we shall see, it was up to the *mustaᵓmin* to decide how to spend or invest his money. Ibn Qudāma (1984, vol. 9, p. 198) states clearly: 'If he conducted actions like selling, granting or anything else, his conduct is correct.' Al-Suyūṭī (1961, vol. 2, p. 582) justifies this on the basis of 'his continuity of ownership'.

Based on this, it was possible for the *mustaʾmin* to buy any land[58] in the Islamic state without restrictions. Therefore we find the scholars debating the consequences of purchasing land in terms of its effect on the *mustaʾmin*'s status and whether the purchase itself entitles him to become *dhimmī* or pay *kharāj*.[59]

Al-Kāsānī (1982, vol. 7, p. 110) stipulates that: 'If the *mustaʾmin* purchased land subject to *kharāj* and he committed to pay the *kharāj* he would become a *dhimmī*.' Shaykhī Zāda looks at a different scenario but even then the *mustaʾmin* is the one who purchases the land. He says: 'If the *mustaʾmin* purchased land on the contract of *muqāsama*[60] and rented it to a Muslim, then the *Imām* took the *kharāj* from the tenant providing that [this *kharāj*] is for the outcome, the *mustaʾmin* will not become a *dhimmī*'(Shaykhī Zāda, 1998, vol. 2, p. 235).[61] What Shaykhī Zāda is saying here is if the *mustaʾmin* did not pay his personal tax he would not become a *dhimmī*.[62]

Elsewhere scholars debated the fate of the land subject to *ᶜushr* after purchase by the *mustaʾmin* and whether it remained land subject to *ᶜushr* or became land subject to *kharāj*. Al-Sīwāsī (n.d., vol. 6, p. 23) reports that according to Muḥammad it remained a land subject to *ᶜushr* while for Abu Ḥanīfa it became a land subject to *kharāj*.

Al-Sarakhsī examines a case wherein the *mustaʾmin* purchases land and hires a Muslim to plant it: 'If the *mustaʾmin* purchased land subject to *ᶜushr* or subject to *kharāj* and gave it to a Muslim on *muzāraᶜa* contract, that would be correct and the outcome [of the land] is divided between them as they agreed' (al-Sarakhsī, n.d., vol. 23, p. 121).

Additionally, the scholars gave the *mustaʾmin* the right to sell the land as well as lease it out without restriction or limitation. Again, while debating the legal status of the *mustaʾmin* in *dār al-Islam* we find them saying: 'If he sold it before the due date for its *kharāj* he would not become a *dhimmī* by its purchase' (Shaykhī Zāda, 1998, vol. 2, p. 235). On the issue of renting, al-Kāsānī (1982, vol. 7, p. 110) asserts: 'And if he rented land subject to *kharāj* and planted it, he will not become *dhimmī* by planting.'[63]

Clearly, the *mustaʾmin* has the right to purchase, sell, lease out and rent land in the Islamic state without restrictions. Moreover, the scholars gave the *mustaʾmin* the right to execute all these dealings by himself or appoint a procurator on his behalf. This agent could be from *dār al-Islam* or *dār al-kufr* (al-Sarakhsī, n.d., vol. 19, p. 138).

From such arguments, it is apparent that the scholars gave full rights to the *mustaʾmin* to engage in various financial activities with virtually no limitation except public security.

When it comes to security and the public interest we find that the scholars do tend to impose restrictions and conditions on the *mustaʾmin*. Al-Shawkānī (1984, vol. 4, p. 563), for instance, bars the *mustaʾmin* completely from purchasing any kind of weaponry: 'The *mustaʾmin* should not be able to purchase the war machine.' He defends this prohibition on security grounds: 'The reason for that is he goes back to *dār al-ḥarb* and this weaponry would strength the disbelievers over the Muslims. Al-Shirwānī (n.d., vol. 4, p. 231) shares this view: 'It is prohibited for the *mustaʾmin* to purchase weaponry.'

Al-Qalyūbī (1998, vol. 2, p. 196) gives examples of the weaponry prohibited for the *mustaʾmin*: 'The war machine is like the sword, shield, horse and boat, either he possessed all or one or some of them.'

However, Ibn Nujaym (n.d., vol. 5, p. 87) eases the ban and imposes conditions to guarantee the security of Muslims:

> If the *ḥarbī* came to [*dār al-Islam*] with a sword and exchanged it with an arrow, spear or a horse, he would not be allowed to get out of [*dār al-Islam*] with it. And so if he exchanged his sword with a better sword, but if the sword was equal to it or worse than it, he would not be barred.

The purpose of these restrictions and conditions was not to harm the *mustaʾmin* or to strip him of his possessions, but rather to protect the national interest and public safety. This is clear from the example offered by Shaykhī Zāda: 'If a *ḥarbī* from the Romans entered to us by *amān* [possessing] horses, weapons or slaves, then he wanted to enter the land of the Turks, the Daylam or any other land of the enemies to sell it to them he would not be allowed to' (Shaykhī Zāda, 1998, vol. 2, p. 234). The danger here is obvious and no state would allow such a threat.

In the following example Shaykhī Zāda makes it clear that the ban was not pointless or intended to harm the *mustaʾmin*: 'If two *mustaʾmin*s of the Romans entered our *dār* by *amān* and one of them has slaves and the other has weapons, then they exchanged their goods or each one of them sold his goods to the other for a certain price, none of them would be banned from getting into *dār al-ḥarb* with the prices they got' (Shaykhī Zāda, 1998, vol. 2, p. 234). So, their possessions would be safe and rather than taking with them weapons that may strengthen the enemy, they can sell them and take the money with them wherever they wish to go.

The amān *of money remains after the personal* amān *expires*

To demonstrate their care for the property of the *mustaᵓmin*, many scholars agreed that if he returned to *dār al-ḥarb* his property would be secure and he would still have the right to recover it. Ibn Taymiyya (1983, vol. 2, p. 181) gives his verdict: 'If a *mustaᵓmin* gives his money to a Muslim as a trust or lends him some money or leaves his money and goes back to settle in *dār al-ḥarb* … the *amān* of his money remains.'[64] This *amān* remains despite the fact that his personal *amān* is nullified as al-Buhūtī explains: 'Because when he entered *dār al-Islam* the *amān* of his money was affirmed, so if his personal *amān* was cancelled by his entering [*dār al-ḥarb*] the *amān* of his money remains valid as it did not enter [*dār al-ḥarb*]' (al-Buhūtī, 1981, vol. 3, p. 108). This means that the Muslim has to pay back the money to *al-ḥārbī* in *dār al-ḥarb* who has theoretically reverted to being his enemy.

On the other hand, if the *mustaᵓmin* was indebted to a Muslim or *dhimmī* in *dār al-Islam* and went back to *dār al-ḥarb* without paying off his debt, they have the right to take their money from his remaining possessions (Ibn ᶜĀbdīn, 2000, vol. 4, p. 173).

In case of death either in *dār al-Islām* or *dār al-ḥarb* there is no difference according to Ibn Qudāma (1984, vol. 9, p. 198): his money should go to his heirs and it is prohibited for the Muslims to take any of it.[65]

Furthermore, Ibn Qudāma disputes al-Shāfiᶜī and Abu Ḥanīfa who say the *amān* of the money expires after it is transferred to the inheritors. He defends his position by saying that: 'The *amān* is an indispensable right attached to the money' and if money is transferred to the inheritors it transfers with it. He also claims that al-Muznī supports his opinion (Ibn Qudāma, 1984, vol. 9, p. 198).

By default, if the *mustaᵓmin* does not have inheritors his inheritance goes to the treasury of the Islamic state according to ᶜUlaysh (1988, vol. 3, p. 175) and others.[66]

The issue of keeping the *mustaᵓmin*'s money even after he has returned to *dār al-ḥarb* and become an enemy is worth pondering. One may jump to the hasty conclusion that this money is permissible to loot as the *musta'min* has become a disbeliever in *dār al-ḥarb*. However, Muslim scholars have even stressed the duty of Muslims to send the *musta'min*'s money to the *ḥarbī* in *dār al-ḥarb*. Ibn ᶜAbdīn (2000, vol. 6, p. 768) claims: 'Getting the money to his inheritors is his right as it is in the majority of the books, so it is prohibited to send it to the Muslim treasury.' Al-Dardīr (n.d., vol. 3, p. 125) also affirms that his money should be sent to his inheritors.

However, al-Suyūṭī (1961, vol. 2, p. 582) and al-Shīrāzī (n.d., vol. 2, p. 264) go further, emphasizing that the money of the *musta'min* should be respected at all times even if this *musta'min* returned to *dār al-ḥarb* as a fighter. Al-Qurāfī (1994, vol. 3, p. 446) judged that: 'If the *musta'min* left some money as a trust with us, then he went back to his country and died or was killed in fighting us, his money should be returned to his inheritors'. The duty of the Muslims, according to al-Qurāfī, is not only to allow him to keep his money but also to get it to him (or his heirs) in *dār al-ḥarb* even after he had been killed fighting the Muslims.

This view was reaffirmed by al-ᶜAbdarī (1977, vol. 3, p. 363): 'If he was killed while he was fighting the Muslims we should send his money which is still with us.'

Moreover, the spoils which the *musta'min* may gain from fighting the Muslims should also be respected when he enters *dār al-Islam* as a *musta'min*, according to al-Dardīr (n.d., vol. 3, p. 126). Nonetheless, Abu al-Ḥasan disliked the idea of Muslims purchasing the spoils from him, for fear that it might encourage him to fight again. Moreover, its purchase by another Muslim meant that the original owner [the Muslim who owned the property before he lost it in the war] would miss the opportunity to get it back, since purchasing it would be the only way to regain it. He explains his position: 'The *ḥarbī* has owned the goods through *amān*, i.e. *amān* has maintained his possession on those goods' (al-Dardīr, n.d., vol. 3, p. 126).

Such generous protection of possessions, and the liberty to transfer the possessions anywhere the refugee liked, is in tune with Article 30 of the Geneva Convention entitled Transfer of Assets.

Nevertheless, to give more protection and security to the possessions of the *musta'min*, the scholars ruled that he who destroys the property of the *musta'min* has to compensate him and pay back what he damaged because his property is protected by the *amān*[67] (al-Kāsānī, 1982, vol. 7, p. 71).

What is more, the state of war that could exist between *dār al-Islam* and *dār al-ḥarb* does not allow the Muslim to loot or to take the money of the disbelievers unlawfully. Al-Zarkashī (1981, vol. 1, p. 354) gives an example of this: 'If a *ḥarbī* borrowed some money from another *ḥarbī* and got to us by *amān* and then converted, he has to reimburse the money, because he took it as a way of reciprocity.'[68]

If a Muslim steals from the *mustaʾmin*, al-Sīwāsī (n.d., vol. 5, p. 462) gives the verdict that it is 'Prohibited to buy the stolen properties because the moneys of the *mustaʾmin* cannot be possessed by theft'.

The punishment of the Muslims in this case was, however, a point of debate between the scholars. Some of them said the punishment should be cutting off his hand as this is the Islamic punishment for theft, according to verse 5:38: 'Now as for the man who steals and the woman who steals, cut off the hand of either of them in requital for what they have wrought, as a deterrent ordained by God: for God is almighty, wise.' Others said the thief should not be punished by cutting off his hand because the property of the *mustaʾmin* is not permanently inviolable, since he is allowed to go back to *dār al-ḥarb*. The scholars of the latter opinion base their judgement on the same argument concerning the killing of the *mustaʾmin* and whether the Muslim should be killed if he had been convicted.[69]

Zufar, the student of Abu Ḥanīfa, affirms that the thief should be punished by cutting off his hands because 'His [the *mustaʾmin*'s] properties in our *dār* are inviolable like the *dhimmī*' (al-Sarakhsī, n.d., vol. 9, p. 181). In another part of his book al-Sarakhsī gives a brilliant explanation of this judgement and replies to those scholars who say the punishment should not be cutting of the hands: 'Cutting off the hands for theft is a right for God the Almighty. Its implementation depends on the crime.' He continues: 'The meaning of the crime is present in stealing the money of the *dhimmī* as well as the *mustaʾmin*' (al-Sarakhsī, n.d., vol. 26, p. 132). In other words, the crime is a crime whether it is against a Muslim, *dhimmī* or *mustaʾmin* and the punishment is for committing the crime in itself regardless of the victim.

After mentioning these two opinions, al-Kāsānī (1982, vol. 7, p. 71) comments: 'His hands should be cut off because he stole a protected money, since the *ḥarbī* has got the protection by *amān* so he is like the *dhimmī*.' In his discussion about the punishment of gangsters who attack caravans, kill and loot, Shaykhī Zāda (1998, vol. 2, p. 402) states that if the people in the caravans were *mustaʾmin*s, the attackers should be punished by the *ḥadd* and must reimburse the money, because the *mustaʾmin*'s property is protected.

On the other hand, Ibn ᶜĀbdīn (2000, vol. 4, p. 84) believes that: 'The thief who steals from the *mustaʾmin* [his hands] should not be cut off.' Al-Zaylaᶜī (1895, vol. 6, p. 104) defends this opinion: 'The money is attaching to the soul, and the money is less important than the soul. So, once [his hands] are cut off for his theft, it would be more adequate to kill the killer [of the *mustaʾmin*], because the soul is greater than the money.' Obviously, he differentiates between the *mustaʾmin* and the *dhimmī* in terms of the value of their lives and possessions, so he believes that the punishment for stealing money from a *mustaʾmin* should not be cutting the hands off the thief.

This opinion, however, has less reasoning and logic than the first. The first opinion accords with the general principles of Islam that call for equality in humanity and more particularly agree with the aims of legislating the *amān*. Making the punishment for stealing his money less than the punishment for stealing from other citizens will make the *mustaʾmin* vulnerable and less protected. Undoubtedly that contradicts with verse 9:6, which obliges Muslims to take good care of the *mustaʾmin*. It also jars with the unprecedented attention and respect the scholars gave to the possessions of the *mustaʾmin*. Finally, the issue of differentiation in rulings between the *dhimmī* and the *mustaʾmin* on the basis that the *dhimmī*'s contract is permanent while the *mustaʾmin*'s is temporary does not stand up to scrutiny. As Zaydān (1982, p. 235) says, the *dhimmī* could cancel his contract and leave to go to *dār al-ḥarb* like the *mustaʾmin*. Even the Muslim could do that. So, the rulings should not be based on what might happen in future but rather should be based on the current situation. In the current situation the *mustaʾmin* has *amān* and any violation of it should be met with the proper sentence.

This profound care for the property of the *mustaʾmin* is quite remarkable. The reasons for this lie in the Islamic principles mentioned in many verses and *ḥadīths* which order Muslims to fulfil their promises and render back the trusts to their owners, such as verse 4:58: 'Behold, God bids you to deliver all that you have been entrusted with unto those who are entitled thereto, and whenever you judge between people, to judge with justice. Verily, most excellent is what God exhorts you to do: verily, God is all-hearing, all-seeing!'

Al-Dāraquṭnī (1966, vol. 3, p. 35) also reports on the authority of Abu Hurayra that the Prophet said: 'Restore deposits to their owners and do not deceive who deceived you.'[70] Ibn Khuzayma (1970, vol. 4, p. 51) reports a narration on the authority of Anas that the Prophet said: 'There is no faith for he who does not keep the trust.' In the account of al-Haythamī (n.d., vol. 1, p. 41) and Abu Yaʿla (1984, vol. 5, p. 247) the Prophet adds: 'And there is no religion for he who does not keep his covenant.'

With regard to the *mustaʾmin*'s right to possess properties in the Islamic state, it is clear that this right is almost absolute with very limited exceptions relating to security and the public interest. Such limitations could be determined by the authorities in the Islamic state according to its situation.

It is also clear that the *mustaʾmin* has the same rights in regard to the protection of his possessions even after returning to his country. Not only that, but he still has the right to manage his properties in *dār al-Islam* through an agent. This coincides precisely with what Hathaway (2005, p. 527) concludes, that 'Non-resident refugees are entitled to the same protection of property rights as is afforded comparably situated non-resident aliens.'

Lastly, after thorough research, it may safely be concluded that the Islamic tradition endorses Article 13 of the Geneva Convention in principle and actually goes further in detailing the rights of the refugee in this regard.

Right of association (Article 15)

Article 15 of the Geneva Convention states that: 'As regards non-political and non-profit-making associations and trade unions the Contracting States shall accord to refugees lawfully staying in their territory the most favourable treatment accorded to nationals of a foreign country, in the same circumstances.'

After examining the history and discussions between the Contracting States of the Convention, Hathaway (2005, p. 891) concludes:

> Overall, the best that can be said for Art. 15 is that it is an important affirmation of the right of refugees – at least once they are lawfully staying, and to the same extent as most-favoured foreigners – to undertake quite a broad range of associational activities, including not only the right to join trade unions, but also to participate in

the activities of a diverse array of associations, including those with cultural, sporting, social, or philanthropic aims.

Obviously, any activities of a political nature are not expressed clearly by this Article. The rationale for this was 'to avoid interstate tension' as well as 'to deny refugees the right to participate in domestic political association', as Hathaway (2005, p. 884) states.

With regard to the Islamic position on this Article it is difficult to find a straightforward opinion from the classical scholars, simply because the association is a modern mode of expressing opinions, gaining or defending rights for a given group. However, we still find general principles in the Islamic tradition that could relate to this Article.

Freedom of expression was and remains an issue of debate between modern Muslim scholars. In his book *The General Freedoms in the Islamic State* al-Ghanūshī discusses the freedoms of Muslims, *dhimmīs* and even atheists. He defends the right of *dhimmīs* and all disbelievers to express their beliefs free from fear of oppression or torture. His justification for this view is based on verse 2:256: 'There shall be no coercion in matters of faith', as well as historical accounts in which non-believers or the digressed groups[71] such as the *khawārij* held public debates with Muslims scholars to dispute the very origins of the Islamic faith, in an atmosphere of religious and intellectual tolerance. Al-Ghanūshī also supports his ideas with reference to many contemporary scholars.

Additionally, when interpreting verse 9:6 many scholars stated that the *mustaʾmin* should stay in *dār al-Islam* as long as it takes for him to understand Islamic principles.[72] They also gave him the full right to ask questions and argue with them about the Qurʾān, the *ḥadīth* and the fundamentals of Islam without restricting his freedom in this regard. Obviously the result of such discussions was not necessarily conversion, but the *mustaʾmin* could adhere to his beliefs and still enjoy the right to stay in *dār al-Islam*.

Therefore, guaranteeing expressive freedom for refugees in *dār al-Islam* by default entails them to join or even establish associations, since they are a means of expression.

Furthermore, we can look at freedom of association from another angle to understand its legitimacy from the Islamic perspective. Tentatively, joining an association could also be to protect one's legitimate rights through collective efforts. In this sense freedom of association is not only permissible but also recommended by the Qurʾān and the *ḥadīth*.

God orders people through the Qurʾanic verse 5:2 to: 'Help one another in furthering virtue and God-consciousness, and do not help one another in furthering evil and enmity; and remain conscious of God: for, behold, God is severe in retribution'.

Rather than applying exclusively to Muslims, al-Akhfash says that this verse is 'an order to all humans to cooperate in goodness and piety' (al-Qurṭubī, 1986, vol. 6, p. 46). Al-Samarqandī (n.d., vol. 1, p. 391) affirms this: 'The verse is general for all people.' Al-Kalbī (1983, vol. 1, p. 167) also endorses this meaning, claiming that the verse is 'a general obligation.'

These interpretations mean that the Muslim, the *dhimmī* and the *mustaʾmin* are all included in its order and are urged to cooperate in everything that is considered a good cause.

Al-Saᶜdı (1984, vol. 1, p. 219) comments on the good cause by defining the meaning of *al-birr*. He says it is 'a general term that includes everything that God loves and is satisfied with [like] all the apparent and covert deeds that relate to God's rights and humans'. So, the good deed here relates not only to the deeds of the hereafter, but also to any well-intentioned endeavour by a human being. The doer of any earthly action that could be considered beneficial to people will also be rewarded on the Judgement Day because the term *al-birr* encompasses it, as al-Rāzī (2000, vol. 5, p. 32) states.

With regard to the Prophetic custom on the issue of cooperation, the Prophet frequently urged Muslims to extend a helping hand to the needy. Al-Hindī (1998, vol. 15, p. 381) reports on the authority of Ibn ᶜAbbās that the Prophet said: 'God will keep helping the man as long as he helps his fellow human.'

In another account the Prophet tells his companions about the great reward for those who help the disadvantaged. He says in the account narrated by al-Mundhirī (1996, vol. 3, p. 263) on the authority of Ibn ᶜAbbās that: 'Whoever gets involved in his brother's need to attain it, [then that] will be better for him than ten years of *Iᶜtikāf*[73]
من مشى في حاجة أخيه وبلغ فيها كان خيرا من اعتكاف عشر سنين.

At the same time the Prophet tries to deter Muslims from supporting each other in doing evil. Ibn Kathīr (1980, vol. 2, p. 7) reports an account of the Prophet saying: 'Whoever walks with an oppressor to help him, knowing that he is an oppressor, then he has gone out of Islam.' This punishment is severe from an Islamic perspective, but indicates the seriousness of the Islamic teachings on resisting oppression and oppressors.

This meaning is precisely repeated in another *ḥadīth* narrated by al-Bukhārī (1986, vol. 6, p. 2550) on the authority of Anas in which the Prophet says: 'Help your brother whether he is oppressed or an oppressor. A man said, O the messenger of God, I help him when he is oppressed but how can I help him if he is an oppressor? [the Prophet] said: stopping him from oppressing is your help.'[74]

Such statements from the Qurʾān, the Prophet and the scholars enable us to generalize that such cooperation is not exclusive to Muslims. Rather, all people are urged to cooperate in good causes and unite in the fight against evil.

In light of this discussion, there is no apparent reason not to extend this verdict to include refugees. On the contrary, in the case of refugees there is a more urgent need to cooperate in removing the barriers which obstruct their normal lives, or protect their rights in the field of work, sport, culture, or to preserve their identity or for any other reason. This could be through establishing their own associations or by joining existing ones. There is no difference as long as legitimate aims are served.

Regarding political activities, the previous principles do not differentiate between the nature of the association and whether it is economic, social, cultural or political. Thus, freedom is still guaranteed for the refugee to express his political opinion through the legal channels provided. Indeed, since political opinion could be the reason behind his flight, it is illogical to deprive him of the right that he fled in search of. Also, according to the above mentioned principles, cooperation in fighting aggression, oppression and tyranny could be more important than cooperation to improve and perfect living conditions for refugees. That is not to say that improving the living conditions of refugees is not important, but that the struggle against tyranny might have priority in certain circumstances.

However, would that mean allowing refugees to join a political association? According to the general principles of cooperation mentioned above, the only condition the scholars put on this issue is that the cooperation may not be based on or advocate 'sin and aggression'. So, in theory the refugee has the right to join or establish a political party that does not contradict the fundamentals of Islam or threaten national security or the public safety.

However, occupying an official political position in the Islamic state is another thing. That is because the refugee was considered by the scholars a foreigner who could stay temporarily in *dār al-Islam* to meet a particular need then go back to his country. According to Zaydān (1982, p. 85) Muslim scholars did not allow the refugee to occupy public positions in the Islamic state. Remarkably, this is exactly what the Civil and Political Covenant states: 'Freedom of association is not tantamount to a right to self-govern, because only citizens of a state have the right to take part in the conduct of public affairs, to vote, and to hold elected offices' (Hathaway, 2005, p. 896).

It is worth noting here that with regard to the nature of the association, whether political or non-political, the Convention does not state the right of the refugee to join or form a political association. However, from the debate above it could be concluded that the Islamic tradition does not object to the refugee joining a political association to serve the struggle against tyranny and oppression.

Access to courts (Article 16)

According to Hathaway (2005, p. 626), the significance of this Article lies in identifying the refugee and granting him the protection and other rights he is entitled to. This right enables him to go to court in order to obtain refugee status under the law. The drafters of the Refugee Convention put primary responsibility for assisting refugees to enforce their rights on the state parties themselves (Hathaway, 2005, p. 628). After much discussion they agreed to codify Article 16 under the title 'Access to courts':

> 1. A refugee shall have free access to the courts of law on the territory of all Contracting States.
>
> 2. A refugee shall enjoy in the Contracting State in which he has his habitual residence the same treatment as a national in matters pertaining to access to the courts, including legal assistance and exemption from cautio judicatum solvı.
>
> 3. A refugee shall be accorded in the matters referred to in paragraph 2 in countries other than that in which he has his habitual residence the treatment granted to a national of the country of his habitual residence.

Access to courts and the Islamic tradition

In principle Muslims are obliged by God in various Qur^ᵓanic verses to be just in judging between people. For example verse 4:58: 'Behold, God bids you to deliver all that you have been entrusted with unto those who are entitled thereto, and whenever you judge between people, to judge with justice. Verily, most excellent is what God exhorts you to do: verily, God is all-hearing, all-seeing!'

In another verse (16:90) God commands fairness and forbids injustice: 'Behold, God enjoins justice, and the doing of good, and generosity towards [one's] fellow-men and He forbids all that is shameful and all that runs counter to reason, as well as envy; [and] He exhorts you [repeatedly] so that you might bear [all this] in mind.'

Moreover, even if a Muslim were to judge people he does not like, he still has to be fair with them, according to the verse (5:8): 'O you who have attained to faith! Be ever steadfast in your devotion to God, bearing witness to the truth in all equity; and never let hatred of anyone lead you into the sin of deviating from justice. Be just: this is closest to being God-conscious. And remain conscious of God: verily, God is aware of all that you do.' Al-Zamakhsharī (n.d., vol. 1, p. 647) maintains that this verse obliges Muslims to act justly even towards disbelievers who are the enemies of God. Ibn Kathīr (1980, vol. 2, p. 6), however, states a general rule: 'Acting equitably is obligatory on everybody towards anybody in any situation.' Al-Saᶜdı (2000, vol. 1, p. 224) endorses this opinion and makes acting justly part of the religion.

In order to motivate Muslims to act justly the Prophet in various *ḥadīths* mentions that they can expect a great reward for doing so. Al-Bayhaqī (1993, vol. 10, p. 87) reports a *ḥadīth* in which the Prophet states: 'The fair people at the Judgement Day will be on a rostrum made of light on the right hand side of God and both His hands are right.' In another account reported by al-Bayhaqī (1991, vol. 10, p. 88) the Prophet states: 'The most loved and the closest to God in the hereafter is the just *Imām*, and the most hated and the most severely punished is the unjust *Imām*.'[75]

Such strong statements in affirming justice and equity in Islamic society are of great relevance to refugees and their right to access courts as stated in Article 16 of the Convention. The fairness and justice Muslims are commanded to abide by do not exclude refugees, even though they might follow another religion.

The importance of such principles in dealing with refugees in particular is clear in regard to the modern tendency to regard refugees as a burden and to try to circumvent the state's legal obligations. The examples of such attempts cited by Hathaway (2005, p. 630) support this opinion.

However, the Muslim scholars touched upon the issue of access to courts for non-Muslims when they discussed the Qurʾanic verse 5:42 and its commands regarding the *dhimmīs* and their right to access Islamic courts in *dār al-Islam*.

Verse 5:42 reads:

> Those who eagerly listen to any falsehood, greedily swallowing all that is evil! Hence, if they come to thee [for judgement] thou mayest either judge between them or leave them alone: for, if thou leave them alone, they cannot harm thee in any way. But if thou dost judge, judge between them with equity, verily, God knows those who act equitably.

This verse and the verse before it (5:41) speaks clearly about the *dhimmīs*. However, the meaning of this verse is apparent in giving the Prophet and any judge after him the choice to judge or not between the *dhimmīs* when they come to him in a dispute (al-Kalbī, 1983, vol. 1, p. 177).

Yet, scholars were at odds in terms of the abrogation of this verse. According to al-Rāzī (2000, vol. 11, p. 186) some of them, like, Ibn ʿAbbās, al-Ḥasan, Mujāhid, ʿIkrima and the school of al-Shāfiʿī said it is abrogated by verse 5:49:

> Hence, judge [between the followers of earlier revelation] in accordance with what God has bestowed from on high, and do not follow their errant views; and beware of them, lest they tempt thee away from aught that God has bestowed from on high upon thee. And if they turn away [from His commandments], then know that it is but God's will [thus] to afflict them for some of their sins.

Thus, the free choice is not valid any more, and the *dhimmīs* in *dār al-Islam* should adhere to the Islamic rulings in their disputes.

Nevertheless, others, such as al-Nakhaʿı, al-Shaʿbī, Qutāda, ʿAṭāʾ, Abu Bakr and Abu Muslim (al-Rāzī, 2000, vol. 11, p. 186), assert that the verse is not abrogated and the choice in judging between them remains.

After examining all the evidence carefully, Zaydān (1982, p. 573) concludes that the overriding opinion is that a Muslim judge has to give a verdict if non-Muslims, whether *dhimmīs* or *mustaʾmins*, decide to go to court.

The relevance of this discussion to Article 16 is that it gives the *mustaʾmin* the right to go to court in *dār al-Islam* and obliges the judge to look at his case and give a suitable verdict. So, he can go to court as a claimant to defend his rights against anybody, or he goes there accused by someone else.

Concrete evidence that the Muslim scholars gave *mustaʾmin* the right to access the courts appears in the scholarly discussion about the illegal *mustaʾmin* in *dār al-Islam*. Throughout their debate it is apparent that any final verdict had to be considered thoroughly. Claimants, proofs, witnesses, judges and deliberations between them were all necessary before arriving at a verdict. So, it is a legal process that may lead to endorsing the stay of the *mustaʾmin* in *dār al-Islam* or invalidate it completely requiring his transfer to his original place.

Ibn Qudāma (1984, vol. 9, p. 281), for instance, goes through the scenario of having a *mustaʾmin* in *dār al-Islam* without *amān* and rules that this *mustaʾmin* should be asked about his *amān*, and if he claims he is a messenger to the Muslims, he should be believed, because 'it is impossible to prove otherwise as the messengers usually come without a previous *amān*'. However, Ibn Nujaym (n.d., vol. 5, p. 109) disagrees with him on this point and says that if he claims to be a messenger, it is necessary to look and see whether he has a letter or not. If he has a letter, then he gets *amān*, if not he will be captured. Nonetheless, al-Nawawī (1984, vol. 10, p. 299) and al-Shirbīnī (n.d., vol. 4, p. 243) propose that if he does not carry a message, he has to swear to prove that.[76]

Al-Ṣāwī (1994, vol. 2, p. 186), however, requires further efforts to verify the conditions surrounding the *mustaʾmin* and suggests looking for any link that may support him, such as the wind which might have forced him to come to *dār al-Islam*. Or, the link could be against him like finding weaponry on him, which might mean he was a fighter and not a *mustaʾmin*.

The scholars were at variance about instances where the *mustaʾmin* claimed that a Muslim had given him *amān*. Al-Shirbīnī (n.d., vol. 4, p. 243) and al-Ramlī (1983, vol. 8, p. 86) say 'he should not be believed without a proof, because [proving it] is feasible'. Yet, al-Ghazālī (1996, vol. 7, p. 58) mentions the two options without weighing any one against the other, and al-Nawawī (1984, vol. 10, p. 299), after mentioning the two possibilities, suggests believing him without proof.

Furthermore, if a Muslim claimed that he had given him *amān*, Ibn ᶜĀbdīn (2000, vol. 4, p. 168) and Shaykhī Zāda (1998, vol. 2, p. 452) judge that this Muslim should not be believed until he brings two witnesses with him.

The significant point here is that the scholars do not reach a verdict hastily. It is a thorough process involving a judge, defendant, prosecutor, witnesses and proofs, which means in effect that a legal process should take place in a court. All the elements of the court are available and at the end there must be a verdict that should be respected by all parties, either to the benefit of the refugee or against him, and that is the essence of Article 16 of the Convention.

The other element to take into account here is that engaging in a legal process costs money. Thus having the right to be heard before the judge to defend himself and table his evidence, the *mustaᵓmin* by default should also have the right to be assisted and given legal aid by the state to pursue the process and be able to cover the expenses including any necessary fees. Otherwise, if we say that he should not be assisted then his right to sue or to be sued becomes meaningless and virtually unattainable. Indeed refugees in most cases are 'unable to enforce their rights without assistance from state or international authorities' (Hathaway, 2005, p. 626). This would then be in contradiction with the principles of justice established in the Islamic legacy.

In light of this it can be safely concluded that Article 16 is in conformity with the Islamic tradition and its principles of justice.

Gainful employment (Articles 17, 18 and 19)

The refugee's right to work was and remains a sensitive issue in all countries whether they are developed or less developed. This is because it affects the local economy and workers in the host state. The sensitivity of this issue is particularly apparent at election time when the impact of migrants on job opportunities for nationals often becomes a talking point.

With regard to 'Wage-earning employment' Article 17 of the Geneva Convention states:

> 1. The Contracting States shall accord to refugees lawfully staying in their territory the most favourable treatment accorded to nationals of a foreign country in the same circumstances, as regards the right to engage in wage-earning employment.

The drafting of this Article, according to Hathaway (2005, p. 742), was not conceived in naivety. Governments were keenly aware of the domestic political and other risks of allowing refugees to compete with their own citizens for employment opportunities. These governments, just recovering from the Second World War, were anxious not to jeopardize their plans for economic recovery by allowing the free entry of refugees into the workforce. Nonetheless, it seems there was 'a clear awareness among the drafters that there are few rights more central to refugee self-sufficiency than the right to work … it was therefore decided that it made more sense to set the right to work at a meaningful high level' (Hathaway, 2005, p. 745).

The drafters of the Convention 'were determined to provide refugees with better than the lowest common denominator of state practice, under which non-citizens are often excluded from the labour market. The drafters clearly recognized, and intended, that Article 17 would require states to grant refugees a preferential access to work opportunities, even though this has not been the case under earlier refugee treaties' (Hathaway, 2005, p. 742).

Gainful employment and the Islamic perspective

Due to the different circumstances, as well as the limited importance of the issue in their times, the early Muslim scholars did not feel the need to formulate or codify the right to work for the *mustaʾmin* in a clear legal text. However, while there was no overall legal ruling, they dealt with a number of related matters separately. For example, they detailed the *mustaʾmin*'s right to trade in *dār al-Islam* with all the surrounding issues relating to it. They also discussed the issue of purchase, selling, letting and renting of land by the *mustaʾmin*. So, generally speaking, they allowed the *mustʾamin* to engage freely in various activities in the area of employment, except in a small number of fields not deemed to be in the public interest. Gathering all these scattered issues will shape the stance of the Islamic tradition on the *mustaʾmin*'s right to work and eventually enable us to compare it with Article 17 of the Geneva Convention.

The right to trade

The sheer volume of texts and discussions by scholars about the *mustaʾmin*'s rights and duties in the field of commerce affirms the conclusion reached in the previous section,[77] that commerce was the practical and tangible purpose of *amān* in the early days[78] of the Islamic state.

Concerning this issue, we do not find the scholars stipulating the right of the *mustaʾmin* to trade. Instead they usually discuss trade-related matters such as the tax imposed on him and the kind of goods he can trade with, and so on. This means the *mustaʾmin*'s right to trade was accepted as a matter of fact and a judgement was not required.

The phrase used by many scholars[79] to impose the amount of tax on the *mustaʾmin* is: 'If a *ḥarbī* trades with us he has to pay [a tax called] *ᶜushr*' (Ibn Mufiḥ, 1979, vol. 3, p. 427). However, this tax was subject to debate between the scholars. Al-Nafrāwī (1994, vol. 1, p. 339) states that even this tax could be altered and reduced if the *Imām* saw fit, or if a different percentage of tax was agreed with the *mustaʾmin* before he entered *dār al-Islam*.

To encourage and facilitate the entrance of the *mustaʾmin* to *dār al-Islam* al-Shāfiᶜī and other scholars went further to abolish the *ᶜushr* tax imposed on the *mustaʾmin* provided he was bringing essential provisions to Muslims. They said: 'If they enter to provide rations needed by people, they are allowed to enter without *ᶜushr*.' Al-Shāfiᶜī substantiates his decision on the grounds that 'their entrance is of benefit to the Muslims' (Ibn Qudāma, 1984, vol. 9, p. 281).

So, according to these opinions the *mustaʾmin* is not only allowed to trade in *dār al-Islam*, but also encouraged to do so. All in all, the *mustaʾmins* had considerable liberty in their commercial activities and the kinds of goods they were permitted to trade in *dār al-Islam*.

The scholars, by and large, widen the scale of trade for the *mustaʾmin*. We find them giving a clear verdict to allow the Muslim and the *mustaʾmin* to be partners in business. Al-Kāsānī (1982, vol. 6, p. 81) states: 'If a *ḥarbī* enters *dār al-Islam* with *amān* and then he gives his money to a Muslim to trade for him on a *muḍāraba*[80] contract, or the Muslim gives his money to him on a *muḍāraba* contract, that will be permissible.'

Other scholars, however, envisaged different scenarios for this partnership and gave solutions for each one. Ibn ᶜĀbdīn (2000, vol. 8, p. 327), for instance, rules that: 'If a *ḥarbī* gives his money to a Muslim on *muḍāraba* and the Muslim then enters *dār al-ḥarb* with a permission from the owner of the money, the contract will be intact.'

Shaykhī Zāda (1998, vol. 4, p. 334) adds that if two *mustaᵓmin*s entered *dār al-Islam* with *amān* and one of them gave money to the other on *muḍāraba* contract and the latter then went to *dār al-ḥarb*, the contract remains unbroken.

Al-Sarakhsī (n.d., vol. 22, p. 129) endorsed the commercial contract between the Muslim and the *mustaᵓmin* even if the agreement was to share the profits equally.

Nevertheless, where farming was concerned, the scholars allowed the *mustaᵓmin* to engage in all sorts of dealings, including purchase, selling, hiring and renting agricultural land. Al-Sarakhsī devotes a section in his book called 'The *muzāraᶜa*[81] contract with the *ḥarbi*' specifically to matters relating to this contract. He says: 'If a *ḥarbī* entered *dār al-Islam* with *amān* and a [Muslim] man gave him his land and seeds on *muzāraᶜa*, [then the contract] is permissible and the harvest at the end of the year should be shared as agreed' (al-Sarakhsī, n.d., vol. 23, p. 121).

Concerning another type of contract al-Dardīr (n.d., vol. 6, p. 235) asserts: 'The Muslim is approved to give his grape trellis to a *dhimmī* or a *muᶜāhid* or *ḥarbī* on a *musāqā*[82] contract providing that he [the Muslim] makes sure that [the *mustaᵓmin*, *muᶜāhid* or the *dhimmī*] does not make the grapes alcohol.'

What is more, the scholars gave the *mustaᵓmin* great liberty in the field of work to the extent that they allowed a Muslim to appoint the *mustaᵓmin* to act on his behalf in a variety of dealings, such as trading, attaining his legal rights and so on (Shaykhī Zāda, 1998, vol. 3, p. 563). This basically means allowing him to work as a solicitor to defend the rights of his clients before the court if need be.

Additionally, the scholars allowed the *mustaᵓmin* to work in financial matters and to be involved in borrowing, lending and depositing money with the Muslims and vice versa (al-Suyūṭī, 1961, vol. 2, p. 582).[83] In practical terms this could be interpreted today as permission to work in the financial markets as an advisor, banker, and so on.

The *mustaᵓmin* also has the right to work as an employee in various fields. Al-Sarakhsī (n.d., vol. 16, p. 56) confirms that: 'If a Muslim hired a *dhimmī* or *mustaᵓmin* to serve him that would be permissible.' Also al-Shirbīnī (n.d., vol. 2, p. 362) permits the *mustaᵓmin* to work in the fields of 'cutting trees, collecting grass and hunting'.

These different permissions might today mean that the *mustaʾmin* is permitted to work in diverse sectors of the market place. To be a trader would by default mean to employ other people, such as accountants, workers, drivers, solicitors, bankers and any other necessary staff. The same applies to allowing the *mustaʾmin* to be a farmer. In other words, he has the right to employ people or to be employed as well as the right to be self-employed.

Restrictions on the mustaʾmin *concerning some kinds of work*

Yet, with this extended freedom granted to the *mustaʾmin* to work in *dār al-Islam*, some scholars introduced restrictions and reservations on particular types of work that could be detrimental to the national interest or in conflict with the identity of the Islamic state.

The scholars, for instance, do not allow the *mustaʾmin* to trade in certain goods with the Muslims because they are forbidden for Muslims, such as pork and alcohol (al-Nafrāwī, 1994, vol. 1, p. 339). However, if there are *dhimmīs* in that area of *dār al-Islam* the *mustaʾmin* can still sell them these goods, according to al-Nafrāwī (1994, vol. 1, p. 339).

Other scholars, such as al-Shawkānī (1984, vol. 4, p. 563), al-Qalyūbī (1998, vol. 2, p. 196) and Ibn Nujaym, (n.d., vol. 5, p. 87) imposed other restrictions on the *mustaʾmin* in regard to his trade in weaponry, especially that carried out with the non-Muslims in *dār al-ḥarb*.

Also, some scholars imposed restrictions on work in excavating treasures especially gold and silver, unless there was permission from the *Imām* (Shaykhī Zāda, 1998, vol. 1, p. 184). Otherwise, anything he finds should be taken from him, because these treasures belong to the people of *dār al-Islam* (al-Samarqandī, 1984, vol. 1, p. 328). In the event that the *Imām* allows him to excavate treasures, he has to pay one-fifth of what he finds to the Muslims (al-Qaffāl, 1980, vol. 3, p. 95). However, if he worked there as an employee with permission, that would be acceptable, according to Shaykhī Zāda (1998, vol. 1, p. 185).

The significance of these opinions is in their influence on contemporary scholars, who face different challenges and circumstances. It could be rightfully said that the *mustaʾmin* is prohibited from working in certain fields due to their sensitive nature. Nonetheless, these limitations and restrictions are the exception, not the rule, and should not be used as an excuse to deprive the refugee of his right to engage in gainful employment.

Based on that, it is clear that there is a large measure of agreement between Article 17 and the Islamic position concerning the same issue. Moreover, in light of these findings, the Islamic tradition could also be in agreement with Articles 18 and 19 of the Convention, because of the very close correspondence of these two Articles with the Article discussed above. Article 18, 'Self-employment', states:

> The Contracting States shall accord to a refugee lawfully in their territory treatment as favourable as possible and, in any event, not less favourable than that accorded to aliens generally in the same circumstances, as regards the right to engage on his own account in agriculture, industry, handicrafts and commerce and to establish commercial and industrial companies.

Remarkably, some of these fields, for example agriculture,were also mentioned by name by Muslim scholars, who asserted that the refugee has the right to engage in them. Also we saw that the scholars stipulated the right of the *mustaʾmin* to establish partnerships and be involved in various contracts either with Muslims, *dhimmīs* or even with his fellow *mustaʾmin*s.

Article 19, 'Liberal professions' reads:

> 1. Each Contracting State shall accord to refugees lawfully staying in their territory who hold diplomas recognised by the competent authorities of that State, and who are desirous of practising a liberal profession, treatment as favourable as possible and, in any event, not less favourable than that accorded to aliens generally in the same circumstances.

Also, this Article, in principle is in line with the Islamic rules and teachings that urge the Muslims to put the best qualified man in the right position according to Qurʾānic verse 28:26: 'Said one of the two [daughters]: "O my father! Hire him: for, behold, the best that thou couldst hire is one who is [as] strong and worthy of trust"'. The qualifications are the capability to do the job, as well as honesty. 'Capability' by default also means the knowledge, experience, and the physical ability to do the work.

The Prophet also recommends that Muslims strive for perfection in their work. In the account narrated by Abu Yaʿlā (1984, vol. 7, p. 349) on the authority of ᶜĀʾisha, the Prophet said: 'If one of you does a job, God loves him to do it just right.'[84]

Thus, it could be said that Article 19 matches to a great extent the principles of the Islamic tradition and could be endorsed by contemporary Muslim scholars.

Welfare (Articles 20, 21, 22, 23 and 24)

To guarantee one of the very basic human rights of refugees the Convention dedicates articles, 20, 21, 22, 23 and 24 of chapter 4 entitled 'Welfare' to the rights of the refugee that will help him benefit from public assistance and ensure he will not be left alone struggling to secure basic needs in his new domicile.

Article 20 addresses the rationing system and the refugee's right to be treated in the same way as a national where this system exists. Article 21 states that the refugee's right to housing and the treatment should be as favourable as possible and, in any event, not less favourable than that accorded to aliens generally in the same circumstances.

Article 22, however, grants the refugee the right to education, access to studies, the recognition of foreign school certificates, diplomas and degrees, the remission of fees and charges and the award of scholarships. Moreover, Article 23 obliges the contracting states to give the refugee the right to public relief on the same level as their own nationals.

Lastly, Article 24 regulates labour legislation and social security.

With regard to the Islamic position towards these Articles, we find well-established principles in the Islamic tradition that oblige Muslims collectively and individually to help the needy and the distressed.

There are numerous *ḥadīth*s in which the Prophet urges his followers to be generous and help the deprived, the destitute, the distressed and anybody who needs help.

Al-Bukhārī (1986, vol. 1, p. 13) narrates an account on the authority of Ibn ᶜUmar that a man asked the Prophet about the best thing in Islam. The Prophet said: 'Feeding, saying the greeting of peace to anybody, whether you know him or not.' In another *ḥadīth* narrated by al-Hindī (1998, vol. 3, p. 168) the Prophet says: 'God loves helping the afflicted.' Ābādı (1995, vol. 14, p. 9) comments on this account that: 'Helping the afflicted is obligatory'. Al-Munāwī (1937, vol. 4, p. 268), however, explains the meaning of *al-malhūf* to include 'the oppressed who ask for help or the grievously distressed'. To support this interpretation he cites a *ḥadīth* that states: 'People are the dependents of God and the most loved ones those who are of help to his dependents', especially when the need is dire, as he comments.

To encourage Muslims to extend their help to whosoever needs it, the Prophet tells his followers about a man[85] who deserved to get into Paradise for going down a well to bring water to a thirsty dog (al-Bukhārī, 1986, vol. 2, p. 833). The amazed companions asked the Prophet: 'Are we rewarded for [doing good] to animals?' and the Prophet said: 'There is a reward [in showing kindness to any creature that has] a fresh [live] liver.'

The Prophet also warns Muslims of the wrong-doing of denying help to the needy, even if the needy were an animal. Ibn Ḥibbān (1993, vol. 2, p. 305) reports on the authority of Ibn ᶜUmar that the Prophet said: 'A woman was punished [in hellfire] for a cat she tied. She neither fed her, nor did she allow her to look for food outside.'[86]

Al-Bukhārī (1989, vol. 1, p. 137) also narrates, on the authority of Jarīt, that the Prophet said: 'God will not show mercy to those who do not show mercy to people.'

It is evident from the above examples that these are very general principles that encompass not only humankind, but other creatures as well. Thus the *mustaᵓmin* is, by default, included in these principles. Al-Suyūṭī (1993, vol. 4, p. 133) in his interpretation of verse 9:6 narrates on the authority of al-Ḍaḥḥāk that Muslims were not only ordered to protect the disbeliever who wants to listen to the word of God [i.e. the *mustaᵓmin*] but also to take care of them financially as long as they are there. Hence, it is the responsibility of the Muslims as individuals and the *Imām* as the head of the state to take financial care of the *mustaᵓmin* and provide him with his material needs.

In addition to the above principles, verse 2:271 of the Qurᵓan may lend itself to support this attitude. It reads: 'If you do deeds of charity openly, it is well; but if you bestow it upon the needy in secret, it will be even better for you, and it will atone for some of your bad deeds. And God is aware of all that you do.' The verse does not differentiate between the needy on the basis of religion. The general terms employed in the verse ensure the poor *dhimmī* is included in its verdict, as Al-Kāsānī (1982, vol. 2, p. 49) maintains. Other scholars like Ibn Rushd (n.d., vol. 1, p. 297) say that: 'The rulings of the *ḥarbī*, when he gets *amān*, are the same like the *dhimmī*.' This means that the poor *mustaᵓmin* is also included.

They also refer to verse 60:8 to support their opinion: 'As for such [of the unbelievers] as do not fight against you on account of [your] faith, and neither drive you forth from your homelands, God does not forbid you to show them kindness and to behave towards them with full equity: for, verily, God loves those who act equitably.'

Abu Ḥanīfa and Muḥammad conclude that spending money of *ṣadaqa*[87] on the *dhimmīs* is a way of showing kindness and we are commanded to do that. They go further to say that had it not been for the *ḥadīth* of Muᶜādh,[88] it would have been permissible to give them *zakāt*[89] as well (al-Kāsānī, 1982, vol. 2, p. 49).

To reinforce his argument in permitting *ṣadaqa* to be spent on the *dhimmīs*, al-Sīwāsī (n.d., vol. 2, p. 267) mentions an account on the authority of Saᶜıd Ibn al-Musayyib that the Prophet gave money of *ṣadaqa* to a Jewish family. He also cites the account of the Prophet who says: 'Give alms to the people of religions' (al-Sīwāsī, n.d., vol. 2, p. 267).

Despite these great principles we still find some scholars who argue that the *mustaᵓmin* is not entitled to financial help from the state. Their rationale is that the *mustaᵓmin* in essence is an enemy and only temporarily allowed to stay in the Islamic state. When the period of his stay expires he goes behind enemy lines. So, helping him will eventually strengthen the enemy camp and this is not acceptable.

Ibn Nujaym (n.d., vol. 2, p. 261) claims that: 'It is a consensus that all the kinds of *ṣadaqa*, whether it is obligatory, mandatory or voluntary are prohibited to the *ḥarbi*.' He justifies this with reference to verse 60:9: 'God only forbids you to turn in friendship towards those who fight against you because of [your] faith, and drive you forth from your homelands, or aid [others] in driving you forth: and as for those [from among you] who turn towards them in friendship; it is they who are truly wrongdoers!' He then comments that the verse is general and it includes the *mustaᵓmin*.

Additionally, al-Kāsānī (1982, vol. 2, p. 49) asserts that the *ṣadaqa* is not permitted to be spent on the *ḥarbī* while it is permitted for the *dhimmī*, because spending it on the *ḥarbī* will help them in fighting us and this is not permissible, while this probability is not available in the case of the *dhimmī*.

Al-Zaylaᶜī (1895, vol. 1, p. 300) also endorses this opinion depending on the verse (60:9). He comments that all the needy of *dār al-ḥarb* are excluded from the poor people in general and the *ḥarbī* in *dār al-Islam* is excluded from it as well.

Moreover, al-Sarakhsī (n.d., vol. 3, p. 111) excludes the *mustaʾmin* from the people eligible for *ṣadaqa* because the *mustaʾmin* is a fighter and we were ordered not to show kindness to those who fight us as God commands in verse 60:9.

So, the apparent reason that opponents would deny the *mustaʾmin* *ṣadaqa* is that he is an enemy and helping him will reinforce the enemy camp and encourage them to fight the Muslims. This assumption, however, is clearly not valid in the case of refugees today, who are usually forced to flee their homes either because of oppression, war, a natural disaster, or other unfortunate circumstances. These people cannot be the enemies of the Islamic state and feeding and sheltering them does not threaten national security, nor will it strengthen the enemy as the scholars feared.

A debate on the sources of money

In addition to the above points, the scholars also debated the sources from which the *mustaʾmin* is eligible for money. Generally speaking the main sources of money in the Islamic state were: the *fayᶜ*,[90] *khums al-ghanīma*,[91] *al-ᶜushūr*,[92] *al-jizya*,[93] *al-ṣadaqāt*,[94] *al-kharāj*,[95] money left by the deceased with no heirs, and natural resources.

The main two sources the scholars debated were the *zakāt* and *ṣadaqa*. The vast majority of scholars do not allow the state to spend the money of *zakāt* on the *dhimmī* or the *mustaʾmin*. When it comes to *ṣadaqa*, some of them allow it and others do not.

According to al-Kāsānī (1982, vol. 2, p. 49), there is consensus among scholars that the *dhimmī* is not eligible to receive *zakāt*: 'It is a consensus that spending money of *zakāt* on the disbeliever is not permitted.' The basis of this verdict is the *ḥadīth*[96] narrated on the authority of Muᶜādh that when the Prophet sent him to Yemen, he ordered him to take the money from their rich people and return it to their poor people. Al-Kāsānī concludes that the *zakāt* is taken from rich Muslims and should be returned only to poor Muslims and not to anybody else, as stated by this *ḥadīth*.

Ibn Nujaym (n.d., vol. 2, p. 261) puts it rather bluntly: 'It is not paid to the *dhimmī* because of Muᶜādh's *ḥadīth*.' Al-Shaybānī (1985, vol. 1, p. 123) and Shaykhī Zāda (1998, vol. 1, p. 329) also come to the same conclusion.

Moreover, al-Sarakhsī (n.d., vol. 2, p. 202) generalizes that any disbeliever [whether a *dhimmī* or a *ḥarbī*], should not take from the money of *zakāt*. Al-Mirghinānī (n.d., vol. 1, p. 113) and al-Ṭaḥḥāwī (1900, vol. 1, p. 473) emphasize that *zakāt* should not be paid to *dhimmī*.

The only scholar who believed it was permitted for *zakāt* to be paid to the *dhimmī* was Zufar, according to al-Sarakhsī (n.d., vol. 2, p. 202). His rationale for this is that: 'The purpose of the *zakāt* is to satisfy the needs of the poor by seeking God's satisfaction, and that has happened.' Yet, Zufar did not explain how to refute the contrary opinion, or how to interpret the straightforward *ḥadīth* of the Prophet narrated by Muᶜādh, which states clearly that *zakāt* should be taken from rich Muslims and returned to poor Muslims.

With regard to the voluntary *ṣadaqa*, al-Sarakhsī (n.d., vol. 3, p. 111) affirms that it is permitted to give the voluntary *ṣadaqa* to the *dhimmī* and says that if we were to use *qiyās*[97] then giving *zakāt* would be allowed, but we dropped *qiyās* here because of Muᶜādh's *ḥadīth*. Nonetheless, it is permitted to give *ṣadaqa* and other alms to them.

Moreover, al-Sīwāsī claims that there is agreement among the scholars about permitting spending of alms on the *dhimmī* (al-Sīwāsī, n.d., vol. 2, p. 267). Al-Sarakhsī and al-Sīwāsī say that the rulings of the *mustaᵓmin* are the same as the *dhimmī* once the *mustaᵓmin* enters *dār al-Islam*. So, these rulings apply to him as well.

Explaining the rationale behind this permission al-Kāsānī (1982, vol. 5, p. 104) states: 'It is permissible to give them *ṣadaqa* as it is permissible to give it to the Muslim. It is, rather, better to give *ṣadaqa* to them because this will attract them to Islam and lead them to convert.'

Al-Shirbīnī (n.d., vol. 3, p. 121) goes further to say that the *ṣadaqa* is allowed to a non-Muslim and supports his view by the *ḥadīth* 'There is a reward [in showing kindness to any creature that has] a fresh [live] liver.' He also reports a scholar called al-Ṣayramī that there is no difference between the *ḥarbī* and the other disbelievers. Al-Ramlī (1983, vol. 6, p. 173) reports the same thing on al-Ṣayramī.

Al-Kāsānī (1982, vol. 2, p. 49) reports that the opponents of this view base their judgement on two things: first, they considered *zakāt* in the same light as *ṣadaqa* and since they are forbidden from receiving *zakāt* they should also be forbidden from receiving *ṣadaqa*. The second thing is that it is not permitted to give *ṣadaqa* to the *ḥarbī* and so it should not be permitted to give it to the *dhimmī*.

This evidence makes it clear that the scholars do not allow *zakāt* to be spent on the *dhimmī* and, by default, on the *mustaᵓmin*. As far as the *ṣadaqa* is concerned, the position of the proponents of spending *ṣadaqa* money on the *dhimmī* is much stronger than the opponents. However, when it comes to the *mustaᵓmin* the case is different.

The interpretation of verses 60: 8–9

Due to their important place in this discussion, an examination of some of the interpretations of these verses will shed more light on the topic.

The reasons for the revelations were disputed by the scholars, according to al-Thaᶜālibī (n.d., vol. 4, p. 292). Some said that those we are commanded to show kindness to are those who have a covenant with the Prophet. Others said they are those who converted in Mecca but did not migrate. Others also said they are the women and children. However, ᶜAbdullah Ibn al-Zubayr said the reason for revelation is the incident that took place between Asmāᵓ Bint Abī Bakr and her mother who came to visit her. Asmāᵓ Bint Abu Bakr refused to welcome her mother because she was a disbeliever. But the Prophet ordered her to accept the gifts from her mother, take good care of her, be generous and show kindness to her.[98]

However, al-Shāfiᶜī (n.d., vol. 2, p. 192) adds another reason for the revelation. He says that some Muslims felt bad when God ordered them to fight against the disbelievers and to cut off relations with them, so they feared that their financial help to their non-Muslim relatives in Mecca would become illegal. Therefore God revealed this verse to allow them to continue sending the money.

This actually means that helping the *ḥarbī* even in *dār al-ḥarb* – let alone *dār al-Islam* – is allowed providing that: 'It is not to support the disbelievers to fight or there is harm that may befall Islam', as Ibn al-Jawzī (1994, vol. 1, p. 56) states.

Al-Qurṭubī (1986., vol. 3, p. 338) emphasizes this interpretation by saying that: 'The apparent meaning of the verses obligates the permission to spend money of all kind of *ṣadaqa* on them, but the Prophet excluded the money of *zakāt* by the *ḥadīth* of Muᶜādh.'

Al-Naḥḥās (1987, vol. 1, p. 713) also confirms that assisting non-Muslim relatives in *dār al-ḥarb* is not prohibited as long as it does not strengthen the fighters by providing them with weapons or horses, and does not expose Muslims to danger.

Al-Ṭabarī agrees with these conditions and states that a Muslim may assist a needy *ḥarbī* in *dār al-ḥarb* even if they are not related by kinship (Ibn al-Jawzī, 1984, vol. 1, p. 239).

Lastly, Ibn ᶜĀbdīn (2000, vol. 2, p. 352) reports that al-Zaylaᶜī confirmed that it is permissible to give *ṣadaqa* to the *mustaʾmin*. He also narrates an account of the Prophet to underline this view. The account explains that when there was a drought in Mecca, the Prophet sent 500 *dīnārs* to Abu Sufyān and Ṣafwān Ibn Umayya to distribute among the poor there.

Though the people of Mecca were obviously enemies in *dār al-ḥarb*, the Prophet sent them money to help the needy at that difficult time. Thus, if it is permitted to help the needy in *dār al-ḥarb*, it would be possible to help those needy when they come into *dār al-Islam*.

The practical way of showing mercy to a *mustaʾmin* is by providing him with social security, housing, medical care and any other thing to guarantee a decent life, free from humiliation and disrespect.

However, the scholars who opposed helping the *mustaʾmin* did not mean needy and vulnerable refugees, but combatants who stay in the Islamic state for a short period of time, then go back to *dār al-ḥarb*. The reason for this prohibition is that the scholars feared this help may strengthen the enemy camp and encourage them to continue fighting the Muslims. This scenario is not relevant in the modern context and does not apply to present refugees.

Despite this understanding some scholars said it was permitted to provide help to the *ḥarbī* in *dār al-ḥarb*, providing that it will not harm Muslims. So, by default helping them in *dār al-Islam* is more appropriate.

In his interpretation of verse 9:6 al-Suyūṭī (1993, vol. 4, p. 133) narrates on the authority of al-Ḍaḥḥāk that the Muslims were not only ordered to protect disbelievers who wanted to listen to the word of God but were also ordered to take care of them financially as long as they were there. In practical terms this means an entitlement to social security benefits, housing, rations when the rationing system exists, public education and any other needs.

Another point here is that the Islamic state has certain peculiarities regarding its financial system owing to its nature and identity. *Zakāt* should be collected from Muslims and spent on Muslims, according to the above-mentioned *ḥadīth*. Other non-Muslim residents in the Islamic state could enjoy financial help from other sources, such as *ṣadaqa*. This issue is minor as long as the help is available for the needy. As Henkin of the United States commented during the discussion to draft Article 23 of the Convention: 'The principle of article (23) was clear: the refugees should be accorded the same treatment with respect to public relief and assistance as was accorded to nationals, and it did not matter how the treatment was accorded, provided the results were the same' (Hathaway, 2005, p. 812).

To sum up, it could be concluded that the Islamic tradition provides strong principles that obligate Muslims individually and collectively to help the needy. These principles are sufficient to rely on in granting the modern refugee the care and material assistance he needs. So there is enough evidence to conclude that the Islamic tradition is in keeping with Articles 20, 21, 22, 23 and 24 of the Geneva Convention.

It is significant that there is also a responsibility on the Islamic state to take care of the refugees financially. Despite the fact that the modern state is dramatically different to the traditional Islamic state with regard to financial resources, the responsibility remains the same and the Islamic state is still obliged by these principles to take care of the refugee financially.

Freedom of movement (Articles 26, 27, 28 and 29)

The issue of movement was dealt with by the Geneva Convention in Art. 26, which states 'Each Contracting State shall accord to refugees lawfully in its territory the right to choose their place of residence and to move freely within its territory subject to any regulations applicable to aliens generally in the same circumstances'.

Despite this, states still have the right to limit freedom of movement 'in two circumstances: during a mass influx, or while investigating the identity of and possible security threat posed by an individual seeking recognition of refugee status' (Hathaway, 2005, p. 705). Otherwise, 'once lawfully in the territory of a state party, refugees should be subject only to whatever restrictions govern the freedom of internal movement and residence of other non-citizens' (Hathaway, 2005, p. 705).

Freedom of movement and the Islamic tradition

Like many other issues relating to the *mustaʾmin*, the Muslim jurisprudents touched upon the issue of movement, not only within the Islamic state but also outside it, as well as the *mustaʾmin*'s residence in *dār al-Islam*. Interestingly, they dealt with the *mustaʾmin*'s right to move outside the state more than they did with his movement inside it, as if the *mustaʾmin* was permitted by default to move freely within the state.

Before elaborating on the issue of movement it is appropriate to mention the issue of residence first, as both issues are very much connected. The issue of nationality is also relevant and will be discussed below, but this debate will shed more light on the relationship between freedom of residence and movement.

To start with, the vast majority of scholars dealt with the *mustaʾmin*'s stay as a temporary period which in any case should not exceed a year. Nevertheless, referring to the Qurʾanic verse (9:6) which deals with the issue of refuge, and the interpretations of the scholars, we find that the verse itself associates the length of the stay with attaining the safety of the *mustaʾmin*. So, it is not a matter of months and years as much as a matter of safety, protection and shelter.

Al-Qummī affirms that: '[Regarding the time of stay], there is nothing in the verse that shows it. It could be left to the judgement of the *Imām*'.[99]

Ṭanṭāwī, who assumes that the *mustaʾmin* comes to learn about Islam, also stresses that the length of stay is left to the *Imām*, and that this period of time should be long enough for the *mustaʾmin* to understand the truths of Islam.[100]

It is clear, then, that the *mustaʾmin* – whether he comes to *dār al-Islam* to trade, learn about Islam or seek protection – has the right to stay there as long as it takes to meet his needs. The other important note is that length of the stay is left to the *Imām* to judge according to his assessment of the need.

However, in terms of his movement outside the state we find the majority of scholars agree that the *mustaʾmin* has the right to travel outside the Islamic state and come back to it without violating his *amān*. The primary condition for endorsing this action is that his travel to *dār al-ḥarb* should not be for the purpose of settling there permanently or for fighting the Muslims.

Ibn Qudāma (1984, vol. 9, p. 198) affirms that: 'If he enters [*dār al-ḥarb*] to settle, his personal *amān* will be nullified.' Ibn Mufliḥ (1979, vol. 3, p. 395) looks at a scenario where a *mustaʾmin* deposits or lends his money to a Muslim or to a *dhimmī* and then travels to *dār al-ḥarb*, to settle there. Ibn Mufliḥ differentiates between the personal *amān* and the *amān* of his money. While his personal *amān* is nullified, according to him, the *amān* of his money remains intact. Ibn Taymiyya (1983, vol. 2, p. 181), however, agrees with Ibn Mufliḥ on the personal *amān* and goes further to say even the *amān* of his money will be cancelled.[101]

Without doubt, if he goes back to *dār al-ḥarb* to fight the Muslims his personal *amān* will be void as Ibn Qudāma (n.d., vol. 4, p. 335) states.

Apart from these two cases the *mustaʾmin* has the right to travel outside *dār al-Islam* for different reasons providing that his intention is to return to *dār al-Islam*. Al-Buhūtī (1981, vol. 3, p. 108) asserts that if the *mustaʾmin* goes back to *dār al-ḥarb* for trading or to fulfil a need, as long as his intention is to go back [to *dār al-Islam*] his *amān* is still valid. Moreover, if he goes back to *dār al-ḥarb* as a messenger his *amān* will be intact, according to al-Suyūṭī (1961, vol. 2, p. 582).

Even more, Ibn Qudāma (1984, vol. 9, p. 198) says that if the *mustaʾmin* goes back to *dār al-ḥarb* on an excursion, his *amān* will still be valid because this is not considered to be in conflict with his intention to stay in *dār al-Islam*.

What is worth noting here is that the Muslim scholars gave the *mustaʾmin* this right of freedom of movement outside the Islamic state after he was lawfully considered a *mustaʾmin*. The Geneva Convention does nearly the same but does not allow the refugee to enter the original country from which he has fled because of fear or other difficult circumstances. The Islamic tradition did not make any exception in this regard and the reason for that could be the fact that the scholars, when debating this issue, thought of the *mustaʾmin* as a trader, not as a conventional refugee.

Regarding internal movement, in general the scholars did not elaborate much about it, except the issue of entering Mecca, as if it were a matter of fact, especially when they discussed the trader *mustaʾmin*, who by the nature of his *amān* needs to travel within the state. Some of them went even further, allowing him to enter Mecca, which is prohibited to disbelievers.

The issue of entering Mecca and settling there was the only issue concerning internal movement that was widely debated by the scholars. This might be because it was a relevant and practical issue at that time.

Although the majority of scholars prohibit the *mustaʾmin* from entering Mecca, we find scholars who object to that ruling. In his interpretation of Qurʾanic verse 9:28: 'O you who have attained to faith! Those who ascribe divinity to aught beside God are nothing but impure: and so they shall not approach the Inviolable House of Worship from this year onwards. And should you fear poverty, then [know that] in time God will enrich you out of His bounty, if He so wills: for, verily, God is all-knowing, wise!'

Al-Jaṣṣāṣ (1984, vol. 4, p. 280) goes through the evidence of his opponents and refutes it, and then he concludes that the *dhimmīs* are allowed to enter Mecca. Al-Sīwāsī (n.d., vol. 2, p. 350) also reports that it was narrated that Abu Ḥanīfa allowed them to enter Mecca.

On the other hand we find scholars who insist that entering Mecca was strictly prohibited, such as Ibn Taymiyya (1983, vol. 2, p. 186), who states: 'As for the *ḥaram* it is strictly prohibited for them to enter it.' The same opinion with slightly different wording is given by al-Nawawī (1997, vol. 7, p. 104) and al-Ramlī (1983, vol. 7, p. 316), who affirm that 'the *dhimmī* is not enabled to enter the *ḥaram*'.

Other scholars, however, put it straightforwardly that the *ḥarbī* is not permitted to enter *Ḥijāz*[102] for trading (al-Shirwānī, n.d., vol. 9, p. 282). Al-Ramlī (n.d., vol. 4, p. 214) also reports on a scholar called al-Balqīnī that he said the same and reports a saying of al-Shāfiᶜī in support of this opinion.

Nevertheless, al-Shirbīnī (n.d., vol. 4, p. 246) makes some exceptions to this verdict. He states that if the *ḥarbī* asks for permission from the *Imām* to enter Mecca, the latter has the right to do so should there be a benefit to the Muslims, like delivering a message, striking a contract of *dhimma* or *ᶜahd* or if this disbeliever brings greatly needed provisions. Otherwise he should not be allowed.

Even in these cases, al-Shirbīnī (n.d., vol. 4, p. 247) asserts that the *ḥarbī* should not stay more than three days there.

In the light of the above discussion, however, it could be safely concluded that the *mustaᵓmin* has the right to stay in the Islamic state until the need that drove him to flee has been removed.

After being lawfully recognized as a *mustaᵓmin* by the state he has the right to travel inside and outside the state, providing that he still wants to come back. In certain cases where the *mustaᵓmin* goes back to his homeland to live there permanently or to fight or to harm the Islamic state he loses his contract of *amān*.

With regard to the restrictions on his movement, the scholars gave the *mustaᵓmin* a great deal of liberty to move outside and inside the state except within Mecca, as the majority of scholars rule. Therefore, it could also be said that the Islamic tradition regarding the freedom of movement granted to refugees is in keeping with Article 26 of the Geneva Convention.

Finally, this freedom of movement granted by the Muslim scholars may have repercussions for the Islamic state trying to make this right a practicable reality. This may mean that the Islamic state should issue travel documents for refugees to enable them to travel, or else this freedom is hypothetical. In this vein it could be concluded that the Islamic tradition is in conformity with Articles 27 and 28 of the Convention that regulate the issue of travel documents for the refugee to facilitate his travel outside the host country.

Refugees unlawfully in the country of refuge (Article 31)

Dealing with the illegal entry of refugees to the country of refuge, Article 31 of the Convention states:

> The Contracting States shall not impose penalties, on account of their illegal entry or presence, on refugees who, coming directly from a territory where their life or freedom was threatened in the sense of article 1, enter or are present in their territory without authorization, provided they present themselves without delay to the authorities and show good cause for their illegal entry or presence.

Refugees, as Goodwin-Gill (1998, p. 152) rightly says, 'have no time for immigration formalities', especially when there is a threat or other unfortunate circumstances that drive them to flee their homes. In this perspective, the significance of this Article becomes more evident.

Article 31 and the Islamic tradition

Unlike other issues concerning the *mustaʾmin*, illegal entry to *dār al-Islam* did not occupy much space in the scholars' discussions. This could be due to the norm that the *ḥarbī* does not enter *dār al-Islam* without getting *amān*, as al-Shirbīnī (n.d., vol. 4, p. 243) states: 'The norm is that the *ḥarbī* does not enter our *dār* without *amān*.' This meant it was not a major issue then and the scholars did not feel the need to give it much attention.

The general rule the scholars adopted in this situation is that the people of *dār al-ḥarb* were not allowed to enter *dār al-Islam* without *amān*, according to Ibn Qudāma (1984, vol. 9, p. 281). The rationale behind this rule is the high probability that the *ḥarbī* could be a spy, as expressed by Ibn ʿĀbdīn (2000, vol. 4, p. 168), especially when we know that the relationship between *dār al-ḥarb* and *dār al-Islam* was one of enmity and war.[103]

However, the jurisprudents had various opinions about the *ḥarbī* who enters *dār al-Islam* without getting *amān* and claims that he is a *mustaʾmin*. While some scholars took the extreme view and invalidated his allegation from the outset, others were at ease with this claim and accepted it to protect his 'blood from spilling' as al-Ramlī (1983, vol. 8, p. 86) explains. A third group, who are the majority, were in the middle and recommended examining him to prove his truthfulness and sincerity.

Starting with the first group: Ibn Nujaym (n.d., vol. 5, p. 109), Shaykhī Zāda (1998, vol. 2, p. 452) and al-Shaybānī (1975, vol. 1, p. 178) affirm that: 'If he [the *ḥarbī*] enters our *dār* without *amān* then he and what he possesses are *fayʾ*.'[104] This meant that he would be enslaved and stripped of his possessions. Whether his possessions went to the Muslim who captured him or to the state treasury is another debate.[105]

Nonetheless, other scholars took a much more tolerant approach, tending to accept the slightest evidence which the *ḥarbī* may give, or even if he did not produce any evidence they were satisfied with his mere claim. Al-Nawawī (1984, vol. 10, p. 299) presumes that if the *ḥarbī* alleges that he entered *dār al-Islam* to listen to the word of God or to deliver a message he ought to be believed and he should not be exposed to any harm regardless of whether he has the letter or not. However, if this *ḥarbī* purports that a Muslim had given him *amān*, al-Shirbīnī (n.d., vol. 4, p. 243) gives a verdict that his *amān* is correct and he should not be harmed because it is probable that his claim is right. To save his blood from spilling, all that al-Ramlī (1983, vol. 8, p. 86) asks from the *ḥarbī*, in case of suspicion, is to swear to the truth of his claim; if he does, then he should be left to stay.

Concerning the third group of scholars, their position was to examine the claimant and judge accordingly. Ibn Qudāma (1984, vol. 9, p. 281) argues that if the *ḥarbī* purports to be a messenger he must show the message he is carrying. If he claims he is a trader he has to show his goods. If he claims that a Muslim gave him the *amān* that Muslim must be consulted to check whether this is true.

Taking the same approach, al-Ghazālī (1996, vol. 7, p. 58) affirms that if the *ḥarbī* claims that he entered *dār al-Islam* to listen to the word of God he has to be believed. In addition if he claims that he is a messenger his claim should be accepted. But if he claims that a Muslim gave him *amān* there are two options: either to trust him or to reject his allegation. Ibn ʿĀbdīn (2000, vol. 4, p. 168) elaborates further on this and states a condition to accept this claim. He states that if the *ḥarbī* alleges that a Muslim gave him *amān* that Muslim has to bring with him two witnesses to prove that he did indeed give the *ḥarbī* his *amān*.

Al-Sīwāsī (n.d., vol. 6, p. 23), however, concentrates on another issue during the test of the *ḥarbī* who claims to be a messenger. He demands verification of the letter which the *ḥarbī* carries to see if it was authentic. If it was, then he should be granted *amān*, otherwise he will be *fayʾ*.

So, the third group of scholars advocate a degree of tolerance towards the *ḥarbī*, but want to verify that he is truthful in his allegations.

In brief, it is significant that the milieu in which the Muslim scholars made their judgements is vastly different from the present day. Despite the state of war between *dār al-Islam* and *dār al-ḥarb*, and the dangerous probability of the *ḥarbī* being a spy against the Muslims, we still find that the majority of scholars granted the illegal *mustaʾmin* the right to stay in *dār al-Islam*. In the modern period, this could actually mean that if refugees fleeing life-threatening dangers seek safety in the Islamic state, they have to be granted the right to stay there.

The principle of examining the genuineness of the refugee's claim does not contradict the above Article. From the examples shown here it is clear that the examination is a lengthy process. This by default entails the right of the refugee to stay in the Islamic state until this process ends – whether it is to the benefit of the refugee, if he succeeds in producing the necessary evidence, or whether it leads to the rejection of his case.

The extreme opinions of some scholars concerning the fate of the *ḥarbī* who fails to defend his case must be put in the relevant context and viewed in light of the state of war between the *dār al-Islam* and *dār al-ḥarb*. Moreover the concepts and the international relations that governed the situation then should be borne in mind when discussing such opinions.

By all means, it can therefore be concluded that the Islamic tradition shares much common ground with Article 31 of the Geneva Convention.

Expulsion (Article 32)

The issue of expulsion is a sensitive one both for refugees and for host states. The Geneva Convention deals with it in Article 32:

> 1. The Contracting States shall not expel a refugee lawfully in their territory, save on grounds of national security or public order.

> 2. The expulsion of such a refugee shall be only in pursuance of a decision reached in accordance with due process of law. Except where compelling reasons of national security otherwise require, the refugee shall be allowed to submit evidence to clear himself, and to appeal to and be represented for the purpose before a competent authority or a person or persons specially designated by the competent authority.

Although the Article gives flexibility to the state to defend its interests and protect its public from the danger posed by a refugee, it still guarantees the refugee the basic right to a fair trial. As Goodwin-Gill concludes, 'Article 32 may yet have both advantages and disadvantages for the refugee.'

The issue of expulsion and the Islamic tradition

One of the most fundamental conditions the Muslim scholars stipulated for the correctness of the *amān* contract is that it should not harm Muslims' interests. Ibn Mufliḥ (1997, vol. 6, p. 228) and al-Mirdāwī (n.d., vol. 4, p. 203) state clearly: '[For the correctness] of the *amān* it must not bring harm to us.'

Brief but straight to the point, al-Dardīr states a rule that should govern the *amān* contract. He says (n.d., vol. 3, p. 124) '[Bringing] benefit is not the condition, but [what is compulsory] is not bringing harm'.

If harm was expected, the *Imām* had the right to terminate the *amān*. al-Zaylaʿī (1895, vol. 3, p. 247) states that the *Imām* is entitled to end the *amān* given by a Muslim if there was harm, in order to safeguard the interests of the Muslims. This opinion is also affirmed by al-Buhūtī (1981, vol. 3, p. 105), who says the *Imām* is not to cancel the *amān* given by a Muslim unless he fears treason on the part of of the one who has been given it.

Al-Qalqashandī (1981, vol. 13, p. 323) also asserts that: 'It is prohibited to terminate [the *amān*] unless harm is expected from the *mustaʾmin*, if this was expected then it is permitted to cancel his *amān*.

Based on this principle many scholars reached the conclusion that if the *mustaʾmin* posed a threat to Muslim interests or showed enmity towards Muslims, or fought against them, then his *amān* should be cancelled.

Al-Buhūtī (1981, vol. 3, p. 108) explains that the scale of the harm that allows the Muslims to terminate his *amān* is treason. Al-Shiīrāzī (n.d., vol. 2, p. 220), however, is satisfied with the fear of treason to terminate it. He states that 'The temporary[106] *amān* is invalidated when treason may be suspected'. Also, al-Qalqashandī gives the example of the *mustaʾmin* being a spy to cancel his *amān*. He says: 'As to its condition … that no harm should accrue to Muslims from the *mustaʾmin*, like his being a vanguard or a spy' (al-Qalqashandī, 1981, vol. 13, p. 322). This example is also used by al-Qurāfī (1994, vol. 3, p. 446) to show a case where the Muslims could invalidate the *amān* of the *mustaʾmin*.

Fighting with Muslims is obviously a valid reason for terminating the *amān*, as stated twice by Ibn Qudāma. He says: 'The condition of the *amān* is not to fight against the Muslims' (n.d., vol. 4, p. 151). Affirming the same point in another book he writes: 'One of the conditions for its correctness is to stop fighting the Muslims' (1984, vol. 9, p. 14). Therefore if the *mustaʾmin* was involved in fighting against the Muslims or is collaborating to do so, his *amān* will certainly be nullified.

Nonetheless, if the Muslims decided to terminate the *amān* of the *mustaʾmin* they have to send him to his place of safety.[107] Al-Nawawī (1984, vol. 10, p. 290) emphasizes this point by saying that: 'Without dispute, if the *amān* of the *musatʾmin* had been terminated he ought to be sent to his place of safety and his belongings should not be exposed to any harm.' Al-Qalqashandī (1981, vol. 13, p. 323) also asserts that if the *amān* is cancelled the *mustaʾmin* should be sent to a place where he will be safe.

From the above discussion it is clear that there are similarities between the Islamic tradition and Article 32 of the Geneva Convention. Both agree that the refugee can be expelled only on the grounds of being a threat to national security and the public interest.

Both also agree that even in these rare cases the refugee should not be sent to a place where he might be subject to persecution. Instead, he must be sent to a place where he feels safe.

Although there are no citations in the Islamic tradition about the fact that refugees should be granted access to a court hearing in the event that their *amān* is terminated, it still can be said that the general Islamic principles of justice and equity will serve the refugee in providing him with a fair hearing as this is a basic norm of fairness which the Islamic legal system should give to the refugee. Moreover, in the previous section it was proved that the *mustaʾmin* has the right to access courts in the

Islamic state to prove his legal status; thus that right can be applied here to defend his stay in the Islamic state.

However, determining what is a threat to national security and the public interest must be left to governmental authorities and courts of law, as these matters vary from one time to another.

Naturalization (Article 34)

The Geneva Convention addresses the issue of naturalization in Article 34, which states: 'The Contracting States shall as far as possible facilitate the assimilation and naturalization of refugees. They shall in particular make every effort to expedite naturalization proceedings and to reduce as far as possible the charges and costs of such proceedings.'

This provision, according to Hathaway (2005, p. 981), is 'without precedent in international refugee law'. It 'sets a duty only to "facilitate" assimilation and naturalization, not an obligation of result … however, despite the minimalist nature of the duties it sets, Art. 34 is breached where a state party simply does not allow refugees to secure its citizenship, and refuses to provide a cogent explanation for inaccessibility' (Hathaway, 2005, p. 987).

The issue of naturalization and the Islamic tradition

The concepts of 'nationality', 'citizenship', 'naturalization' and their relation and implementation in the traditional Islamic state is quite a major issue, and one that is still hotly debated by modern scholars.[108] This debate is not my specific focus, but it is necessary to discuss it briefly in order to contextualize the opinions of the early scholars.

In the book *Citizenship and Democracy in the Arab Countries* a group of historians, legal experts and Muslim scholars debate the issue of citizenship in the Islamic state and other related issues. One of the papers, presented by El-Afendī, deals with the concept of citizenship whether it is based on religion or race. After explaining the historical context of the issue and comparing it to modern times, he concludes that the term 'Muslim' was used in the Islamic tradition to indicate the equivalent of the modern term 'citizen' (Nāfi^{c} *et al.*, 2003, p. 56). The reason for this, according to the author, is that the religious and political identity which shaped early Islamic society was an essential requirement to guarantee the full rights of a given person in that society. However, the status of non-members [non-Muslims] depended on their contractual relationship with the original group [the Muslims] (Nāfi^c^ *et al.*, 2001, p. 57). In other word, due to the religious nature of the Islamic state citizenship was granted automatically to Muslims while non-Muslims living there had to prove their commitment to the Islamic state by paying *jizya*. In return their protection was guaranteed by the Muslim army.

As El-Afendī points out (Nāfi^c^ *et al.*, 2001, p. 61), this concept has changed through the course of time, and modern scholars including Fatḥī ^c^Uthmān, Fahmī Huwaydī, Ṭāriq al-Bishrī, Salīm al-^c^Awwā, Kamāl Abu al-Majd and others have developed new ideas about giving equal citizenship to all citizens of the Islamic state regardless of religion.

Going back to the early Muslim scholars, then, it goes without saying that the term 'naturalization' was not used, since this is a modern term that came into use after the advent of the national state. However, the core of the issue of naturalization was discussed by the Muslim scholars in the legal tradition. In their debates we find that they clearly differentiate in their rulings between foreigners who come to *dār al-Islam*, like the *musta^ɔ^min*, and the residents there such as Muslims and *dhimmīs*. As evident above, Muslim scholars accorded duties and allocated rights to the *musta^ɔ^min* which were different from the rights and duties of the *dhimmī* and the Muslim. The scholars also debated the circumstances under which the *musta^ɔ^min* could be treated like a *dhimmī*, i.e. a member of the society.

In principle the scholars did not allow the *musta^ɔ^min* to stay long in *dār al-Islam*, as stated bluntly by al-Kāsānī (1982, vol. 4, p. 37): '[The *Imām*] should not enable [the *musta^ɔ^min*] to stay long in *dār al-Islam*.' Shaykhī Zāda (1998, vol. 2, p. 45) and al-Ḥaṣkafī (1966, vol. 4, p. 168) clarify the length of stay by saying: 'The *musta^ɔ^min* should not be allowed to stay for a year in our *dār*.'

The reason for this limitation as explained by these scholars (Shaykhī Zāda, 1998, vol. 2, p. 45), (al-Ḥaṣkafī, 1966, vol. 4, p. 168) and al-Zayla^c^ī (1895, vol. 3, p. 268) is the suspicion that the *musta^ɔ^min* may harm the Muslims by spying on behalf of the disbelievers.

Nonetheless, other scholars argued the year limitation and left it to the *Imām* to decide upon it as he deemed fit to the interests of the Muslims. Al-Shaybānī (1985, vol. 1, p. 321) states that: 'The *Imām* should approach [the *musta^ɔ^min*] once he enters [*dār al-Islam*] and give him a certain period of time to stay, depending on his opinion.' Going even further, al-Shawkānī (1984, vol. 4, p. 567) refutes the whole idea of limiting the period to a year and says: 'There is no justification for restricting the period to a year. It is permissible for the *Imām* to give the period to [the *mustaʾmin*] which he thinks is right even though it might be long.' Al-Jaṣṣāṣ (1984, vol. 4, p. 273) does not agree with the idea of limiting the period to a year, but at the same time refuses to allow the *Imām* to let the *mustaʾmin* stay in *dār al-Islam* without an excuse or a valid reason which requires his stay. He affirms that: '[The *mustaʾmin*] should not be left to stay more than he requires for fulfilling his need'.

The circumstances that entitle the mustaʾmin *to become a* dhimmī

The *dhimmī*, as we saw in Chapter 3, is a citizen in the Islamic state. So, when the scholars spoke about the *mustaʾmin* becoming a *dhimmī* that meant in effect he became a citizen, to use the modern term.

The circumstances that enable the *mustaʾmin* to become a *dhimmī* in *dār al-Islam* vary. Some scholars make the length of stay a valid reason to be treated like a *dhimmī*. So, if he stays more than a year he becomes a *dhimmī*, provided that there is agreement between the *mustaʾmin* and the *Imām* on this, from the first day of his stay. Al-Rāzī (1996, vol. 1, p. 187) asserts that when the *mustaʾmin* enters *dār al-Islam* he should be told that if he stays a year he becomes *dhimmī*. However, if he deliberately stays a year then he automatically becomes a *dhimmī* [even if he was not told this at the beginning of his stay]. Affirming this opinion, Shaykhī Zāda (1998, vol. 2, p. 234) and al-Zaylaʿī (1895, vol. 3, p. 268) add that the period should be measured from the day of agreement between the *mustaʾmin* and the *Imām* and not from the day of entrance. Thus, the agreement and the date it comes into force are essential preconditions for becoming a *dhimmī*. Al-Ḥaṣkafī (1966, vol. 4, p. 168) asserts that if the *mustaʾmin* stays a year or two before the *Imām* tells him the condition he will not become a *dhimmī*. Emphasizing the same point, al-Shaybānī (1985, vol. 1, p. 321) says that if the *mustaʾmin* stays years without the *Imām* approaching him, then he will not be a *dhimmī*.

Relating to the period of time, some commentators state that verse 9:6 does not stipulate any kind of limitation on the length of time the *mustaʾmin* who comes to learn about Islam can stay. Al-Rāzi (2000, vol. 2, p. 182) states: 'There is no evidence in the verse that shows the limits of the period [*al-mustaʾmin* could stay], however, it may only be known by customary practice. Once there are remarks from him that he is a seeker for the truth and researcher for the decisive evidence he should be permitted to stay. And when it appears that he rejects the truth and wants to gain time by lies, then no account should be taken of him [and his *amān* be ended].'

Al-Qummī also reaffirms this: 'As regarding the time of reflection, there is nothing in the verse that shows it. It might be left to the discretion of the *Imām*.'[109]

Hence, it means that the process is not automatic – nor is it compulsory. It is a two-way process where the *Imām* has to make the offer, including the period of stay, to the *mustaʾmin*, and on the other hand the *mustaʾmin* has the full right to agree or not on becoming a *dhimmī*. If he declines, he still has to adhere to the agreed period of stay.

Other scholars, however, made paying *kharāj*[110] a valid reason for the *mustaʾmin* to become a *dhimmī*. Ibn Nujaym (n.d., vol. 5, p. 110) clearly states: 'He becomes a *dhimmī* by the adherence to pay *kharāj*.' Even if the *kharāj* of the land which the *mustaʾmin* had purchased becomes due in less than a year of its purchase the *mustaʾmin* becomes a *dhimmī*, according to al-Kāsānī (1982, vol. 7, p. 110). Al-Sīwāsī (n.d., vol. 6, p. 23), moreover, rules that his commitment to pay the *kharāj* of the purchase land will be enough to make him eligible to become a *dhimmī*. Thus purchasing a piece of land subject to *kharāj* and committing to pay it is a valid reason for becoming a *dhimmī*.

Nonetheless, some of the scholars went even further to say that the mere purchase of land subject to *kharāj* is a valid reason to become a *dhimmī*, according to al-Zaylaʿī (1895, vol. 3, p. 268). Others[111] still believe that the mere purchase is not enough until the *kharāj* is imposed on it (al-Zaylaʿī, 1895, vol. 3, p. 268).

Another possible reason for becoming a *dhimmī* is the marriage of a *mustaʾmina*[112] to a *dhimmī*. Al-Kāsānī (1982, vol. 7, p. 110) and al-Zaylaʿī (1895, vol. 7, p. 110) state that: 'If a *ḥarbiyya*[113] marries a *dhimmī* she becomes a *dhimmiyya*[114] due to her commitment to stay with him.' They justify this on the grounds that: 'A woman is attached to the man in his residence'. If she marries a Muslim, by default she will become a *dhimmiyya*, as Shaykhī Zāda states (1998, vol. 2, p. 453). However, if a *mustaʾmin* marries a *dhimmiyya* he will not become a *dhimmī* because this is not a commitment from his side to stay with her, as she is attached to him in his residence and not vice versa, according to al-Shaybānī (1985, vol. 1, p. 321) and al-Kāsānī (1982, vol. 7, p. 110).

This justification is quite interesting as it symbolizes the whole issue of naturalization. If we look carefully at all previous cases where the *mustaʾmin* is eligible to become a *dhimmī* we find that there is a common factor between them, namely loyalty and adherence to the Islamic state. In the first case we find that if the *mustaʾmin* stays in *dār al-Islam* according to the conditions set by the *Imām* then he is allowed to become a *dhimmī*, even if he stays there a month or so as stated by Shaykhī Zāda (1998, vol. 2, p. 453). So, the point is not the length of stay as much as showing willingness to adhere to Islamic principles and rules.

We can say the same regarding the second case, which is purchasing land subject to *kharāj*. The discussions evidently show that the scholars were looking for any sign from the *mustaʾmin* that reflected his willingness to adhere to Islamic regulations, such as purchasing land or commitment to pay *kharāj*.

Concerning the third case, the justification the scholars gave for excluding the *mustaʾmin* who marries a *dhimmiyya* from becoming a *dhimmī* is significant; it illustrates that the lack of his commitment to stay in *dār al-Islam* is behind that exclusion. Al-Kāsānī (1982, vol. 7, p. 110) states clearly that 'the husband is not a follower to the woman, so his marriage to her is not evidence of his satisfaction to stay in our *dār*, hence, he will not become a *dhimmī*'. This is confirmed by al-Sarakhsī (n.d., vol. 10, p. 84), who says: 'He [the *mustaʾmin*] by this marriage [to the *dhimmiyya*] did not [show his] satisfaction to stay in our *dār* perpetually.' Moreover, al-Mirghinānī (n.d., vol. 2, p. 154) gives the same explanation in different wording: 'The *mustaʾmin* can divorce her [the *dhimmiyya*] and go back to his country, thus he is not committed to stay [in *dār al-Islam*].'

In other words, the Muslim scholars were very keen to give the *mustaʾmin* the right to become a *dhimmī*, i.e. a citizen. They were satisfied with any sort of evidence that indicated the sincere desire of the *mustaʾmin* to assimilate to Islamic society and become a citizen, either by purchasing land, agreeing to stay for a period of time in the Islamic state or marrying a *dhimmī* or a Muslim.

This keenness and flexibility of the Islamic legal scholars to grant the *mustaʾmin* the right to stay permanently and become a *dhimmī* is in accord with the spirit of Article 34, which calls upon the contracting state to facilitate the assimilation and naturalization of refugees.

Recommendations

Based on the findings of this research it could be safely said that the Islamic tradition concerning the *mustaʾmin* provides very strong grounds to claim that the Muslims in their history welcomed non-Muslim aliens in their countries and provided them with the needed protection. By analogy this tradition could be interpreted into contemporary laws to apply to refugee status in modern times. However, when deducing such laws the difference between the Caliphate and modern national states should be noted and present in minds of the scholars and legal experts, since the rulings, the circumstances and the nature of the two are different. Because of this difference the issue of *dhimma* should be revisited by the scholars in order to give them full citizenship in terms of equal rights and duties as their Muslim fellows in the modern Islamic state.

Most importantly, the Islamic tradition and the Geneva Convention have very close similarities. The suggestion made by Bognetti and quoted in Wansbrough (1971, p. 34) that 'European medieval safe conduct must have owed a good deal to Islamic law' raises a very interesting point here. If it were to be proven that the European medieval safe conduct was the ancestor of the 1951 Geneva Convention then it might be claimed that the Islamic tradition exerted a strong influence over the present international law concerning refugees and that the 1951 Geneva Convention owes a great deal to the Islamic tradition. Obviously this requires further study, which I recommend, to examine the relationship between medieval safe conduct and international law concerning refugees, especially the 1951 Geneva Convention, to establish to what degree the Islamic tradition influenced both.

Armed with these findings my recommendation to Arab and Islamic governments is to endorse the 1951 Geneva Convention relating to the status of refugees and if necessary make reservations concerning certain Articles taking account of the internal circumstances of each state. I know that many Muslim states do have the judiciaries and suitable institutions to adopt this judgement; however, this should not be an excuse, since these states have to undergo a serious reform in many areas, and certainly signing the Convention and dealing with the issue of refugees in the right way is one of the main and important issues.

Thus, I disagree with those, such as Elmadmad, who call for the drafting of an Arab or Islamic Convention relating to refugees. I believe the Geneva Convention is fully in tune with the Islamic tradition and the Arab and Islamic states should sign it.

NOTES

Introduction

1 (http://www.unhcr.se/en/News/State_World_Refugees_2006_publ.html)/ [accessed July 2009]

2 (http://www.unhcr.org/cgi-bin/texis/vtx/search?page=search&docid=45ebd9544&query=the%20re-emergence%20of%20racism/ [accessed July 2009]

3 Ibid.

4 Ibid.

5 (http://www.unhcr.org/cgi-bin/texis/vtx/home?id=search)/ [accessed July 2009]

6 (http://www.unhcr.org/cgi-bin/texis/vtx/search?page=search&docid=45ebd9544&query=the%20re-emergence%20of%20racism/ [accessed July 2009]

7 According to Khalīf (1959, p. 11) and Ḍayf (1960, p. 38) this period encompasses mainly the last 150 years before the advent of Islam.

Chapter 1

1 Samākayn: name of stars, see al-Thaᶜālibī (1982, vol. 1, p. 65).

2 See also al-Qālī (1980, vol. 1, p. 41).

3 Al-Qālī (1980, vol. 1, p. 239).

4 Al-Maydānī (1987, vol. 1, p. 285) states that he was the subject of the parable: أحمى من مجير الجراد 'More protective than the protector of locusts'.

5 See also Smith, 1903, p. 50.

6 See an example of this in al-Qālī (1980, vol. 2, p. 57).

7 See al-Balādhurī, 1996, vol. 1, p. 49.

8 See al-Aṣfahānī, 1983, vol. 3, p. 57. The tent was a *ḥaram*, i.e. a sacred place where their women (*ḥarīm*) lived, which enjoyed the maximum security and safety. This custom is still respected in contemporary Arab tribes in many parts of the Arab world including Yemen, Egypt and Jordan.

9 See al-Aṣfahānī, 1983, vol. 10, p. 18.

10 See Mubarrad, 1956, p. 131.

11 See al-Sharīf, 1965, p. 44.
12 See al-Maydānī (1987, vol. 2, p. 444) and Ibn Ḥabīb (1942, p. 194).
13 'Walk like a bobwhite' [quail] يمشي مثل الحجل (al-Fayrūzabādī, n.d, vol. 1, p. 1356).
14 See also al-Wāqidı, 1966, p. 167.
15 See al-Nuwayrī (1988, p. 1700) and al-Andalusī (1987, vol. 6, p. 70).
16 *Ṣuraḥā*ʾ is the plural of *Ṣarīḥ* and it means the true-blooded member of the tribe. See Ibn Ḥazm (1948, p. 198) and al-Aṣfahānī (1983, vol. 3, pp. 57–9).
17 See al-Aṣfahānī, 1983, vol. 16, p. 172.
18 See also al-Aṣfahānī, 1983, vol. 9, p. 93.

Chapter 2

1 'One night I asked a youngster from Quraysh to look after my sheep so I could go to Mecca and party there like the other people. Once I got to the first house in Mecca I heard music, then I asked: what is that? They said: somebody is getting married, so I sat to watch them, then God made me sleep and I slept and nothing woke up except the heat of the sun next day. (He tried to do the same in another day [and] the same happened to him)' (al-Tabarī, 1986, vol. 1, p. 520).
2 The foot in *al-Maqām* is the footprint of the prophet Ibrāhīm, near the Kaᶜba.
3 *Ṣamīm* means *ṣarīḥ*, i.e. the true-blooded man of the tribe. The Arabs were very proud of being in this hierarchical class. Abu Hilāl al-ᶜAskarī (al-Nuwayrī, 1988, p. 568) praised a man after being classified *ṣarīḥ* saying:
قد زاد في عدد الكرام كريمُ   محضٌ صريحٌ في الكرام صميمُ
The number of nobles increased by a noble one
a clear, indigenous and true-blooded amongst the nobles.
4 In the narration of al-Ṭabarī (n.d., vol. 1, p. 555) it was Abu Jahl who asked this question (are you a *mujīr* or a follower?) and when al-Muṭᶜim replied Abu Jahl said: قد أجرنا من أجرت 'We grant *jiwār* to whom you grant'.
5 See Ibn Hishām (1990, vol. 2, p. 164), Ibn ᶜAbd al-Barr (1982, vol. 1, p. 48), Ibn Kathīr (n.d., vol. 3, p. 66).
6 The seventh month in the Hijrī Date.
7 Traditionally, once her husband died, his son from another woman or one of his close relatives could place his cloak around her and do anything he liked with the woman. He could marry her, make her marry someone else or even prevent her from marrying again. God forbade this in the Qurʾanic verse 4:19. See on this subject: al-Qurṭubī (1952, vol. 5, p. 94), al-Bukhārī (1987, vol. 4, p. 1670) and Ibn Kathīr (1980, vol. 1, p. 466).
8 There are various accounts of this event. Some of the accounts state that ᶜAlī Ibn Abī Ṭālib was the person who suggested the *hijra* should be the start point of dating, while other accounts cite that it was the Prophet himself who decided to calculate dates from his arrival in Medina, and used this date when he sent letters to the Christians of Najrān inviting them to convert to

Islam. For full details of these accounts see al-Ṭabarī, (n.d., vol. 2, pp. 3–6), al-Suyūṭī (1978, vol. 1, p. 19–23), Ibn al-Jawzī (1939, vol. 4, p. 228), Ibn Sa^c^d (n.d., vol. 3, p. 281) and Ibn Kathīr (n.d., vol. 3, p. 206).

9 From these nine, there were two men from Banī Awf who were known by the name of al-Qawāqil. They were called this because they used to give *jiwār* to whoever asked for it, and when they did so they would give the *mustajīr* an arrow and tell him قوقل i.e. 'walk proudly in Medina' (Ibn Kathīr, n.d., vol. 2, p. 280).

10 This was the last famous battle between al-Aws and al-Khazraj; al-Awas and its allies won a victory over al-Khazraj and its allies. See al-Shaybānī (1994, vol. 1, p. 538).

11 Ibn Sa^c^d called it *Bya^c^at al-^c^Aqaba al-Ākhira.*

12 He called upon al-Khazraj only, although al-Aws were present, because the Arabs used to call both al-Awas and al-Khazraj 'al-Khazraj', either because al-Khazraj were in the majority or because they were the more powerful tribe.

13 In the narration of Ibn Sa^c^d he added: 'By God we all protect him, irrespective of whether we follow him or not. Those who do not follow him protect him out of lineage and honour.'

14 A place where Quraysh used to meet to take crucial decisions, as Ibn Isḥāq says; see Ibn Hishām, 1990, vol. 3, p. 5.

15 These tribes eventually converted to Islam and were the last in Medina to convert. For details see Ibn Kathīr (n.d., vol. 5, p. 221) and Ibn Ḥibbān (1975, vol. 1, p. 136).

16 These shouts are for calling for help from the tribe when one is in danger; the tribesmen are obliged to answer this call in terms of the blood-feud. This sacred duty of helping one's fellow tribespeople was an important means of survival in the harsh environment. See Watt (1994, p. 261).

17 It is remarkable how closely the speech of Ibn Ubayy resembles the utterances of many contemporary extreme right-wing parties in the developed countries regarding immigrants. The logic and even the wording are similar. These parties speak about immigrants who come to their countries to take over their jobs and enjoy the benefits and the wealth of their countries. They call for moves to reduce their numbers, if not prevent them completely from entering their countries. Moreover, one can detect a kind of racist attitude within many of these extreme right-wing parties as they consider themselves superior to any other foreigners living with them in their countries, exactly as Ibn Ubayy thought. He believed that he was superior and honourable, and the migrating Muslims meaner and inferior.

18 See also Ibn Ḥajar (n.d., vol. 8, p. 650).

19 See al-Andalusī (1987, vol. 2, p. 45), Ibn Sa^c^d (n.d., vol. 2, p. 87) and al-Shayybānī (1991, vol. 5, p. 372).

20 When the Prophet entered Mecca triumphantly, some members of the Quraysh tried to save themselves in different ways. Al-Ḥārith Ibn Hishām

and Zuhayr Ibn Umayya (al-Ḥalabī, n.d., vol. 3, p. 41) sought *jiwār* of Um Hāni', who granted it. Her brother ᶜAlī Ibn Abī Ṭālib came across and saw the two men. Astonished as to how his sister could give *jiwār* to non-Muslims, he decided to kill them, but she confronted him and refused to hand the two men over to him. She then rushed to the Prophet and told him what had happened. The Prophet said: 'We give *jiwār* to whom you have given *jiwār* to, and we secure whom you have secured. He [Alī] should not kill them.' See also al-Ḥalabī (1979, vol. 3, p. 41), Ibn Kathīr (n.d., vol. 4, p. 281) and Ibn Saᶜd (n.d., vol. 2, p. 144).

Chapter 3

1 This is also evident from the following discussions of the scholars and their definitions of *dār al-ḥarb* and *dār al-Islam*. See the sources below.

2 Some scholars consider *dār al-ᶜahd* to be part of *dār al-Islam*, as we shall see later.

3 See for example, al-Ṭabarī (n.d., vol. 5, p. 207), Ibn al-Arabī (n.d., vol. 2, p. 441), al-Shawkānī (n.d., vol. 1, p. 218), Ibn Qudāma (1984, vol. 1, p. 208), Ibn Taymiyya (n.d., vol. 19, p. 217) and al-Shāfil (1973, vol. 4, p. 193).

4 See al-Ṭabarī (n.d., vol. 6, p. 213), al-Qurṭubī (n.d., vol. 13, p. 339), al-Shawkānī (n.d., vol. 3, p. 410), al-Buhūtī (n.d., 1981, vol. 3, p. 43), Ibn Ḥazm (n.d., vol. 7, p. 284), al-Mubārkfūrī (n.d., vol. 8, p. 304), al-Suyūṭī (1961, vol. 2, p. 511) and Ibn Qudāma (1984, vol. 1, p. 211).

5 Al-Shāfil (1979, vol. 2, p. 13), al-Ṭabarī (n.d., vol. 6, p. 217), Ibn Kathīr (n.d., 1980, vol. 1, p. 442), Ibn al-Jawzī (1983, vol. 6, p. 281), al-Mirdāwī (n.d., vol. 6, p. 358), Ibn Mufliḥ (1979, vol. 6, p. 156), al-Shāfil (1973, vol. 4, p. 160), al-Nawawī (1997, vol. 2, p. 82), al-Shīrāzī (n.d., vol. 1, p. 25), al-Shaybānī (1975, vol. 1, p. 237), Ibn ᶜĀbdīn (2000, vol. 8, p. 387), al-Sīwāsī (n.d., vol. 6, p. 109), al-Sadı (1984, vol. 1, p. 309), al-ᶜAbdarī (1977, vol. 3, p. 375), Ibn ᶜAbd al-Barr (2000, vol. 8, p. 224), al-Qurṭubī (n.d., vol. 1, p. 291), al-Dāraquṭnı (1966, vol. 4, p. 112), Ibn Ḥibbān (1993, vol. 1, p. 343), Ibn Ḥajar (n.d., vol. 1, p. 52), Abu al-Faraj (1979, vol. 4, p. 419) and al-Ṭaḥḥāwī (1978, vol. 3, p. 245).

6 Al-Jaṣṣāṣ (1984, vol. 3, p. 228), al-Ṭabarī (n.d., vol. 5, p. 223), al-Shawkānī (n.d., vol. 1, p. 506), al-Shāfil (1973, vol. 7, p. 333), al-Sadı (1984, vol. 2, p. 726), al-ᶜAbdarī (1977, vol. 4, p. 160), al-Dusūqī (n.d., vol. 2, p. 482), al-Maghribī (1977, vol. 3, p. 382), al-Nasā'ī (1991, vol. 2, p. 297), Ibn Ḥazm (n.d., vol. 9, p. 302), al-Ḥākim (1990, vol. 3, p. 15), Ibn Ḥibbān (1993, vol. 15, p. 471), Ibn Abī Shayba (1988, vol. 6, p. 505) Abd al-Razzāq (1982, vol. 5, p. 196) al-Zuraī (n.d., vol. 1, p. 270) and al-Fayrūzabādī (n.d., vol. 1, p. 1276).

7 *Aṣḥāb* means members of the same school (Bosworth *et al.*, 1995, vol. 8, p. 830).

8 The first *amān* is the *amān* the Muslims give to all the residents in the Islamic state, including the *dhimmīs* who live there.

9 See al-Shirwānī (n.d., vol. 6, p. 204) and al-Shirbinī (n.d., vol. 2, p. 362).

10 See Ibn Mufliḥ (1979, vol. 3, p. 379).

11 Al-Buhūtī reaffirmed this in another book (1981, vol. 3, p. 96).
12 See al-Suyūṭī (1961, vol. 2, p. 566).
13 See Chapter 2, under heading 'The migration to Medina', for more details.
14 See examples of this in Ibn Kathīr (n.d., vol. 7, p. 247), al-Shaybānī (1994, vol. 3, p. 365), Ibn Khaldūn (1984, vol. 4, p. 675) and al-Ṭabarī (n.d., vol. 3, p. 375).
15 On the authority of Abu Hurayra that the Prophet said: 'Every child is born with innate character [faith of Islam] but his parents convert him to Judaism, Christianity or Magianism, as the animal delivers a perfect animal, do you find it mutilated?' Then Abu Hurayra said: Read if you like (Allah's nature with which He has created human beings. No change let be in the creation of Allah) (Q. 30:30).
16 The verses are (2:218), (3:195), (4:34/89/97/100), (8:72/74/75), (9:20/100/117), (16:41/110), (19:46), (22:58), (23:67), (24:22), (25:30), (29:26), (33:6/50), (59:8/9), (60:10), (73:10), (74:5).
17 The verses that could fall in this category are: (2:218), (3:195), (9:20/100/117), (16:41/110), (22:58), (24:22), (33: 50), (59:8).
18 Casewit in his paper titled '*Hijra* as history and metaphor: a survey of Qur'anic and *ḥadīth* sources' cites more examples to support this meaning and convincingly draws comparison between the *hijra* of the Prophet and the *hijra* of other prophets such as Noah and Abraham.
19 See the story of Ādam in *sūrat al-Baqara* (2:30–39).
20 See the *ḥadīth* narrated by al-Bukhārī (1987, vol. 5, p. 2358) on the authority of Ibn ᶜUmar that the Prophet put his hand on his shoulder and said: 'Be in this life as a foreigner or a passer-by'.
21 See also Siddiqī, 1969, Chaudhry, 1995, ᶜAmāra, 2003 and Doi, 1981.
22 Regarding the amount of *jizya*, the scholars differed as no fixed amount is mentioned in the verse which obligated *jizya* (9:29). Some of them said it was one *dinār* annually on each adult, others said it is 48 *dirhams*, while others said the amount should be agreed between the *Imām* and the *dhimmīs* (al-Jaṣṣāṣ, 1984, vol. 4, p. 290). However, women, children, monastics, the elderly and the poor *dhimmīs* were not subject to *jizya* (al-Buhūtī, 1981, vol. 3, p. 120) and (Ibn Mufliḥ, 1979, vol. 3, p. 407).
23 This *ḥadīth* was narrated in different formats by many scholars like al-Nasāʾı (1990, vol. 2, p. 279), Abu Dāwūd (n.d., vol. 3, p. 44), Ibn Ḥanbal (n.d., vol. 3, p. 224) and Ibn Jārūd (1987, vol. 1, p. 260).
24 Regarding the detailed rulings of the *dhimmīs* in *dār al-Islam*, the Muslim scholars debated these rulings in depth and naturally they differed in many of these details. Such debates are scattered throughout the books of jurisprudence, like the one mentioned above.
25 For details of these conditions see Hoyland (2004, pp. 104–6), al-Zarkashī (2002, vol. 3, p. 229), Ibn Sālim (n.d., vol. 1, p. 100) and Ibn Yūsuf (1969, vol. 1, p. 104).
26 Al-Shirbinī (1994, vol. 2, p. 572) says the same thing.

27 See for example; al-Shaybānī (189 AH) (n.d., vol. 9, p. 56), al-Shāfil (204 AH) (1979, vol. 2, p. 64), al-Bukhārī (256 AH) (1987, vol. 6, p. 2733), al-Ṭabarī (310 AH) (1984, vol. 10, p. 80), al-Jaṣṣāṣ (370 AH)) (1984, vol. 4, p. 273), al-Bayhaqī (458 AH) (1993, vol. 8, p. 31), al-Qurṭubī (1986, vol. 1, p. 209), Ibn Mufliḥ (1979, vol. 3, p. 389), al-Anṣārī (1997, vol. 2, p. 306), al-Shirbinī (n.d., vol. 4, p. 236), al-Buhūtī (1982, vol. 3, p. 104), al-Suyūṭī (1961, vol. 2, p. 577) al-Shawkānī (1973, vol. 7, p. 155).

28 All the books I could find in libraries and online.

29 *Ibāḍiyya* is one of the main branches of the kharijites. The sect takes its name from that of one of those said to have founded it, Abd Allāh Ibn Ibāḍ al-Tamīmī. This sect is spread nowadays in Oman, East Africa and southern Algeria (Lewis, 1971, vol. 3, p. 648).

30 *Zaydiyya* is a branch of Shiᶜa, arising out of the abortive revolt of Zayd Ibn Ali al-Ḥusayn in Kūfa, in 122 AH. During the preparations for the revolt, some of the Kūfan Shīᶜa withdrew their support from Zayd in protest against his refusal to condemn unconditionally the early caliphs preceding Ali, and backed Zayd's nephew Jafar al-Ṣādiq. The *Zaydiyya*, as moderates, did not classify the Sunnī Muslims generally as infidels. In political terms, however, they were in contrast to the radical but quietest Imāmiyya, militant, espousing revolt against the illegitimate Sunnī rulers as a religious duty (Bearman *et al.*, 2002, vol. 6, p. 478).

31 See also al-Zamakhsharī (n.d., vol. 2, p. 230), al-Ṭabarī (1984, vol. 10, p. 70), al-Rāzī (2000, vol. 15, p. 176) and al-Qurṭubī (n.d., vol. 8, p. 70).

32 Some scholars shed doubts on the authenticity of this book and its reference to Ibn ᶜAbbās. See for example Abu Shuhba (1971, p. 69) and al-Dhahabī (2000, vol. 1, p. 56).

33 Another name for *Surāt al-Tawba.*

34 (http://www.altafsir.com/Tafasir.asp?tMadhNo=0&tTafsirNo=12&tSoraNo=9&tAyahNo=6&tDisplay=yes&UserProfile=0)/ [accessed July 2009]

35 (http://www.altafsir.com/Tafasir.asp?tMadhNo=3&tTafsirNo=31&tSoraNo=9&tAyahNo=6&tDisplay=yes&UserProfile=0)/ [accessed July 2009]

36 These months were the period that God gave to disbelievers before declaring the state of war against them in the verses prior to this verse (9:1–5).

37 (http://www.altafsir.com/Tafasir.asp?tMadhNo=0&tTafsirNo=14&tSoraNo=9&tAyahNo=6&tDisplay=yes&UserProfile=0)/ [accessed July 2009]

38 The issue of 'freedom of movement' for the *mustaᵓmin* will be discussed in Chapter 4 when comparing the Geneva Convention 1951 to the Islamic tradition.

39 (http://www.altafsir.com/Tafasir.asp?tMadhNo=4&tTafsirNo=3&tSoraNo=9&tAyahNo=6&tDisplay=yes&UserProfile=0)/ [accessed July 2009]

40 (http://www.altafsir.com/Tafasir.asp?tMadhNo=4&tTafsirNo=38&tSoraNo=9&tAyahNo=6&tDisplay=yes&UserProfile=0)/ [accessed July 2009]

41 (http://www.altafsir.com/Tafasir.asp?tMadhNo=0&tTafsirNo=36&tSoraNo=9&tAyahNo=6&tDisplay=yes&UserProfile=0)/ [accessed July 2009]

42 (http://www.altafsir.com/Tafasir.asp?tMadhNo=0&tTafsirNo=37&tSoraNo=9&tAyahNo=6&tDisplay=yes&UserProfile=0)/ [accessed July 2009]
43 (http://www.altafsir.com/Tafasir.asp?tMadhNo=0&tTafsirNo=50&tSoraNo=9&tAyahNo=6&tDisplay=yes&UserProfile=0)/ [accessed July 2009]
44 (http://www.altafsir.com/Tafasir.asp?tMadhNo=0&tTafsirNo=42&tSoraNo=9&tAyahNo=6&tDisplay=yes&UserProfile=0)/ [accessed July 2009]
45 (http://www.altafsir.com/Tafasir.asp?tMadhNo=0&tTafsirNo=56&tSoraNo=9&tAyahNo=6&tDisplay=yes&UserProfile=0)/ [accessed July 2009]
46 Abrogation literally means ablation or cancellation. In the Qurʾān to abrogate a verse means to remove it, replace it by another verse or to replace the verse verdict by another verdict.
47 Al-Hawwārī (3 AH), Al-Baghawī (510 AH), al-Zamakhsharī (538 AH), Al-Qurṭubī (642 AH), Ibn al-Bāzarī (738 AH), al-Khāzin (741 AH), Abu Ḥayyān (745 AH), al-Aqam (Zaydī, 9 AH), Al-Qummī, Ibn Adil (880 AH), al-Biqāı (885), Al-Thaālibī (928 AH), al-Shawkānī (1250 AH), al-Alūsī (1270 AH), Iṭfayyish (1332 AH), al-Ṭabāṭbāʾī (14 AH) and Quṭb (14 AH).
48 (http://www.altafsir.com/Tafasir.asp?tMadhNo=0&tTafsirNo=56&tSoraNo=9&tAyahNo=6&tDisplay=yes&UserProfile=0)/ [accessed July 2009]
49 See al-Bāqillānī (n.d., p. 17) and al-Kirmānī (1976, vol. 1, p. 1).

Chapter 4

1 See section entitled 'The definition of the term *mustaʾmin*', Chapter 3.
2 See also Ibn Khuldūn, 1984, vol. 3, p. 356 and al-Ṭabarī, n.d. vol. 5, p. 358
3 See also al-Nāṣirī, 1997, vol. 3, p. 93.
4 Some narrations name him as Maqīs Ibn Ṣubabah. See al-Nasāʾı, 1994, vol. 7, p. 106, al-Ṭaḥḥāwī, 1978, vol. 3, p. 330, Ibn Abī Shayba, 1988, vol. 7, p. 404, al-Hindī, 1998, vol. 10, p. 233.
5 In the narration of Ibn Ḥajar (n.d., vol. 4, p. 61) he states that there were ten people the Prophet did not give *amān* to: six men and four women. However, the majority of the accounts cite that they were four men and two women.
6 In the narration of Ibn Ḥajar (1992, vol. 2, p. 604), the Prophet sent the men to teach the tribes of ᶜAḍal and Qārah the principles of Islam.
7 This account was also narrated by Abu Yaᶜla (1984, vol. 2, p. 101), al-Maqdisī (1989, vol. 3, p. 249) and al-Haythamī (1986, vol. 6, p. 169).
8 In the account narrated by al-Suyūṭī (1993, vol. 1, p. 571), his wife came to the Prophet and asked him to give ᶜIkrima *amān*, then he came to the Prophet and converted to Islam.
9 See Ibn Saᶜd (n.d., vol. 4, p. 299), Ibn Abī Shayba (1988, vol. 7, p. 404), al-Bazzār (1984, vol. 3, p. 350) and al-Nasāʾı (1991, vol. 2, p. 302).
10 See for example, al-Nasāʾı (1991, vol. 2, p. 302, al-Ṭaḥḥāwī (1978, vol. 3, p. 330), al-Hindī (1998, vol. 10, p. 233), al-Bazzār (1988, vol. 3, p. 350), and Ibn ᶜAbd al-Barr (1991, vol. 4, p. 1539).
11 In the narration of Ibn Abī Shayba (1988, vol. 7, p. 399), his cousin Numayla

killed him between al-Ṣafā and al-Marwā near the Kaᶜba.

12 The name of the place.

13 They are: al-Tabrīzī (1985, vol. 2, p. 1163), al-Sajistānī (n.d., vol. 3, p. 65), al-Bayhaqī (n.d., vol. 7, p. 159), al-Maqdisī (1989, vol. 2, p. 69), al-Zaylaᶜī (1938, vol. 3, p. 280), Ibn Ḥajar (n.d., vol. 2, p. 85), al-Qārī (2001, vol. 7, p. 485), al-Naysābūrī (1990, vol. 2, p. 136), Ibn Ḥusām al-Dīn (1998, vol. 10, p. 214) and al-Shawkānī (1973, vol. 8, p. 175).

14 Al-Qārī (2001, vol. 7, p. 485) says this is an expression of the fanaticism or the refusal of the Quraysh to face the truth.

15 Ibn Jārūd (1987, vol. 1, p. 275), al-Ṭabarānī (1994, vol. 4, p. 316) and al-Fākihī (1993, vol. 5, p. 72).

16 For the full details of this account see Ibn Hishām (1990, vol. 4, pp. 290–93), al-Ṭabarī, (n.d., vol. 2, p. 125), Ibn Kathīr (n.d., vol. 4, p. 176) and al-Ḥalabī (1979., vol. 2, p. 719).

17 The majority of the scholars say the woman was Um Kulthūm; however, others say she was Subayᶜa Bint al-Ḥārith. See al-Rāzī (2000, vol. 29, p. 265) and Abu al-Suᶜūd (n.d., vol. 8, p. 239).

18 Some scholars, such as al-Bayhaqī (1989, vol. 9, p. 229), argue that women were not included in the *ṣulḥ* in the first place. He reports the account as follows: 'So Suhayl said: on the condition that any man from us comes to you, although he is following your religion, you have to return him to us'. Then al-Bayhaqī commented that this is evidence that women were not included in this condition.

19 (http://www.altafsir.com/Tafasir.asp?tMadhNo=7&tTafsirNo=57&tSoraNo=9&tAyahNo=6&tDisplay=yes&UserProfile=0)/) [accessed July 2009]

20 Also narrated by Ibn Qāniᶜ (1997, vol. 2, p. 202), al-Aṣbahānī (1984, vol. 9, p. 24), al-Qaḍāᶜī (1986, vol. 1, p. 130), al-Hindī (1998, vol. 4, p. 156) and al-Manāwī (1937, vol. 6, p. 19).

21 He means if the *mustaᵓmin* was killed by another *mustaᵓmin*.

22 See al-Shirbinī (1994, vol. 2, p. 410), al-Nawawī (1984, vol. 5, p. 279) and al-Ramlī (1983, vol. 6, p. 239).

23 Like Ibn Shibrima, al-Thawrī, al-Awzāᶜī and al-Shāfiᶜī.

24 See also Ibn Jārūd (1987, vol. 1, p. 200), al-Nasāᵓī (1991, vol. 4, p. 220), al-Bayhaqī (1991, vol. 8, p. 29), al-Dāraquṭnī (1966, vol. 3, p. 98) and al-Tirmidhī (n.d., vol. 4, p. 25).

25 *Muᶜāhid* is the person who has a covenant with the Muslims. It applies for both the *dhimmī* and *mustaᵓmin*.

26 See also what the scholars said about the interpretation of verse 9:6 in Chapter 3.

27 See Hathaway 2005, pp. 98–107.

28 *Ḥadd* is the technical term for the punishments of certain acts which have been forbidden or sanctioned by punishments in the Qurᵓān and have thereby become crimes against religion (Lewis *et al.*, 1971, p. 20).

29 The female of *mustaʾmin*.
30 *Qadhf*: false accusation of unlawful intercourse (Lewis *et al.* 1971, p. 20).
31 See also Nizam *et al.*, 1990, vol. 2, p. 149.
32 *Ta^{c}zīr*: an Islamic legal term meaning discretionary punishment, e.g. by the *qāḍī* [the judge] for the offences for which no *ḥadd* punishment is laid down (Bearman *et al.*, 2000, p. 406).
33 ^{c}*Ushr* is a tax on the land owned by Muslims, or a tax on the commercial goods to be paid by Muslim, *dhimmī*, or *ḥarbī* merchants from non-Muslim countries (*dār al-ḥarb*) (Bearman *et al.*, 2000, p. 917).
34 He means when the Muslims go to *dār al-ḥarb*.
35 See also al-Tirmidhī n.d., vol. 5, p. 734.
36 See also Ibn Ḥibbān (1993, vol. 2, p. 119), Ibn Rāhawayh (1991, vol. 1, p. 369) and Ibn Ḥanbal (n.d., vol. 2, p. 284).
37 See also al-Haythamī (n.d., vol. 1, p. 37) and Ibn al-Mubārak (1986, vol. 1, p. 16).
38 See also al-Naḥḥās (n.d., vol. 4, p. 215), Ibn ^{c}Abd al-Wāḥıd (1989, vol. 9, p. 43) and Ibn Abī Shayba (1988, vol. 7, p. 89).
39 See Chapter 1.
40 See also Ibn Ḥusām al-Dīn 1998, vol. 16, p. 13.
41 See also al-Zayla^{c}ī (1993, vol. 3, p. 349) and al-Suyūṭī (1993, vol. 7, p. 579).
42 The *ju^{c}lān* is plural of *ju^{c}l* which is a small animal with a bad smell (Ibn Manẓūr, 1956, vol. 11, p. 112).
43 See also al-Ṣan^{c}ānī (1982, vol. 9, p. 447) and Abu ^{c}Uwāna (n.d., vol. 4, p. 73).
44 See the section entitled 'The migration to Medina' in Chapter 2.
45 See also the section entitled 'Naturalization', Chapter 4.
46 See Ibn ^{c}Ābdīn (2000, vol. 4, p. 169), al-Shirbinī (1994, vol. 2, p. 410), al-Nawawī (1984, vol. 5, p. 279) and al-Ramlī (1983, vol. 6, p. 239).
47 See also al-Ṭabarī (1984, vol. 3, p. 14) and al-Nasafī (n.d., vol. 1, p. 125).
48 See also al-Rāzī, 1979, vol. 4, p. 77.
49 See also Ibn Abī Shayba, 1988, vol. 3, p. 108.
50 See for example Ibn Nujaym (n.d., vol. 5, p. 81), al-Mirghinānī (n.d., vol. 1, p. 214) and al-Kāsānī (1982, vol. 2, p. 311).
51 See section entitled 'Personal status', Chapter 4, below.
52 See also al-Kāsānī (1982, vol. 7, p. 147) and Ibn Nujaym (n.d., vol. 8, p. 519).
53 Also narrated by Ibn Sa^{c}īd al-Umawī (n.d., vol. 1, p. 72) and Ibn Hibatullah (1995, vol. 2, p. 50).
54 See Hathaway, 2005, pp. 210–23.
55 The female of *ḥarbī*.
56 The famous students of Abu Ḥanīfa (al-Sīwāsī, n.d., vol. 3, p. 386).
57 See also al-Zayla^{c}ī (1895, vol. 2, p. 159) and Ibn Nujaym (n.d., vol. 8, p. 519).
58 In the Islamic state land was divided into categories, such as *al-arāḍī al-^{c}Ushriyya* and *arādı al-kharāj*, and each one had subcategories. See al-Smarqandī (1984, vol. 1, p. 320) and Ibn ^{c}Ābdīn (2000, vol. 2, p. 334).

59 *Kharaj* is the tax imposed on the person and the output of the land. See al-Sīwāsī, n.d., vol. 6, p. 31.
60 A kind of contract between landlord and tenant. See al-Sarakhsī, n.d., vol. 23, p. 34.
61 See also al-Kāsānī, 1982, vol. 7, 110.
62 This point is discussed in more detail later in this chapter.
63 See also Shaykhī Zāda *et al.* (1990, vol. 2, p. 235).
64 See also Ibn Mufliḥ (1997, vol. 6, p. 229).
65 See also Ibn Taymiyya (1983, vol. 2, p. 181), al-Buhūtī (1996, vol. 1, p. 654), al-Sīwāsī (n.d., vol. 6, p. 23), Ibn ᶜĀbdīn (2000, vol. 6, p. 768), Shaykhī Zāda (1990, vol. 2, p. 235) and al-Shaybānī (1975, vol. 1, p. 174).
66 Such as Ibn Qudāma (1984, vol. 9, p. 198), Ibn Taymiyya (1983, vol. 2, p. 181) and al-Buhūtī (1996, vol. 1, p. 654).
67 Ibn ᶜĀbdīn (2000, vol. 4, p. 113)
68 See also Ibn Qudāma (n.d., vol. 4, p. 336), al-Shīrāzī (n.d., vol. 2, p. 264) and Ibn al-Sayyid (n.d., vol. 4, p. 204).
69 See previous section entitled 'The safety of the *mustaᵓmin*'.
70 See also al-Ḥākim al-Naysābūrī (1990, vol. 2, p. 53) and al-Qūdāᶜī (1986, vol. 1, p. 432).
71 Groups that have different views regarding the mainstream ideology of the Sunni Muslims, such as al-Khawārij, etc.
72 See section entitled 'The interpretation of verse 9:6 and its relation to *amān*', in Chapter 3.
73 *Iᶜtikāf* is a particularly commended pious practice consisting of a period of retreat in a mosque, the vow for which stipulates a certain number of days in accordance with the believer's own wish. He must not leave it, save for the performance of his natural functions and his ablutions. During the retreat he will practise fasting, ritual prayer and recitation of the Qurᵓān (Lewis *et al.*, 1978, vol. 4, p. 280). The reward for this is great in Islam, as the Prophet says: 'Who make one day of *iᶜtikāf* God will distance him from the hellfire by three trenches [each one of them] is further than the two ends of the world' (al-Suyūṭī, 1993, vol. 1, p. 486).
74 Also narrated by Ibn Ḥibbān (1993, vol. 11, p. 571) and al-Bayhaqī (1989, vol. 6, p. 94).
75 Narrated also by Ibn Ḥanbal (n.d., vol. 3, p. 22) and Ibn Jaᶜd (1990, vol. 1, p. 295).
76 This debate shows the meticulous attention that Muslim scholars paid to the honouring of diplomatic customs between nations.
77 See section entitled 'Movable and immovable property', above.
78 The clearest manifestation of this could be seen in the Mamlūk period. See Wansbrough, 1971, pp. 20–35.
79 See for example al-Mirdāwī (n.d., vol. 4, p. 243), al-Buhūtī (1970, vol. 2, p. 19), Ibn Qudāma (n.d., vol. 1, p. 157), Ibn Mufliḥ (1997, vol. 6, p. 253),

al-Buhūtī (1981, vol. 3, p. 100) and al-Khiraqī (1982, vol. 1, p. 133).

80 A *muḍāraba* contract is a contract between two people whereby one provides the funds and the other provides the labour and the revenue earned from the project will be shared on an agreed percentage. See al-Mirdāwī (n.d., vol. 5, p. 427) and Ibn Nujaym (n.d., vol. 7, p. 263).

81 *Al-muzāraᶜa* is an agricultural contract between the owner of the land and the worker to share the harvest according to a certain percentage. See al-Kāsānī, 1982, vol. 6, p. 175.

82 *Al-musāqā* is a contract between the owner of the field and another person in terms of which the latter carries out all the work necessary to farm the field, including irrigation, and the harvest is shared according to an agreed percentage. See al-Ḥusaynī (1994, vol. 1, p. 291) and Ḥaydar (n.d., vol. 3, p. 504).

83 See also Ibn Mufliḥ (1997, vol. 6, p. 229) and al-Buhūtī (1996, vol. 1, p. 654).

84 Also narrated by al-Bayhaqī (1989, vol. 4, p. 334), al-JīrāḥI (1984, vol. 1, p. 513) and al-Numayrī (1996, vol. 1, p. 67).

85 In the narration reported by Muslim (n.d., vol. 4, p. 1761) it was a prostitute of Banī Israel who gave water to the dog, and God forgave all her sins for that good deed.

86 This incident was also narrated by Muslim, n.d., vol. 4, p. 1760.

87 *Ṣadaqa* means voluntary alms (Bosworth *et al.*, 1995, vol. 8, p. 708).

88 On the authority of Muᶜādh, he said when the Prophet sent him to Yemen, he ordered him to take money from the rich Muslims and give it to the poor people there خُذْهَا من أغْنِيَائِهِمْ وَرَدَّهَا في فُقَرَائِهِمْ (al-Shaybānī, 1985, vol. 1, p. 123); see also al-Ṭaḥḥāwī, 1987, vol. 4, p. 372, Ibn Ḥajar, 1964, vol. 3, p. 112 and al-Zaylaᶜı, 1938, vol. 2, p. 398. From this *ḥadīth* the scholars concluded that *zakāt* should only be taken from Muslims and returned to poor Muslims only; i.e., all non-Muslims are not allowed to take from the money of *zakāt*.

89 *Zakāt* is the obligatory payment by Muslims of a determinate portion of specified category of their lawful property for the benefit of the poor and other enumerated classes (Bosworth *et al.*, 2002, vol. 6, pp. 406–7).

90 *Al-fayʾ* is the possessions of the disbelievers which are obtained by Muslims other than through war (Ibn Qudāma, 1984, vol. 6, p. 312).

91 One-fifth of the war spoils (Ibid).

92 The tax that is paid by the non-Muslim traders who enter *dār al-Islam* (Ibid).

93 *Al-jizya* is the poll-tax that, in traditional Muslim law, was levied on non-Muslims in the Muslim state (Lewis *et al.*, 1965, p. 559).

94 *Al-ṣadaqāt* refers to the monies that Muslims give to charity seeking the reward of God. They are two kinds; the first is obligatory and is called *zakāt* and the other one, which is voluntary, is known as *ṣadaqa*.

95 *Kharaj* is the tax imposed on the person and the output of the land (al-Sīwāsī, n.d., vol. 6, p. 31).

96 This *ḥadīth* was also narrated by al-Shaybānī (1985, vol. 1, p. 123), al-Ṭaḥḥāwī

(1978, vol. 4, p. 372), Ibn Ḥajar (1964, vol. 3, p. 112), Ibn Ḥajar (n.d., vol. 1, p. 266) and al-Zayla^{c}ı (1938, vol. 2, p. 398).

97 *Qiyās* is reasoning by analogy; it is the fourth source of Muslim law (Bosworth *et al.* 1986, vol. 5, p. 238).

98 Abu al-Su^{c}ūd (n.d., vol. 8, p. 238), al-Suyūṭī (1993, vol. 8, p. 130) and al-Zamakhsharī (n.d., vol. 4, p. 515) support this account. Nonetheless, Ibn ^{c}Abbās says the disbelievers mentioned in the verse were a tribe of Banī al-^{c}Abbās who were driven forcibly to fight in the Badr expedition (al-Rāzī, 2000, vol. 29, p. 263).

99 http://www.altafsir.com/Tafasir.asp?tMadhNo=4&tTafsirNo=38&tSoraNo=9&tAyahNo=6&tDisplay=yes&UserProfile=0)/ [accessed July 2009]

100 http://www.altafsir.com/Tafasir.asp?tMadhNo=7&tTafsirNo=57&tSoraNo=9&tAyahNo=6&tDisplay=yes&UserProfile=0)/ [accessed July 2009]

101 Regarding the *amān* of money see section above, 'Movable and immovable property'.

102 *Ḥijāz* is the area that encompasses Mecca, Medina, Yamāma, Khaybar, Yanbu^{c} and Fadak (Ibn Taymiyya, 1983, vol. 2, p. 186).

103 See section '*Dār al-ḥarb* and *dār al-Islam*', Chapter 3.

104 *Fayʾ* is the spoils which the Muslims get from disbelievers other than through war (Ibn Taymiyya, n.d., vol. 28, p. 276).

105 See Ibn ^{c}Ābdīn (2000, vol. 4, p. 135), Ibn Nujaym (n.d., vol. 5, p. 109) and al-Sīwāsī (n.d., vol. 6, p. 23).

106 The word 'temporary' is used here to distinguish this *amān* from the *dhimmī* contract, which is permanent.

107 For more details about the place of safety and what the scholars said about it, see the section entitled 'Prohibition of expulsion or return: "*refoulement*"', above.

108 See Nāfi^{c} *et al.*, 2001 to find an example of such a debate.

109 (http://www.altafsir.com/Tafasir.asp?tMadhNo=4&tTafsirNo=38&tSoraNo=9&tAyahNo=6&tDisplay=yes&UserProfile=0)/ [accessed July 2009]

110 *Kharāj* is the tax imposed on the person and the output of the land. See al-Sīwāsī (n.d., vol. 6, p. 31).

111 Shaykhī Zāda (1998, vol. 2, p. 451) and al-Shaybānī (1985, vol. 1, p. 321) also agree with this condition.

112 *Mustaʾmina* means the female of *mustaʾmin*.

113 The female of *ḥarbī*.

114 The female of *dhimmī*.

BIBLIOGRAPHY

NB: names beginning with Al- and Ibn- are alphabetized as separate groups within the overall alphabetical listing, so that all names beginning with Al- and Ibn- respectively are grouped together.

Ābādı, M., 1995. *Awn al-Mabūd* (2nd edn). Beirut: Dār al-Kutub al-Ilmiyya.

Abd al-Razzāq, A., 1982. *Muṣannaf Abd al-Razzāq* (2nd edn). Beirut: al-Maktab al-Islāmī. ed. Ḥ. al-Aẓamī.

Abu Dāwūd, S., n.d. *Sunan Abī Dāwūd*. Beirut: Dār al-Fikr (ed M. Abd al-Ḥamīd).

Abu Ḥayyān, M., 1983. *Al-Baḥr al-Muḥıṭ* (2nd edn). Beirut: Dār al-Fikr.

Abu Shuhba, M., 1971. *Al-Isrāʾılıyyāt wa al-Mawḍūāt fī Kutub al-Tafsīr* (4th edn). Cairo: Maktabat al-Sunna.

Abu al-Suᶜūd, M., n.d. *Tafsīr Abī al-Suʾūd*. Beirut: Dār ʾIḥyāʾ al-Turāth.

Abu al-Suᶜūd, M., n.d. *Irshād al-Aql al-Salīm ʾIlā Mazāyā al-Qurʾān al-Karīm*. Beirut: Dār ʾIḥyāʾ al-Turāth.

Abu Uwāna, Y., n.d. *Musnad Abī Uwāna*. Beirut: Dār al-Marifa.

Abu Yalā, A., 1984. *Musnad Abī Yalā*. Damascus: Dār al-Maʾmūn li al-Turāth (ed Ḥ. Asad).

Al-ᶜAbdarī, M., 1977. *Al-Ṭāj wa al-Iklīl* (2nd edn). Beirut: Dār al-Fikr.

Al-Ābī, A. M., 1989. *Nathr al-Durr*. Cairo: al-Hayʾa al-Miṣriyya al-Āmma li al-Kitab (eds S. Ḥamīd & Ḥ. Naāṣṣr).

Al-Adawī, A., 1991. *Ḥāshiyat al-Adawī*. Beirut: Dār al-Fikr (ed Y. al-Biqāı).

Al-Alūsī, Sh., n.d. *Rūḥ al-Maānī fī Tafsīr al-Qurʾān al-Aẓım wa al-Sab al-Mathānī*. Beirut: Dār ʾIḥyāʾ al-Turāth.

Al-Andalusī, A., 1984. *Ṭabāʾi al-Nisāʾ*. Cairo: Maktabat al-Qurʾān.

—— 1987. *Al-Iqd al-Farīd*. Cairo: Dar al-Kutub al-Ilmiyya (ed M. Qumayḥa).

Al-Aqam, A., 2002–2007. *Tafsīr al-Aqam*. [e-book]. Jordan: Royal Āl al-Bayt Institute for Islamic Thought. Available from: http://www.altafsir.com/ [cited April 2006].

Al-Aṣbahānī, A., 1984. *Ḥiliyat al-Awliyyāʾ* (4th edn). Beirut: Dār al-Kitāb al-Arabī.

Al-Aṣfahānī, F.A., 1983. *Kitab al-Aghānī*, Beirut: Dar al-Thaqāfa and Tunis: al-Dar al-Tūnisiyya li al-Nashr (ed lajna min al-Udabāʾ).

Al-Aṣfahānī, H., 1961. *Muḥaḍarāt al-Udabāʾ wa Muḥawarāt al-Shuarāʾ wa al-Bulaghāʾ*. Beirut: Dar Maktabat al-Ḥayāt.

Al-Aṣfahānī, H., n.d. *Al-Mufradāt fī Gharīb al-Qurʾān*. Beirut: Dār al-Marifa (ed M. Kılānī).

Al-Aynı, B., n.d. *Umdat al-Qārī*. Beirut: Dār ʾIḥyāʾ al-Turāth.

Al-Baghawī, Ḥ., 2002–2007. *Mālim al-Tanzīl*. [e-book]. Jordan: Royal Āl al-Bayt Institute for Islamic Thought. Available from: http://www.altafsir.com/ [cited April 2006].

Al-Baghdādı, A. U., 1998. *Khizānat al-Adab wa-Lubb Lubāb Lisān al-Arab*. Beirut: Manshūrāt Muḥammad ᶜAlī Bayḍūn, Dar al-Kutub al-Ilmiyya (ed M. Ṭarīfı).

Al-Balādhurī, A.Y., 1996. *Kitāb Jumal min Ansāb al-Ashrāf*. Beirut: Dar al-Fikr (eds S. Zakkār & R. Ziriklī)

Al-Baᶜlī, A., 2002. *Kashf al-Mukhadarāt wa al-Riyāḍ al-Muzhirāt li Sharḥ Akhṣar al-Mukhtaṣarāt*. Beirut: Dār al-Bashāʾir al-Islāmiyya ed. M. al-Ajamī.

Al-Bāqillānī, M., 1997, *Ijāẓ Al-Qurʾān* (5th edn) Egypt: Dār al-Maārif (ed A. Ṣaqir).

Al-Bayḍāwī, n.d. *Tafsīr al-Bayḍāwī*. Beirut: Dār al-Fikr.

Al-Bayhaqī A., n.d. *Marifat al-Sunan wa al-Āthār*. Beirut: Dār al-Kutub al-Ilmiyya (ed S. Ḥasan).

—— 1989. *Sunan al-Bayhaqī al-Ṣughrā*, Medina: Maktabat al-Dār (ed M. al-Aẓamī).

—— 1993. *Sunan al-Bayhaqī al-Kubrā*. Mecca: Maktabat Dār al-Bāz (ed M. Aṭā).

Al-Bazzār, A., 1988. *Musnad al-Bazzār*. Beirut: Muʾassasat Ulūm al-Qurʾān (ed M. Zaynullah).

Al-Biqāı, I., *Naẓm al-Durar fī Tanāsub al-Āyāt wa al-Suwar*. [e-book]. Jordan: Royal Āl al-Bayt Institute for Islamic Thought. Available from: http://www.altafsir.com/ [cited April 2006].

Al-Buhūtī, M., 1970. *Al-Rawḍ al-Muraba*. Riyadh: Maktabat al-Riyāḍ al-Ḥadītha.

—— 1981. *Kashshāf al-Qinā*. Beirut: Dār al-fikr (ed H. Hilāl).

—— 1996. *Sharḥ Muntahā al-ʾIrādāt* (2nd edn). Beirut: Ālam al-Kutub.

Al-Bujayramī, S., n.d. *Ḥāshiyat al-Bujayramī*. Diyār Baker: al-Maktaba al-Islāmiyya.

Al-Bukhārī, I., 1989. *Al-Adab al-Mufrad* (3rd edn). Beirut: Dār al-Bashāʾir al-Islāmiyya (ed M. Abd al-Bāqī).

Al-Bukhārī, M., 1986. *Ṣaḥıḥ al-Bukhārī* (3rd edn). Beirut: Dār Ibn Kathīr (ed Muṣtafa al-Baghā).

Al-Dāraquṭnī, A., 1966. *Sunan al-Dāraquṭnı*. Beirut: Dār al-Marifa (ed A. al-Madanī).

Al-Dardīr, n.d. *Sharḥ Mukhtaṣar Khalīl*. Beirut: Dār al-Fikr.

Al-Dhahabī, M., 2000. *Al-Tafsīr wa al-Mufassirūn* (7th edn). Cairo: Maktabat Wahbi.

Al-Dusūqī, M., n.d. *Ḥāshiyat al-Dusūqī*. Beirut: Dār al-Fikr (eds A. Shākir, A. Hārūn & M. Alīsh).

Al-Fākihī, M., 1993. *Akhbār Makka* (2nd edn) Beirut: Dār Khaḍir, ed. A. Duhaysh.

Al-Farāhīdı, K.A., 1980. *Al-Ayn*. Baghdad: Wizarat al-Thaqāfa wa-al-Ilam (ed M. al-Makhzūmī & I. al-Sāmirrā'ı).

Al-Fayrūzabādī, I., 1982. *Al-Tanbīh fī fiqh al-Shāfi'ī*. Beirut: Ālam al-Kutub (ed I. Ḥaydar).

Al-Fayrūzabādī, M., n.d. *Al-Qāmūs al-Muḥıṭ*. Beirut: Mu'assasat al-Risāla.

Al-Ghamrāwī, M., n.d. *al-Sirāj al-Wahhāj*. Beirut: Dār al-Marifa.

Al-Ghanūshī, R. 1993. *Al-Ḥuriyyāt al-Āmma fī al-Dawla al-Islāmiyya*. Beirut: Markaz Dirāsāt al-Wiḥda al-Arabiyya.

Al-Ghazālī, M., 1992. *Al-Mustaṣfā fī Ilm al-Uṣūl*. Beirut: Dār al-Kutub al-Ilmiyya (ed M. Abd al-Shāfī).

—— 1996. *Al-Wasīṭ fī al-Madhhab*. Cairo: Dār al-Salām (eds A. Ibrāhīm & M. Tāmir).

l-Ḥākim, M., 1990. *Al-Mustadrak Alā al-Ṣaḥıḥayn*. Beirut: Dār al-Kutub al-Ilmiyya (ed M. Aṭā).

Al-Ḥalabī, A., 1979. *Al-Sīra al-Ḥalabiyya fī Sīrat al-Amīn al-Ma'mūn*. Beirut: Dār al-Marifa.

Al-Ḥamawī, Y. A., 1993. *Mujam al-Udabā': Irshād al-Arīb ilā Marifat al-Adīb*. Beirut: Dar al-Gharb al-Islāmī (ed I. Abbās).

Al-Ḥaṣkafī, M., 1966. *Al-Durr al-Mukhtār Sharḥ Tanwīr al-Abṣār* (2nd edn). Beirut: Dār al-Fikr.

Al-Hawwārī, H., 2002–2007. *Tafsīr Kitāb Allah al-'Azīz*. [e-book]. Jordan: Royal Āl al-Bayt Institute for Islamic Thought. Available from: http://www.altafsir.com/ [cited April 2006].

Al-Haythamī, A. n.d. *Mawārid al-Ẓam'ān*. Beirut: Dār al-Kutub al-Ilmiyya (ed M. Abd al-Razzāq).

—— 1986. *Mujamma al-Zawā'id*. Beirut: Dār al-Rayyān li al-Turāth.

Al-Hindī, A., 1998. *Kanz al-Ummāl*. Beirut: Dār al-Kutub al-Ilmiyya (ed M. al-Dimyāṭı).

Al-Ḥusaynī, A., 1994. *Kifāyat al-Akhyār fī Ḥal Ghāyat al-'Ikhtiṣār*. Damascus: Dār al-Khayr (eds A. Biltājī & M. Sulaymān).

Al-Jaṣṣāṣ, A., 1984. *Aḥkām al-Qur'ān*. Beirut: Dār 'Iḥā' al-Turāth (ed M. Qamḥāwī).

Al-Jīrāḥī, I., 1984. *Kashf al-Khafā'* (4th edn). Beirut: Mu'assasat al-Risāla (ed M. al-Qallāsh).

Al-Jumaylī, R., 1972. *Muḥaḍarāt fī Tarīkh al-Arab fī al-Jāhiliyya wa Aṣr al-Dawa al-Islāmiyya*. Beirut.

Al-Kalbī, M., 1983. *Al-Tashīl li Ulūm al-Tanzīl* (4th edn). Lebanon: Dār al-Kitāb al-Arabī.

Al-Kāsānī, A., 1982. *Badā'i al-Ṣanā'i* (2nd edn) Beirut: Dār al-Kitāb al-Arabī.

Al-Kāshānī, M., 1985. *Kitāb al-Wāfı*. Asfahan: Maktabat al-Imām. ed. Ḍiyāʾ al-Dīn.

Al-Khāzin, A., n.d. *Lubāb al-Taʾwīl fi Maānī al-Tanzīl*. Cairo: Dār al-Kutub al-Arabiyya al-Kubrā.

Al-Khiraqī, U., 1982. *Mukhtaṣar al-Khiraqī* (3rd edn). Beirut: al-Maktab al-Islāmī (ed Z. al-Shāwīsh).

Al-Kirmānī, M., 1976. *Asrār al-Tikrār fi al-Qurʾān* (2nd edn). Cairo: Dār al-Itiṣām (ed A. Aṭā).

Al-Maqdisī, M., 1989. *Al-Aḥādıth al-Mukhtāra*. Mecca: Maktabat al-Nahḍa al-Ḥadītha (ed A. Duhaysh).

Al-Marzubānī, M. I., 1935. *Mujam al-Shuarāʾ*. Cairo: Maktabat al-Qudsī.

Al-Marzūqī, A. M., 1953. *Sharḥ Dıwān al-Ḥamāsa*. Cairo: Lajnat al-Taʾlīf wa al-Tarjama wa al-Nashr (eds A. Amīn & A. Harūn).

Al-Maydānī, A. M., 1987. *Mujamma al-Amthāl*. Beirut: Dar al-Jīl (ed M. A. Ibrāhīm).

Al-Mirdāwī, A., n.d. *Al-Inṣāf*. Beirut: Dār ʾIḥyāʾ al-Turāth (ed M. al-Faqī).

Al-Mirghināni, A., n.d. *Al-Hidāya Sharḥ Bidāyat al-Mubtadī*. Diyār Baker: al-Maktaba al-Islāmiyya.

Al-Mubārakfūrī, M., n.d. *Tuḥfat al-Aḥwadhī*. Beirut: Dār al-Kutub al-Ilmiyya.

Al-Munāwī, A., (1031), 1937. *Fayḍ al-Qadīr*. Egypt: al-Maktaba al-Tijāriyya.

Al-Mundhirī, A., 1996. *Al-Targhīb wa al-Tarhīb*. Beirut: Dār al-Kutub al-Ilmiyya (ed I. Shams al-Dīn).

Al-Nafrāwī, A., 1994. *Al-Fawākih al-Dawānī*. Beirut: Dār al-Fikr.

Al-Naḥḥās, A. 1984. *Maānī al-Qurʾān*, Mecca: Jāmiat Um al-Qurā (ed M. al-Ṣābūnı).

—— 1987. *Al-Nāsikh wa al-Mansūkh*. Kuwait: Maktabat al-Falāḥ (ed Muḥammad Abd al-Salām).

—— n.d. *Irāb al-Qurʾān*. Beirut: Ālam al-Kutub (ed Z. Zāhid).

Al-Nasafı, A., 2002–2007 *Madārik al-Tanzīl wa Ḥaqāʾq al-Taʾwīl* [e-book]. Jordan: Royal Āl al-Bayt Institute for Islamic Thought. Available from: http://www.altafsir.com/ [cited April 2006].

Al-Nasāʾī, A., 1991. *Sunan al-Nasāʾī al-Kubrā*. Beirut: Dār al-Kutub al-Ilmiyya (eds A. al-Bandārī & S. Ḥasan).

Al-Nāṣirī A., 1997. *Al-Istiqṣā Li Akhbār Duwal al-Maghrib al-Aqṣā*. Al-Dār al-Bayḍāʾ: Dār al-Kutub.

Al-Nawawī, Y., 1972. *Sharḥ al-Nawawī Alā Ṣaḥıḥ Muslim* (2nd edn). Beirut: Dār Iḥyāʾ al-Turāth.

—— 1984. *Rawḍat al-Ṭālibīn wa Umdat al-Muftın* (2nd edn). Beirut: al-Maktab l-Islāmī.

—— 1987. *Taḥrīr Alfāẓ al-Tanbīh*. Damascus: Dār al-Qalam (ed A. al-Daqar).

Al-Nawawī, Y., 1997. *Al-Majmū*. Beirut: Dār al-Fikr.

Al-Naysābūri, M., 1990. *Ṣaḥıḥ Muslim*. Beirut, Dār Iḥyāʾ al-Turāth (ed M. Abd al-Bāqī).

Al-Numayrī, U., 1996. *Akhbār al-Madīna*. Beirut: Dār al-Kutub al-Ilmiyya (eds A. Dandal & Y. Bayān).
Al-Nuwayrī., 1988. *Nihāyat al-Arab fī Funūn al-Adab*. Al-Dār al-Bayḍāˀ: Maṭbaat al-Najāḥ al-Jadīda (ed M. Aḥmad).
Al-Qaffāl, M., 1980. *Ḥilyat al-Ulamāˀ*. Beirut: Muˀassast al-Risāla (ed Y. Darādika).
Al-Qālī, I., 1980. *Al-Amālī*. Beirut: Dar al-Āfāq.
Al-Qalqashandī, 1981. *Ṣubḥ al-Ashā fī Ṣināat al-ˀInshā*. Damascus: Wazārat al-Thaqāfa (ed A. Zakkār).
Al-Qalqashandı, A., 1958. *Nihāyat al-ˀArab fī Marifat Ansāb al-Arab*. Baghdad: Maṭbaat al-Naja.
Al-Qalyūbī, A., 1998. *Ḥāshiyat al-Qalyūbī*. Beirut: Dār al-Fikr (ed Maktab al-Buḥūth wa al-Dirāsāt).
Al-Qaraḍāwī, Y., 1977. *Non-Muslims in the Islamic Society*. Egypt: Dār Gharīb li al-Ṭibāa.
Al-Qārī, A., 2001. *Mirqāt al-Mafātıḥ*. Beirut: Dār al-Kutub al-Ilmiyya (ed J. Ītānī).
Al-Qawnawī, Q., 1985. *Anīs al-Fuqahāˀ*. Jedda: Dār al-Wafāˀ (ed A. al-Kubaysī).
Al-Qazwīnī, M., 1998. *Sunan Ibn Māja*. Beirut: Dār al-Fikr (ed M. Abd al-Bāqī).
Al-Quḍāī, M., 1986. *Musnad al-Shihāb* (2nd edn). Beirut: Muˀassasat al-Risāla.
Al-Qummī, Ḥ., 2002–2007. *Gharāˀb al-Qurˀān wa Raghāˀb al-Furqān*. 2002–2007 [e-book]. Jordan: Royal Āl al-Bayt Institute for Islamic Thought. Available from: http://www.altafsir.com/ [cited April 2006].
Al-Qurāfī, A., 1994. *Al-Dhakhīra*. Beirut: Dār al-Gharb (ed M. Ḥajjī).
Al-Qurṭubī, M., 1986. *Al-Jāmi li Aḥkām al-Qurˀān*. Cairo: Dār al-Shab.
Al-Qushayrī, A., *Laṭāˀf al-Ishārāt*. 2002–2007 [e-book]. Jordan: Royal Āl al-Bayt Institute for Islamic Thought. Available from: http://www.altafsir.com/ [cited April 2006].
Al-Ramlī, M., 1983. *Nihāyat al-Muḥtāj*. Beirut: Dār al-Fikr.
Al-Rāzī, M., 1979. *Al-Maḥṣūl fī Ilm Uṣūl al-Fiqh*. Riyadh: Jāmiat al-Imām Muḥammad (ed Ṭ. al-Ilwānī).
—— 1994. *Mukhtār al-Ṣiḥāḥ*. Beirut: Maktabat Lubnān Nāshirūn (ed M. Khāṭir).
—— 1996. *Tuḥfat al-Mulūk*. Beirut: Dār al-Bashāˀr al-Islāmiyya (ed A. Aḥmad).
—— 2000. *Al-Tafsīr al-Kabīr*. Beirut: Dār al-Kutub al-Ilmiyya.
Al-Sadī, Abd al-Raḥmān, 2000. *Tafsīr al-Sadī*. Beirut: Muˀassasat al-Risāla (ed Ibn Uthaymīn).
Al-Sadī, A., 1984. *Fatāwā al-Sadī*. Amman: Dār al-Furqān, Beirut: Muˀassasat al-Risāla (ed S. al-Nāhī).
Al-Ṣafadī, K. A., 1931. *Al-Wāfı bi al-Wafayāt*. Istanbul: Maṭbaat al-Dawla (ed H. Ritter).
Al-Samarqandī, A., 1984. *Tuḥfat al-Fuqahāˀ*. Beirut: Dār al-Kutub al-Ilmiyya.
Al-Samarqandī, N., n.d. *Tafsīr al-Samarqandī (Baḥr al-Ulūm)*. Beirut: Dār al-Fikr.
Al-Ṣanānī, A., 1982. *Muṣannāf Abd al-Razzāq* (2nd edn). Beirut: al-Maktab al-Islāmī. ed. Ḥ. al-Aẓamī

Al-Ṣanānī, M., 1959. *Subul al-Salām* (4th edn). Beirut: Dār Iḥyā᾽ al-Turāth (ed M. al-Khūlī).

Al-Sarakhsī, Sh., n.d. *Al-Mabsūṭ*. Beirut: Dār al-Marifa.

Sarkīs, I., 1979. *Madkhal ilā al-Adab al-Jāhilī*. Beirut: Dār al-Ṭalīa.

Al-Ṣāwī, A., 1994. *Bulghat al-Sālik li Aqrab al-Masālik*. Beirut: Dār al-Kutub al-Ilmiyya (ed M. Shāhīn).

Al-Shāfiī, M., 1973. *Al-Um* (2nd edn) Beirut: Dār al-Marifa.

—— 1979. *Aḥkām al-Qur᾽ān*. Beirut: Dār al-Kutub al-Ilmiyya (ed A. Abd al-Ḥaqq).

Al-Shanqīṭī, M., 1995. *Aḍwā᾽ al-Bayān*. Beirut: Dār al-Fikr. ed. Maktab al-Buḥūth wa al-Dirāsāt.

Al-Sharīf, A., 1965. *Makka wa al-Madīna fī al-Jāhiliyya wa ᶜAhd al-Rasūl*. Cairo: Dar al-Fikr al-Arabī, Mukhaymar Press.

Al-Shawkānī, M., 1973. *Nayl al-Awṭār*. Beirut: Dār al-Jıl.

—— 1984. *Al-Sayl al-Jarrār*. Beirut: Dār al-Kutub al-Ilmiyya (ed M. Zāyid).

—— n.d. *Fatḥ al-Qadīr al-Jāmi Bayna Fannay al-Riwāya wa al-Dirāya min Ilm al-Tafsīr*. Beirut: Dār al-Fikr.

Al-Shaybānī, A., 1991. *Al-Āḥād wa al-Mathānī*. Riyadh: Dār al-Rāya (eds B. Fayṣal & A. al-Jawābra).

—— 1994. *Al-Kāmil fī al-Tārīkh* (2nd edn). Beirut: Dār al-Kutub al-Ilmiyya.

Al-Shaybānī, M. n.d. *Al-Mabsūṭ*. Karachi: Idārat al-Qur᾽ān wa al-Ulūm (ed A. al-Afaghānī).

—— 1975. *Al-Siyar*. Beirut: al-Dār al-Muttaḥida (ed M. Khadūrī).

—— 1985. *Al-Jāmi al-Ṣaghīr*. Beirut: Ālam al-Kitāb.

Al-Shīrāzī, I., n.d. *Al-Muhadhdhab*. Beirut: Dār al-Fikr.

Al-Shirbinī, M., n.d. *Mughnı al-Muḥtāj*. Beirut: Dār al-Fikr.

—— 1994. *Al-Iqnā fī Ḥal Alfāẓ Abī Shujā*. Beirut: Dār al-Fikr (ed Maktab al-Buḥūth wa al-Dirāsāt).

Al-Shirwānī, A., n.d. *Ḥawāshī al-Shirwānī*. Beirut: Dār al-Fikr.

Al-Sīwāsī, M., n.d. *Sharḥ Fatḥ al-Qadīr* (2nd edn). Beirut: Dār al-Fikr.

Al-Subkī, A., n.d. *Fatāwā al-Subkī*. Beirut: Dār al-Ma᾽rifa.

Al-Suyūṭī, J. 1978. *Al-Shamārīkh fī Ilm al-Tārīkh*. Kuwait: al-Dār al-Salafiyya (ed M. al-Shaybānī).

Al-Suyūṭī, M. 1961. *Maṭālib Ulī al-Nuhā*. Damascus: al-Maktab al-Islāmī.

—— 1985. *Kifāyat al-Ṭālib al-Labīb fī Khaṣā᾽ṣ al-Ḥabīb*. Beirut: dār al-Kutub al-Ilmiyya.

—— 1993. *Al-Durr al-Manthūr*. Beirut: Dār al-Fikr.

Al-Ṭabarānī, S., 1983. *Al-Mujam al-Kabīr* (2nd edn). Musil, Iraq: Maktabat al-Zahrā᾽ (ed) Ḥ. al-Salafı.

—— 1994. *Al-Mujam al-Awsaṭ*. Cairo: Dār al-Ḥaramayn (ed Ṭ. al-Ḥusaynī).

Al-Ṭabarī, M., n.d, *Ṭārīkh al-Ṭabarī*. Beirut: Dār al-Kutub al-Ilmiyya.

Al-Ṭabarī, M., 1984. *Tafsīr al-Ṭabarī*. Beirut: Dār al-Fikr.

Al-Ṭabarsī, F., 1980. *Majma al-Bayān fī Tafsīr al-Qur᾽ān*. Beirut: Dār Maktabat al-Ḥayāt.

Al-Ṭabāṭbāʾī, M., 1971. *Al-Mīzān fī Tafsīr al-Qurʾān* (2nd edn). Beirut: Muʾasasat al-Al-Alamī

Al-Tabrīzī, M., 1985. *Mishkāt al-Maṣābīḥ* (3rd edn). Beirut: al-Maktab al-Islāmī (ed M. al-Albānī).

Al-Ṭabāṭbāʾī, M., 2002–2007. *Taysīr al-Tafsīr*. [e-book]. Jordan: Royal Āl al-Bayt Institute for Islamic Thought. Available from: http://www.altafsir.com/ [cited April 2006].

Al-Ṭaḥḥāwī, A., 1900. *Ḥāshiyat al-Ṭaḥḥāwī Alā Marāqī al-Falāḥ* (3rd edn). Egypt: al-Maṭbaa al-Kubrā.

—— 1978. *Sharḥ Maānī al-Āthār*. Beirut: Dār al-Kutub al-Ilmiyya (ed M. al-Najjār).

Al-Thaālibī. A., n.d. *Al-Jawāhir al-Ḥisān fī Tafsīr al-Qurʾān*. Beirut: Muʾassasat al-Alamī.

—— 1982. *Yatımat al-Dahr fī Maḥāsin Ahl al-Aṣr*. Beirut: Ḍār al-Kutub al-Ilmiyya (ed M. Qamḥiyya).

Al-Tirmidhī, M., n.d, *Sunan al-Tirmidhī*. Beirut: Dār Iḥyāʾ al-Turāth (eds A. Shākir & others).

Al-Ṭūsī. M., 1960. *Al-Tibyān fī Tafsīr al-Qurʾān*. Iraq: Maktabat Qaṣīr (ed A. Qaṣīr).

Al-ᶜqaylī, M., 1983. *Ḍuafāʾ Al-ᶜqaylī*. Beirut: Dār al-Maktaba al-Imiyya (ed A. Qalajı).

Al-Wāqidı, M., 1966. *Kitāb al-Maghāzī*. London: Oxford University Press (ed M. Jones).

Al-Zamakhsharī, M. U., 1979. *Asās al-Balāgha*. Beirut: Dar Ṣādir.

—— U., 2001. *Rabī al-Abrār wa Fuṣūṣ al-Akhbār*. Cairo: Dar al-Kutub wa al-Wathʾāiq al-Qawmiyya (ed M. Qurna).

—— n.d. *Al-Kashshāf An Ḥaqāʾiq al-Tanzīl*. Beirut: Dār ʾIḥyāʾ al-Turāth.

Al-Zarkashī, M., 1981. *Khabāyā al-Zawāya*. Kuwait: Wazārat al-Awqāf (ed A. al-Ānı).

—— 2002. *Sharḥ al-Zarkashī Alā Mukhtaṣar al-Khiraqī*. Beirut: Dār al-Kutub al-Ilmiyya (ed A. Ibrāhīm).

Al-Zaylaı, A., 1938. *Naṣb al-Rāya*. Egypt: Dār al-Ḥadīth (ed M. al-Bannūrī).

Al-Zaylaı, J., 1993. *Takhrīj al-Aḥādıth wa al-Āthār*. Riyadh: Dār Ibn Khuzayma(ed A. al-Sad).

Al-Zaylaı, U., 1895. *Tabyın al-Ḥaqāʾiq*. Cairo: Dār al-Kutub al-Islāmī.

ᶜAmāra, M., 2003. *Al-Islām wa al-Aqalliyyāt; al-Māḍı wa al-Ḥāḍir wa al-Mustaqbal*. Cairo: Maktabat al-Shurūq al-Dawliyya.

Āqil, N., 1969. *Tārīkh al-Arab al-Qadīm wa Aṣr al-Rasūl*. Damascus.

Arnaout, G. 1987. *Asylum in the Arab-Islamic Tradition*. Geneva: office of the United Nation High Commissioner for Refugees.

Asad, N., 1962. *Maṣādir al-Shir al-Jāhilī wa Qīmatuha al-matuha al-Tārīkhiyya* (2nd edn). Cairo: Dār al-Maārif.

Askarī, A., 1987. *Jamharat al-Amthāl*. Beirut: Dār al-Fikr.

Aṭfiyyash, M., *Hamayān al-Zād Ilā Dār al-Maād*. [e-book]. Jordan: Royal Āl al-Bayt Institute for Islamic Thought. Available from: http://www.altafsir.com/ [accessed April 2006]

Bdawī, A., 1979. *Dirāsāt al-Mustashriqīn ḥawla Ṣiḥḥat al-Shir al-Jāhilī*. Beirut: Dār al-Ilm lilmalāiyyn.

Bearman, P.J. *et al.*, 2000. *The Encyclopaedia of Islam*. New edition, Leiden: Brill.

Bearman, P.J. *et al.*, (eds) 2002. *The Encyclopaedia of Islam*. New edition. Leiden, E.J Brill.

Bosworth, C.E. *et al.*, (eds) 1986. *The Encyclopaedia of Islam*. Leiden: E.J. Brill.

Bosworth, C.E. *et al.*, (eds) 1995. *The Encyclopaedia of Islam*. Leiden: E.J. Brill.

Bosworth, C.E. *et al.*, (eds) 2002. *The Encyclopaedia of Islam*. New edition. Leiden: E.J. Brill.

Burhānbūrī. N. and a group of scholars. 1990. *Al-Fatāwā al-Hindiyya*. Beirut: Dar al-Fikr.

Casewit, D. 1998. 'Hijra as history and metaphor: a survey of Qurʾanic and *ḥadīth* sources', *The Muslim World*, LXXXVIII (2), pp. 105–128.

Chaudhry, M., 1995. *Non-Muslim Minorities in an Islamic State*. Lahore: Impact Publication International.

Chimni, B.S. (ed) 2000. *International Refugee Law A Reader*. New Delhi/ Thousand Oaks/ London: Sage Publications.

Crone, P., 1994. 'The First-Century Concept of Hijra', *Arabica: Journal of Arabic and Islamic Studies*. Leiden: Brill. XLI, pp. 352–387.

Ḍayf, Sh., 1960. *Tārīkh al-Adab al-Arabī*. Cairo: Dār al-Maārif.

Doi, A., 1981. *Non-Muslims under Sharīa [Islamic Law]*. (2nd edn) USA: International Graphics.

Dresch, P., 1993. *Tribe Government and history in Yemen*. Oxford: Clarendon Press.

Elmadmad, K. 1991. 'An Arab Convention on Forced Migration: Desirability and Possibilities', *International Journal of Refugee Law* (3): pp. 461–481.

Feller, E., Turk, V. and Nicholson, F. (eds) 2003. *Refugee Protection in International Law UNHCR's Global Consultation on International Protection*. Cambridge: Cambridge University Press.

Goodwin-Gill, G., 1996. *The refugees in International Law* (2nd edn). Oxford: Clarendon.

Guillaume, A., 2006. *The life of Muhammad* (20th impression). Oxford: Oxford University Press.

Guterres, A., 2007. 'Statement by Mr. António Guterres, United Nations High Commissioner for Refugees, to the League of Arab States' [online] http://www.unhcr.org/admin/ADMIN/45ed1ea64.html [accessed August 2007]

Ḥamīdullah, M., 1974. 'Significance of the Hijra', *Cultures* VII (4) pp. 25–38.

Ḥammada, F. 1980. *Maṣādīr al-Sīra al-Nabawiyya wa Taqwīmuhā*, al-Dar al-Bayḍāʾ: Dār al-Thaqāfa.

Hathaway, J., 1991. *The Law of Refugee Status*. Toronto: Butterworths

—— 2005. *The Rights of Refugees under International Law*. Cambridge: Cambridge University Press.

Ḥaydar, A., n.d. *Durar al-Ḥukkām Sharḥ Majallat al-Aḥkām*. Beirut: Dār al-Kutub al-Ilmiyya (tr F. al-Ḥusaynī).

Hoyland, R., 2004. *Muslims and Others in Early Islamic Society*. UK: Cromwell Press.

Ḥusayn, Ṭ., 1926. *Fī al-Shir al-Jāhilī*. Cairo: Dār al-Nahr.

—— 1927. *Fī al-Adab al-Jāhilī*. Cairo: MaṬba^{c}at al-I^{c}timād.

Ḥusayn, M., n.d, *Naqḍ Kitāb fī al-Shir al-Jāhilī*. Beirut: al-Maktaba al-Ilmiyya.

Ibn ^{c}Abd al-Barr. Y., 1967. *Al-Tamhīd*. Morocco: Wazārat Umūm al-Awqāf (eds M. al-Alawī & M. al-Bakrī).

—— n.d. *Al-Durar fī Ikhtiṣār al-Maghāzī wa al-Siyar* (2nd edn). Cairo: Dār al-Maārif (ed Sh. Ḍayf).

—— 2000. *Al-Istidhkār*. Beirut: Dār al-Kutub al-Ilmiyya (eds S. Muḥammad & M. Muawwaḍ).

Ibn ^{c}Abd al-Wāḥıd, M., 1989. *Al-Aḥādıṭh al-Mukhtāra*. Mecca: Dār al-Nahḍa al-Ḥadītha (ed A. Duhaysh).

Ibn ^{c}Ābdīn, M., 2000. *Rad al-Muḥtār Alā al-Dur al-Mukhtār (Ḥāshiyat Ibn ^{c}Ābdīn)*. Beirut: Dār al-Fikr.

Ibn Abī Ḥadīd, A., 1959–1963. *Sharḥ Nahj al-Balāgha*. Cairo: Īsā al-Bābī al-Ḥalabī (ed M. Ibrāhīm).

Ibn Abī Shayba, A., 1988. *Muṣannaf Ibn Abī Shayba*. Riyadh: Maktabat al-Rāshīd (ed K. al-Ḥūt).

Ibn ^{c}Ajība, A., 2002–2007. *Al-Baḥr al-Madīd fī Tafsīr al-Qur$^{\circ}$ān al-Majīd*. [e-book] Jordan: Royal Āl al-Bayt Institute for Islamic Thought. Available from: http://www.altafsir.com/ [accessed April 2006]

Ibn al-Arabī, M., n.d. *Aḥkām al-Qur$^{\circ}$ān*. Beirut: Dār al-Fikr (ed M. Aṭā).

Ibn al-Athīr, A.M., 1884. *Al-Kāmil fī al-Tārīkh*, Cairo: al-Maṭbaa al-Azhariyya.

Ibn al-Bāzarī, H., 1984. *Nāsikh al-Qur$^{\circ}$ān wa Mansūḥihī* (3rd edn). Beirut: Mu$^{\circ}$assasat al-Risāla (ed Ḥ. al-Ḍāmin).

Ibn Ḍuwayyān, I., 1984. *Manār al-Sabīl* (2nd edn). Riyadh: Maktabat al-Maārif (ed I. al-Qalajī).

Ibn al-Jad, A., 1990. *Musnad Ibn al-Jad*. Beirut: Mu$^{\circ}$assasat Nādir (ed A. Ḥaydar).

Ibn al-Jawzī, A., 1939. *Al-Muntaẓam*. Beirut: Dār Ṣādir.

Ibn al-Jawzī, A., 1983. *Zād al-Masīr fī Ilm al-Tafsīr*. Beirut: al-Maktab al-Islāmī.

Ibn al-Jawzī, A., 1984. *Nawāsikh al-Qur$^{\circ}$ān*. Beirut: Dār al-Kutub al-Ilmiyya.

Ibn al-Jawzī, A., 1994. *Al-Muṣaffā Min Ilm al-Nāsikh wa al-Mansūkh*. Beirut: Mu$^{\circ}$assasat al-Risāla.

Ibn al-Jawzī, A., 1997. *Kashf al-Mushkil*. Riyadh: Dār al-Waṭan (ed A. al-Bawwāb).

Ibn al-Mujāwir, Y., 1954. *Ṣifat Bilād al-Yaman*. Leiden: E. J. Brill (ed Ḥ. al-Qāḍī).

Ibn al-Mubārak, A., 1986. *Musnad Ibn al-Mubārak*. Riyadh: Maktabat al-Maārif (ed Ṣ. al-Sāmirrā$^{\circ}$ī).

Ibn al-Sayyid, M., n.d. *Iānat al-Ṭālibīn*. Beirut: Dār al-Fikr.

Ibn al-Shiḥna, M., 1973. *Lisān al-Ḥukkām fī Marifat al-Aḥkām* (2nd edn). Cairo: al-Bābī al-Ḥalabī.

Ibn Āshūr, M., 2000. *Tafsīr al-Taḥrīr wa al-Tanwīr*. Beirut: Muᵓasasat al-Tārīkh.
Ibn ᶜAṭiyya, A., 2002–2007. *Al-Muḥarrar al-Wajız fī Tafsīr al-Kitāb al-ᶜAzīz*. [e-book]. Jordan: Royal Āl al-Bayt Institute for Islamic Thought. Available from: http://www.altafsir.com/ [accessed April 2006]
Ibn Durayd, M., 1958. *Al-Ishtiqāq*. Cairo: Maṭbaat al-Sunna al-Muḥammadiyya (ed A. Harūn).
Ibn Ḥabīb, J., 1942. *Kitāb al-Muḥabbar*. Haydarabad: al-Dakkan, Maṭbaat Jamiyyat Dāᵓirat al-Maārif al-Uthmaniyya (ed I. Shtaytir).
—— 1985. *Al-Munammaq fī Akhbār Quraysh*. Beirut: Ālam al-Kutub (ed K. Fāriq).
Ibn Ḥajar, A., 1964. *Talkhīṣ al-Ḥabīr*. Medina (ed Abdullah al-Madanī).
—— 1992. *Al-Iṣāba fī Tamyız al-Ṣaḥāba*. Beirut: Dār al-Jīl (ed A. al-Bajāwī).
—— n.d. *Al-Dirāya fī Takhrīj Aḥādıth al-Hidāya*. Beirut: Dār al-Marifa (ed A. al-Madanī).
—— n.d. *Fatḥ al-Bārī*. Beirut: Dār al-Marifa (ed M. al-Khaṭīb).
Ibn Ḥamīd, A., 1988. *Musnad Abd Ibn Ḥamīd*. Cairo: Maktabat al-Sunna (eds Ṣ. al-Sāmirrāᵓī & M. al-Ṣaīdī).
Ibn Ḥanbal, A., n.d. *Musnad Aḥmad Ibn Ḥanbal*. Egypt: Muᵓassasat Qurṭuba.
—— 1988. *Masāᵓil al-Imām*. Delhi: al-Dār al-Ilmiyya (ed F. Muḥammad).
Ibn Ḥazm A., n.d. *al-Muḥallā*. Beirut: Dār al-Āfāq al-Jadīda (ed Lajnat ᵓIḥyāᵓ al-Turāth).
Ibn Ḥazm, A.A. 1948. *Jamharat Ansāb al-Arab*. Cairo: Dar al-Maārif.
Ibn Hibatullāh, A., 1995. *Tārīkh Madīnat Dimashq*. Beirut: Dār al-Fikr (ed U. al-Umarī).
Ibn Ḥibbān, M., 1975. *Al-Thiqāt*. Beirut: Dār al-Fikr (ed Sh. Aḥmad).
—— 1993. *Ṣaḥıḥ Ibn Ḥibbān* (2nd edn). Beirut: Muᵓassasat al-Risāla (ed S. Arnaᵓūṭ).
Ibn Hishām, A., 1990. *Al-Sīra al-Nabawiyya*. Beirut: Dar al-Jıl (ed Ṭ. Sad).
Ibn Ḥujja, A., 1987. *Khizānat al-Adab wa Ghāyat al-Arab*. Beirut: Dār al-Hilāl (ed I. Shaqyū).
Ibn Ḥumayd, A., 1988. *Musnad Abd Ibn Ḥumayd*. Cairo: Maktabat al-Sunna (ed Ṣ. al-Sāmirrāᵓī).
Ibn Ḥusām al-Dīn, A., 1998. *Kanz al-Ummāl*. Beirut: Dār al-Kutub al-Ilmiyya (ed M. al-Dimyyāṭı)
Ibn Isḥāq, M., n.d. *Sīrat Ibn Isḥāq*, Morocco: Mahad al-Abḥāth wa al-Dirāsāt li al-Tarīb (ed M. Ḥamīdullah).
Ibn Isḥāq, Y., n.d. *Musnad Abī Uwāna*. Beirut: Dār al-Marifa.
Ibn Jabr, M., 1976. *Tafsīr Mujāhid*. Pakistan: Mujamma al-Buḥūth al-Islāmiyya (ed A. al-Sūratı).
Ibn Jārūd, A., 1987. *Al-Muntaqā*. Beirut: Muᵓassasat al-Kitāb (ed A. al-Bārūdı).
Ibn Jinnī, A., 1913. *Al-Khaṣāᵓiṣ*. Cairo.
Ibn Kathīr, I., 1980. *Tafsīr Ibn Kathīr*. Beirut: Dār al-Fikr.
—— n.d, *al-Bidāya wa al-Nihāya*. Beirut: Maktabat al-Maārif.

Ibn Khaldūn, A.M., 1900. *Al-Muqaddima* (3rd edn) Beirut.
Ibn Khaldūn A., 1984, *Tārīkh Ibn Khaldūn*. Beirut: Dār al-Qalam.
Ibn Khuzayma, M., 1970. *Ṣaḥıḥ Ibn Khuzayma*. Beirut: al-Maktab al-Islāmī (ed M. al-Aẓamī).
Ibn Manẓūr, M., 1956. *Lisān al-Arab*. Beirut: Dār Ṣādir and Dār Beirut.
Ibn Mufliḥ, I., 1979. *Al-Mubdi*. Beirut: al-Maktab al-Islāmī.
Ibn Mufliḥ, M., 1997. *Al-Furū*. Beirut: Dār al-Kutub al-Ilmiyya.
Ibn Nujaym, Z., n.d. *Al-Baḥr al-Rāʾq* (2nd edn). Beirut: Dār al-Marifa.
Ibn Qāni, A., 1997. *Mujam al-Ṣaḥāba*. Medina: Maktabat al-Ghurabāʾ al-Athariyya (ed Ṣ. al-Miṣrātı).
Ibn Qayyim al-Jawziyya, M., 1961. *Aḥkām Ahl al-Dhimma*. Damascus: Maṭbaat Jāmiat Dimashq (ed Ṣ. Ṣāliḥ).
Ibn Qudāma, A., 1984. *Al-Mughnı*. Beirut: Dār al-Fikr.
—— n.d. *Al-Kāfı fī Fiqh Ibn Ḥanbal*. Beirut: al-Maktab al-Islāmī.
—— n.d. *Umdat al-Fiqh*. Ṭāʾif: Maktabat al-Ṭarafayn (eds A. al-Abdalī & D. al-Utaybī).
Ibn Rāhawayh, I., 1991. *Musnad Isḥāq Ibn Rāhawayh*. Medina: Maktabat al-Īmān (ed A. al-Blūshī).
Ibn Rushd, M., n.d. *Bidāyat al-Mujtahid wa Nihāyat al-Muqtaṣid*. Beirut: Dār al-Fikr.
Ibn Saᶜd, M., n.d. *Al-Ṭabaqāt al-Kubrā*. Beirut: Dār Ṣādir.
Ibn Saīd. A., n.d. *Musnad Aḥmad Ibn ᶜAlī Ibn Saıd*.
Ibn Salām, Q., 1987. *Al-Amwāl*. Beirut: Dār al-Fikr (ed K. Harrās).
Ibn Sālim, M., n.d. *Zād al-Mustaqni*. Mecca: Maktabat al-Nahḍa al-Ḥadītha (ed A. al-Hindī).
Ibn Taymiyya, A., 1983. *Al-Muḥarrar fī al-Fiqh* (2nd edn). Riyadh: Maktabat al-Maārīf.
—— 1996. *Al-Ṣārim al-Maslūl Alā Shātim al-Rasūl*. Beirut: Dār Ibn Ḥazm (eds M. Ḥilwānī & M. Shūdarī).
—— n.d. *Majmū al-Fatāwā* (2nd edn). Maktabat Ibn Taymiyya (ed A. al-Najdı).
Ibn Yūsuf, M., 1969. *Dalīl al-Ṭālib* (2nd edn). Beirut: al-Maktab al-Islāmī.
Khafājī, M., 1973. *Al-Shir al-Jāhilī*.Beirut: Dār al-Kitāb al-Lubnānī.
Khalīf, Y., 1959. *Al-Shuarāʾ al-Ṣaālīk* (2nd edn). Cairo: Dar al-Maārif.
Lewis *et al.*, 1965. *The Encyclopaedia of Islam*. New edition. Leiden: Brill.
Lewis *et al.*, 1971. *The Encyclopaedia of Islam*. New edition. London: Luzac & Co., Leiden: E. Brill.
Lewis *et al.*, 1978. *The Encyclopaedia of Islam*. New edition. Leiden: Brill.
Mawdūdī, S., 1982. *Rights of Non-Muslims in Islamic States* (7th edn). Lahore: Islamic Publication Ltd (ed & tr K. Ahmad).
Moinuddin. H., 1987. *The Charter of the Islamic Conference and legal framework of economic co-operation among its member states*. Oxford: Clarendon.
Mubarrad, M., 1956. *Al-Kāmil fī al-Lugha wa al-Adab wa al-Naḥw wa al-Taṣrīf*. Cairo: Maktabat Nahḍat Miṣr (eds M. Ibrāhīm & A. Shaḥāta).

Nāfi, B. *et al.*, 2003. *Al-Muwāṭana wa al-Dımuqrāṭiyya fī al-Buldān al-Arabiyya.* Beirut: Markaz Dirāsāt al-Wiḥda al-Arabiyya.
Nicholson, F., and Twomey, P. (eds) 1999. *Refugee Rights and Realities: Evolving International Concepts and Regimes.* Cambridge: Cambridge University Press.
Niẓām. N., 1990. *Al-Fatāwā al-Hindiyya.* Beirut: Dār al-Fikr.
Peristiany, J. G., 1966. *Honour and Shame: the Values of Mediterranean Society.* Chicago: the University of Chicago Press.
The Qurā˒n.
Quṭb, S., 1967. *Fī Ẓilāl al-Qur˒ān* (5th edn). Beirut: Dār Iḥyā˒ al-Turāth al-Arabī.
Rubin, U., 2003. 'The Life of Muḥammad and the Qur˒ān: The Case of Muḥammad's Hijra', *Jerusalem Studies in Arabic and Islam*, 28, pp. 40–64.
Shalabī, A., 1974. *Mawsūat al-Tārīkh al-Islāmī wa al-Ḥaḍāra al-Islāmiyya* (7th edn). Cairo: Maktabat al-Nahḍa al-Maṣriyya.
Shaykhī Zāda, A., 1998. *Mujamma al-Anhur fī Sharḥ Multaqā al-Abḥur.* Beirut: Dār al-Kutub al-Ilmiyya.
Siddıqī, A., 1969. *Non-Muslims under Muslim Rule and Muslims under non-Muslim Rule.* Karachi: Jamiyat Falaḥ.
Smith, W.R., 1903. *Kinship and Marriages in Early Arabia.* Boston: Beacon Press.
Spencer, R., 2005. *The Myth of Islamic Tolerance: How Islamic Law Treats Non-Muslims*, Amherst, New York: Prometheus Books.
Ṭanṭāwī, A., 2002–2007. *Al-Wasīṭ fī Tafsīr al-Qur˒ān al-Karīm* [e-book]. Jordan: Royal Āl al-Bayt Institute for Islamic Thought. Available from: http://www.altafsir.com/ [accessed April 2006]
ᶜUlaysh, M., 1989. *Minaḥ al-Jalīl.* Beirut: Dār al-Fikr.
UNHCR, 2007. *UN Refugee Agency Launches 'The State of the World's Refugees'* [online]. Available from: http://www.unhcr.se/en/News/State_World_Refugees_2006_publ.html [accessed July 2009]
Van Krieken, P.J. & Asser, T.M.C. (eds), 1999. *Refugee Law in Context: The Exclusion Clause.* The Netherlands: the Huge Press.
Wansbrough, J., 1971. 'The safe-Conduct in Muslim Chancery Practice', *Bulletin of the School of Oriental and African Studies*, University of London, 34, pp. 20–35.
Watt., M., 1994. *Muḥammad at Medina* (3rd edn). Oxford: Oxford University Press.
Ye'or, B., 1985. *The Dhimmī: Jews and Christianity under Islam* (trs David Maisel, Paul Fenton & David Littman). London: Rutherford.
Zakı, A., 2006. *Al-Islam al-Siyāsī wa al-Muwāṭana wa al-Aqalliyyāt.* Cairo: Maktabat al-Shurūq.
Zaydān, A., 1982. *Aḥkām al-Dhimmiyın wa al-Musta˒minın fī Dār al-Islām.* Beirut: Mu˒assasat al-Risāla & Maktabat al-Quds.

INDEX

Names beginning with Al- and Ibn- are alphabetized as separate groups within the overall alphabetical listing, so that all names beginning with Al- and Ibn-respectively are grouped together as in the Bibliography.

www.ingramcontent.com/pod-product-compliance
Ingram Content Group UK Ltd.
Pitfield, Milton Keynes, MK11 3LW, UK
UKHW021905150926
475560UK00003B/186

9 781848 853904